*Hi Simon + Barba[ra]
Thanks for your S[upport]
Lez*

Rednecks
There's a New Sheriff in Town

by

Lez Bromfield

Lez Bromfield

DORRANCE PUBLISHING CO., INC.
PITTSBURGH, PENNSYLVANIA 15222

*Cover picture 'Harry' my father
Lez*

The contents of this work, including, but not limited to, the accuracy of events, people, and places depicted; opinions expressed; permission to use previously published materials included and conclusions drawn from the author-presented information; and any advice given or actions advocated are solely the responsibility of the author, who assumes all liability for said work and indemnifies the publisher against any claims stemming from publication of the work.

All Rights Reserved
Copyright © 2011 by Lez Bromfield

No part of this book may be reproduced or transmitted, downloaded, distributed, reverse engineered, or stored in or introduced into any information storage and retrieval system, in any form or by any means, including photocopying and recording, whether electronic or mechanical, now known or hereinafter invented without permission in writing from the publisher.

Dorrance Publishing Co., Inc.
701 Smithfield Street
Pittsburgh, PA 15222
Visit our website at *www.dorrancebookstore.com*

ISBN: 978-1-4349-1243-5
eISBN: 978-1-4349-3957-9

Dedication

To Barbara (Barbs), my late wife, who believed in me.

To Family and Friends: My wife, Lynell, who takes care of me and always encourages me; my fantastic sons Wayne, Sean, and Rafe, who never let me down; my daughters-in-law, who are like daughters, Lori and Colette; my grandchildren, Colin (C.G.), Brittni, Alexis, Danielle, and Jordan; Harry, my big brother, who taught me to spell; Shirley, my sister and my friend; and also to Craig, Vanessa, Murray, Ross and Jeff Malone.

To 'Special' Friends: Bunny (Strong Man) and Toy Digue, Gordon and Lyn Baker, Wolfgang and Daisy Losken, Michael and Nancy Kucera.

Preface

Who are the 'Rednecks' specifically? Who are the Rednecks of the world? They abound in every nation, but are not referred to as rednecks, except in the USA and South Africa

The South African population of 48 million includes 4 million white descendants from, essentially the very same stock of Europeans, which migrated to early America.

South Africa needs a break!

Since the abolishment of Apartheid, all the peoples of South Africa have emerged from the 'Dark Continent' syndrome and are clawing their way out of that artificial darkness into the 'rainbow' country that emerged under the leadership of Mr. Mandela. So give them a break!

The world, particularly Americans, focus on this beautiful country and its colorful people, which has suddenly emerged out of the darkness because of the recent World Football Cup (generally referred to as Soccer). Can you believe that? Now that the world has seen people from every corner of the globe play a sport together in South Africa and not be murdered in the streets, they have suddenly found religion.

Hey, guys, did you know that the World Rugby competition was held in South Africa in 1995 and that South Africa won the cup as memorialized by the movie *Invictus*?

Recently a South African golfer won the British Open by seventeen strokes and the commentators were derelict in their duty to learn the correct pronunciation of this champion's name. The golfer was an Afrikaner (descendant of a Dutch immigrant); his caddy, a fellow-South African, was black. They hugged on the eighteenth hole.

Examine the distinguished records of South Africans in every field of endeavor. How many people know that the South African pilots supporting the UN in Korea earned 55 USA, DFC's, including many other medals of honor from participating nations?

Learn more. Read this work, ostensibly written 'tongue in cheek,' but which reveals a glossary of gems regarding the trials and tribulations of a society that has finally emerged out of a world of distrust to reach out for a better life for all its inhabitants.

For further information: Read the book.

Enjoy,
Author

Certain "auto related" pictures depict some of the "unusual" antics of South African rednecks in the 50's and 60's.

Rednecks
There's a New Sheriff in Town

Things have got to change! For far too long now, the American Southern folk have laid claim to the term 'redneck.' Ask any self-respecting Yankee to describe the term and y'all could bet good money that the answer would include something like, 'corn liquor' or 'NASCAR.' What do they know? They don't even know how to spell 'likker,' never mind drink it. And none of them...not a one of them...have ever heard of Smoky Tukeyington, the NASCAR rear wheel tire changer working for the number 111 car. As I have said, they know nothing about real rednecks and their southern lifestyles. So, is it any wonder that they eat hot dogs without grits? Makes you think...don't it? One of them ripe New Yorkers even went so far as to say that the North won the Civil War. Take a number, Clarence. I rest my case.

However, I am ready to make another case...a really serious case that challenges the American southerner's claim for the title of 'redneck.' Before I start a rebellion far greater than the Civil War or find myself strangled by my 'Southern Belle' wife, allow me the opportunity to clarify the term 'redneck' as I understand it. I hasten to add that when the term 'redneck' is used in derogatory terms, it deserves no place in these United States of America or anywhere else. "You can put that hangman's noose away now, Miss Nellie."

As someone from another planet who has taken (yep, 'taken'...nobody gave her to me) himself a homegrown southern gal for a wife, "To have and to hold and 'allow' her to drive my pickup truck whenever she is not busy in the kitchen," I am not what I seem to be. Miss Nellie hates the term 'redneck'...but the fact of the matter is that she 'are' married to one. I need to 'splain!

But first, have you noticed how in almost all countries (and I have spent time in many), one can detect some form or other of profiling that lends itself to stereotyping of others within their community? It comes in many forms, some of which that come to mind include differences in lifestyle, politics, recreation, ethnic backgrounds, and others. There are bound to be other forms in many societies with which I am not familiar, but you know what I mean! The strange thing about these phenomena is that those individuals who cast aspersions on others or who make unkind jokes about them, never ever express these sentiments when in the company of these much-maligned folk. Why is that? Here's my take. Just imagine someone going up to Hulk Hogan and telling him that all wrestling is fake and that the female spectators are not sexually aroused by their antics. I don't know anybody who would be brave enough to besmirch the reputations of those women spectators. Get the point? For those ladies who don't get pumped up for whatever reason (some women do not believe that wresting sexually arouses them...mainly those who are married to these guys), allow me to give one further example...just one more. My friend Donald Singleton told a lady in a bar that he thought it was unladylike for her to sit on a bar stool with her mini skirt drawn up to her 'unko.' The lady, who was actually Oscar, sent him to slumber land with a mighty left hook. The moral of the story: Don't hit on a left-handed cross-dresser in a gay bar. We will talk more about left-handed people down the line. Stay tuned.

Now back to my personal challenge regarding the American Southerner's claim to the exclusive rights to the term 'redneck.' You may be forgiven for wondering why anybody would want to challenge these folk for the title, let alone someone actually wanting to be known as a redneck!

It's not so much 'wanting' that title but it may come as a surprise to learn that early South African history actually records the fact that some of its citizens were openly referred to as 'rooi neks,' the Afrikaan's translation for the English word 'redneck.' The Afrikaners, the mainly Dutch-speaking farmers against whom the British fought during the Anglo-Boer War (the Boer War) coined the word 'rooi nek' to describe the newly arrived British settlers. These English-speaking intruders were all fair-skinned, which when exposed to the merciless African sun, burnt a delicate red like a tender steak exposed to a relentless flame...in this case, the hot African sun. These poor souls who had never been exposed to 'real' sunshine while living in England (think Manchester where it rains every day), were now experiencing the fierce African sun. Added to this, was the fact that during the Boer War the British officers wore a tunic, which included a starched bright red collar...perfect target for the sharp-shooting Boer commandos. These two facts make a strong case for declaring early South Africans as the original 'documented' rednecks.

Having established the fact that the term 'redneck' may not be the exclusive domain of the American southerners, we can move on...but not before taking a fresh look at the real meaning of the word 'redneck' in the American context. Who 'really' are these people? In simple terms, they are the descendants of immigrants who settled in the southern parts of early America. I hasten to add that no simple term can do justice to these early settlers whose love of God and country molded them into patriotic Americans and loyal Southerners.

These are not the rednecks that have, on occasions, been portrayed by Hollywood idiots as 'li'l Abner characters. No, sir, not even the likes of Hulk

Hogan scares them. If you don't believe me, go into the mountains around Blue Ridge City, Georgia, and pick on one of them rednecks. I have some advice for you. If you have the guts to refer to them as a redneck…you had better smile. The undertakers prefer to work on a corpse that has a smile.

On the other hand, name one person in distress needing relief that has ever been turned down by these folk. Briefly, although they don't take kindly to rudeness, they can always be relied on to defend their country, their honor, and their kin. You have been warned!

A Note to All Readers: If, after reading this book, you have not been 'mentally' challenged, I will gladly refund the cost of this book. Simply return it to my home address, but include 'mailing and shipping charges' of $199.99. To expedite refunds…no personal checks please…only bank certified checks. Do not send cash…you just can't trust anybody anymore.

I made the same offer to readers of my previous book, "How to Befriend My Wife's 'Rock Hudson' LOOK-ALIKE GYNECOLOGIST." I was most distressed, disturbed, and personally saddened by the fact that a few of those readers had not enjoyed that publication and demanded a refund.

I bear no ill feelings. "Bless your hearts, y'all." Due to circumstances beyond your control, after all refunds had been received, I hastily relocated to my newly acquired 'little old' penthouse in Miami, Florida, the one located above the revolving restaurant, A dizzy of a place!

Confession: In all honesty, not everyone who requested a refund mailed $199.99 in a bank certified check. You can't fool everybody. Some honest readers sent cash, which included the small change, which proves that some still do trust everybody. "Bless their hearts."

What to expect in this book?

I feel the need to tell y'all a little of what can be expected when reading this book. It may be possible that even at this early stage, the reader will be able to just simply return this book for a normal refund, thus saving the $0.99 handling charge. On the 'udder' hand, after reading this book, you will have gained special knowledge that will enable you to understand everything that anybody will ever tell you. (Provided they speak English…er, American.) Nobody will ever again be able to bamboozle you! Stay tuned.

Confession 2: This book was written by an ex-Colonial 'rooi nek,' which is Afrikaans for 'redneck' (clarification to follow). The writer is an ex-South African, who obviously was not born in the American South, but who could not get here quick enough. My purpose for writing is several-fold:

> First: To provide some tongue-in-cheek, light relief to this otherwise somber existence.

Second: To provide a basic understanding of Colonial South Africans, which is necessary to understand the characters that will emerge 'large as life' to challenge others for the title of 'redneck' in the rest of this book. This will necessitate the inclusion of some basic history that may seem somewhat serious for a book of this nature. But, on the other hand, even the light South African humor will not be fully appreciated without some knowledge of the background of the character. It is my hope that those more serious issues will not detract from the overall reading experience.

That said…as I am about to challenge the American Southerner for the title of 'redneck,' I feel that it is only fair that I introduce one, only one, American redneck story to illustrate the strength of the American argument in favor of their cause.

Thereafter, I will introduce the South African redneck challenge. I will relate the American story, after which we can analyze, dissect, and absorb the contents to give it every opportunity to defend itself against the onslaught from the 'other' south…South Africa.

So, where do we go from here? I'm going to relate an amazing elephant story, which I hope will help the reader to appreciate the strong case for Americans to challenge the South African onslaught on their legacy as the rightful heir in question. In addition, I intend to introduce some basic rules for a fuller life. You may be surprised. Prepare yourself. Here goes…

In 1987, an American by the name of Donny Mango was vacationing in South Africa after graduating from Community College. On a hike through the bush, he came across a young bull elephant standing with one leg raised in the air. The elephant seemed distressed, so Donny approached it very carefully.

The huge animal did not move, so Donny got down on one knee, inspected the elephant's foot, and discovered a large piece of wood deeply embedded in it. As carefully and as gently as possible, Donny worked the wood out with his knife, after which the animal gingerly put down his foot. The elephant turned to face the man, and with a rather curious look on his face, stared at him for several tense moments. Donny froze, thinking of nothing else but being trampled.

Eventually, the elephant trumpeted loudly, turned, and walked away.

Donny never forgot that elephant or the events of that day.

Twenty years later, Donny was walking through the zoo in Ashville, North Carolina, with his teenage son. As he approached the 'Asian Elephant' enclosure, one of the creatures turned and walked over to where Donny and his son Claude were standing. The large bull elephant stared at Donny, lifted his front foot off the ground and slowly put it down again. The elephant did that several times, and then trumpeted loudly, all the while staring at the man.

Remembering the encounter in 1987, Donny could not help wondering if this was the same elephant. Donny summoned up his courage, climbed over the railing, and made his way carefully into the enclosure. He walked right up to the elephant and stared in wonder.

The elephant trumpeted once again, wrapped its trunk around one of Donny's legs, and slammed him against the railing, killing him instantly.

Probably not the same cotton picking elephant!

Now that is a redneck story that would be hard to top! But, before we move on to South African redneck tales…let's take a hard look at the elephant story. What can we 'other' people learn from it? My contention is that something should be learned from everything…otherwise the story would have no significance.

Okay, what did we learn? Hopefully, some basic rules for a fuller life. If not, let's carefully analyze the elephant story to test that theory.

Now, if Donny were really small, he would have done two things before climbing over the rail separating 'normal' folk from Dumbo. First, he would have taken a closer look at the elephant to compare the big gray brute with the image of the one he had stored in his brain since his elephant experience in South Africa. Then, after careful comparison, he would have asked himself a question, *Could this be the same elephant?*…and…*Could this 'African' elephant have sauntered over from Africa to India where he was captured and brought to the North Carolina Zoo?* Knowing Donny as I do, it would have taken his brain at least four hours to 'carefully compare,' in which case, he would not have died in vain because on that day the zoo would have closed within an hour and, if he stayed, he would have been escorted off the property and never had the opportunity to climb over the rail. But, giving our boy the benefit of the doubt, I must assume that his fog shrouded brain had actually made the comparison and decided that this could very well be the same creature from which he had removed that nasty twig from the festering wound during his South African visit. Then his brain would not have asked the 'obvious' question regarding the possibility of whether that elephant could have trekked from South Africa and crossed several countries during a walk of thousands of miles. Not to mention some long-distance swimming! And finally, the million-dollar question: Could such a smart elephant like this then be captured and shipped from India to America? Seems to me that more questions than answers have been generated!

Or, maybe one further observation, assuming that the late Donny Mango had noticed the difference in the elephant, would he have still climbed over the protective rail? Remember that Donny was no dummy. He completed his two-year "Auto Body Repair Course" in just four years at High Dogwood Community College. And, also of interest, his adopted sister Shirletta made the Dean's list at that prestigious girls 'finishing school' in South Africa, which was funded by Oprah (?) before the sex scandal. These were two smart kids.

Two things are very obvious:

First: Donny did not compare the image of the African elephant he helped in South Africa with this Asian variety in the American zoo. If he had, he would have surely noticed the obvious (oops!) difference in the size of the ears. Everybody in the universe knows that the African elephant's ears are much larger than those of the Indian elephant (?), or is it the other way around?

Second: It is not only the size of the ears that are different. The African elephant, Loxodonta, is much larger in every respect when compared with the Asian, Elephas Maximus. The jolly ol' Elephas Maximus grows to a height of nine feet, weighs in at between three to five tons, and has tusks up to six feet in length. On the 'udder' hand, the bigger African variety, Loxodonta, grows to thirteen feet, weighs in between six and eight tons with ten-foot tusks! So, which one would you chose to ride? There is a reason why you don't find 'elephant jockeys' in Africa.

Anyway the (?) after any statement reflects that there is a factual basis for the statement 'one way or another.' I know for a fact that their ear sizes are markedly different…it is not my job to prove which way around it turns out…simply to tell you that this is a fact 'cause they are different. Did you notice the question marks (?) in previous pages? If not, you may want to page back…could be a learning experience.

Before leaving our Loxodonta and Elephas Maximus friends, I need to bring some very interesting elephant behavior to your attention. Elephants form deep bonds and live in tight groups of related females referred to as a 'herd.' The herd is led by the oldest and often the biggest female in the herd, called a 'matriarch.' No guy elephants in these herds. So, where are the 'guy' elephants? These greedy good ol' boys fall way behind the girly group and neglect their courting instincts in order to eat. I hope that I never get that hungry! But, sooner or later, they 'rise' to the mating call during the rainy season and take off after the girls. (Remember that the first one there gets the pretty one.). The heavy rains slow down the girls to an amble and the big boys surf onto the scene. That is the reason that elephants only mate in the rain! (?) This is nature's way of keeping things cool!

Because everything is different these days, one needs to be equipped with some human devices that would enable us to recognize the differences, how to accept these differences, and finally how to adapt to them. The phrase 'adapt or die' comes to mind. It is my intention to introduce you to the main secret 'human devices' right now! Others will follow. So for now…

Ask questions like, Who?…What?…When?…Where?…How?…Why? Say what?…etc., etc. Those are just a few examples that come to mind…I may add a few along the way. But, for now, the last thing that I want to do is overwhelm the reader.

However, I hasten to add for the third time that when asking a question you need to understand two things. First, you need to ask the correct, intelligent question; and second and more critical, you need to be sure the timing is right. Timing is something that we learn through personal experience and I will cover this subject comprehensively in Chapter Sixty-Sex.

Did you pick up the fact that our elephant story had its beginning in South Africa? Hold that thought, not your breath. You are not a humpback whale...(later).

While holding that thought, breathe easy, Albert, allow me to introduce two important subjects that must be mastered and understood along your journey to perfection. The first relates to "Words of Wisdom," hereafter referred to as 'WOW.' The second relates to "Question with Boldness," hereafter referred to as 'QWB.'

Examples of 'WOW' and 'QWB' will be introduced without warning along the way to test the effectiveness of the learning process. What the heck, let's throw in a couple now!

WOW: NEVER, UNDER ANY CIRCUMSTANCES, TAKE A SLEEPING PILL AND A LAXATIVE ON THE SAME NIGHT!

Now *there* are words of wisdom for you...but, unless you have learnt something important from them, you are missing the point. Ask yourself, "What have I learnt?" Billy Braselton told Slim Applegate that "WOW" taught him how to spell 'laxative.' Now, he can write a note for his son Billy Jr. to take to Rite Aid when he has a headache.

QWB: WHY DID KAMIKAZE PILOTS WEAR CRASH HELMETS? Some advice: Before answering, take two precautions. First: Take a breath. Don't hold it, you are not a humpback whale...later story.

Second: Don't jump to conclusions. Heard that somewhere before...maybe Fort Hood?

Having done the aforementioned and giving due consideration to all that has been written on similar subjects, how about this! Unlike those Japanese fighter pilots who attacked Pearl Harbor, these kamikaze twits could not open their cockpit canopies, not even to throw out hand grenades. (See page 10...not now...later.) So, they wore crash helmets to add to the force of the impact 'if and when' they hit their targets. Talk about headaches! Ask Billy. He said that the last thing that those kamikaze pilots needed was a laxative! Previously sealed coded WW II records that were recently released and decoded by Native American translators state clearly the dress code of the kamikaze pilots:

"*%# (^#%$+)&%#*%) # ^#*(^#@&*##*()^&%@#$%&-*(*%%%^^&**&

&^^^#^@!&)&$%#^"

Decoded thus, "By command of the Emperor of Japan: All honorable kamikaze pilots will wear a neck scarf, a crash helmet, and a diaper." Note: No mention of a uniform. Remember in those days pilots caught short in those heavy flight coveralls did not have time to undo seventeen buttons in an emergency. No zippers in them days. No wonder they preferred to remain unseen and locked in the cockpits. Oh, I forgot to mention that the kamikaze flying manual did not give landing instructions. Is it not truly amazing what you can learn from one simple QWB? The real secret is to analyze each and every word.

Like Roger Whittaker once, or twice, sang: "I must look at life from all sides now." The lesson is clear. We too, must look from all sides now.

Something really interesting concerning the recruitment of the kamikaze pilots came to light during the decoding. Only young single men were recruited, for obvious reasons; they would not leave a wife and/or children. However, one of the decoders, Little Big Horse son of big Big Horse discovered that the Wing Captain Komonandingdem who led the first attack was, in fact, a married man. It seems that he would do anything to get away from the little woman.

Chapter Sixty-Sex

The Right Question at the Right Time

I could start by giving an example of someone asking the wrong question or an example of someone asking a question at the wrong time. But, what the heck, let's look at an example of someone asking the 'wrong question at the wrong time,' commonly referred to as the 'big one'!

The setting is Pearl Harbor just moments before the Japanese air attack. Sergeant Maloe has just completed a training exercise in hand grenade tossing. He has dismissed the squad except for Billy Banderbush, whom he had asked to remain 'after class' for extra hand grenade tossing practice, because the last grenade he tossed ended up ten feet behind the protective bunker instead of twenty feet ahead of the bunker. Billy had scared the crap out of the rest of the training detail, all of who had wet their pants, except for Private Finton G. Westerbottom, who spoiled the almost perfect record. But, in fairness to Finton, he suffered from a nervous stomach.

Picture the scene as Sergeant Maloe hands Billy the grenade with the pin still intact, instructs him to follow the set of instructions laid out by the military manual, which states something like this: Take a firm grip of the grenade, take a breath, exhale slowly, select your target, remove the pin, count to three, lob the grenade, and duck behind the protective bunker." (?)

Just at that point, three things happened: First, Billy asked the sergeant, "Hey, Sarge, did you know that your wife is having an affair with Sergeant Cooper?" Second, the two men noticed a group of Japanese fighter planes heading for their position. And, Third, Sergeant Maloe pointed out the fast approaching enemy planes, pulled the pin on the grenade that Billy was clutching, and instructed him, "Don't throw it, yet. Put it on the floor and save it for the enemy." With that the sergeant hauled himself out of the bunker, headed for the next bunker, and dove in.

Billy Banderbush's remains were accorded a military burial and he was posthumously awarded a medal for bravery, "For valiantly attempting to bring down an enemy aircraft with a single hand grenade," As Sergeant Maloe had recommended in his written report.

Talk about asking the wrong question at the wrong time. Oh, I forgot to mention that Sergeant Cooper's body was also discovered several days after the attack on Pearl Harbor. There was not much left to bury. The Board of Inquiry had no option, but to assume that the Japanese pilots must have had a few American hand grenades, because the autopsy report indicated that an American hand grenade had detonated in his mouth. It must have bounced right in there!

I feel the need to point out the fact that the Billy Banderbush event occurred in America. On the other hand, the elephant story originated in South Africa and, as I am about to compare rednecks from both countries, I will now swing your attention to the South African setting.

American readers will see the South Africans as those 'other' people and the South Africans also see Americans as those 'other' people. So let's hook them up.

But, First...
WOW: NEVER TEST THE DEPTH OF THE WATER WITH BOTH FEET!
QWB: IF ELECTRICITY COMES FROM ELECTRONS, DOES MORALITY COME FROM MORONS?

We and Those 'Other' People

Much has been written, for pure reading pleasure, about 'how things have changed over the years in America.' Maybe even 'what has changed.' All good and well, but what about asking the same questions of those immigrants who experienced similar…or, maybe not so similar…adjustments in other countries and in other cultures before arriving in America? Important questions like what children did for fun and, even more interestingly, what did adults do for fun?

In recent years, people of all persuasions, shapes, sizes, and different cultures have started new lives in America and have had to adjust to differences both big and small. Ever think to ask these newcomers about the differences? If you did, the answers all have to do with differences in the more serious areas such as banking, weather, transport…to mention a few of the most common. But, what about sports, entertainment, church, etc.? Consider sports for instance; the average male immigrant from the UK has played soccer, cricket, and rugby, all of which are most un-American, not embraced, understood, or accepted this side of the pond, seldom covered, and NEVER discussed without a certain distain. After all, speaking of cricket…who on earth would play a game over five days and still end up with a draw? That's just a taste, but this and similar subjects will bubble up in following chapters.

Soooo, what follows are personal experiences taken from diary notes and old newspaper clippings that have languished in a box for so many years that they have matured to the extent that various shades of gray are prominent. The period in question includes those uncertain years during WW II and will take the reader to present day. It must be acknowledged that during the earlier troubled times when the free world fought with valor and tremendous sacrifice, much can and will be written. Even in those times of turmoil and suffering, life went on. It had to, if for no other reason but to reflect the human spirit and the will to overcome.

Immigrants had arrived in America from virtually every country in the world, all carrying with them memories of the land they left behind. Memories, good or bad, but so important and so generally cherished that they linger forever in the minds of those who have moved on for whatever reasons. When visiting Ellis Island, and hearing from guides and seeing the history portrayed in photographs, and casting the eye over the exhibits of those who arrived in mainly distressed circumstances, I was moved to tears. Mainly, because I was embarrassed by the fact that my family and I had a comparatively easy experience when immigrating…not that it was a breeze (later)! The immigration experience is an eye-opener even to the most prepared. Much has been documented and written about immigrants from countries familiar to the general American populace, but little has been written or known of those who have 'quietly' moved in from South Africa.

What are the first questions posed to the South African immigrant? Basically, two subjects are usually raised related to either wild animals or about Apartheid. I must warn the reader at the outset that neither subject will be covered for two reasons:

> First: There are almost no wild animals left roaming around freely in South Africa. If you want to see some, you will have to go to a game reserve or zoo and pay for the experience. A fact is that more deer are killed by automobiles in America, than the number shot by American hunters on safari in South Africa.

> Second: Apartheid no longer exists in South Africa. Does it exist in other places? Maybe that is a question best asked of the United Nations.

Lighthearted books are written about various people or cultures and their peculiar brand of humor or lifestyle, despite the apparent injustices that exist within their communities. Were it not for some light relief, we would be depriving one another of some of the most basic of human interactions. For the moment, let's move on from 'man's injustices to man' in whatever form. What country is without its skeletons hidden in closets?

The American Indian, Native American wars are over. The war against England is over. The Civil War is over. WW II is over. Slavery in America is over. Apartheid in South Africa is over. Korea is over. Vietnam is over. Desert Storm is over…so are many other hurtful conflicts. We need to move on and one way of adding pleasure to the journey is to bring on some humor. Not to suggest that life is without pain, sorrow, or regret…not at all. For without some pain, there is little gain.

Allow me… "You cannot truly laugh, until you have truly cried." In the final analysis of life, we will all have to decide which tears are the strongest…'the tears of sorrow and regret, or the tears of joy and hope.' Over to you… Enjoy.

The time has come to introduce those South African characters that, in my opinion, are ready to challenge the American version of redneck. What better way than to introduce members of my own family including me, because it is only fair that all are not judged without including myself and my own family.

Experience has taught me that humor is best presented and accepted by others, in the manner in which it is intended, by making fun of oneself. My family and I will not be spared. Are we rednecks? You be the judge…here we go.

Rare "White" Lions in South Africa.

Yours Truly...

I was born in 1937 in the small seashore town of Port Shepstone, beside the Zululand border on the southeast coast of South Africa. Two of my grandparents were Scottish, one English, and the fourth was French. But, as I was born to parents who themselves were born in South Africa, I was a genuine South African…one might say, 'the real Mc Coy.'

How I Solved WW II...
and Met Tommy Tickle-Toes

What are my earliest recollections? Around five years of age, for sure, because I remember a friend of my father telling him in the butcher shop, "Harry, my friend, I just heard that the Japanese attacked the Americans at Pearl Harbor. They bombed the crap out of the American fleet!" He heard it on the radio and expected that America would go to war.

I watched my father's reaction and waited for his reply. I knew that he had heard something very important because his friend Tom was a policeman and I was told that if ever I was lost, I should ask a policeman how to get home...so a policeman must have been very smart. But, my father was smart too. After all, he owned his own small butcher shop. Not many people in our small town of a few thousand residents owned their own business. So, I listened with interest to my father's reply.

"Well, Tom, looks like the Yanks will soon be fighting next to our boys against the Germans."

Whoa...all this information was too much for a five year old to understand. The Japlonese, whoever they were, bombed the Americans, so now the Yanks, whoever they were, were going to help us fight the Germans, whoever they were. Who were the Japlonese and who were the Yanks?" I figured it out. The Yanks were 'pissed off Americans,' and they could fight! I had seen them fighting the Red Indians in a movie on Saturday, but now it seemed that these bad Japlonese had stuck their noses into America's business. It took me some time, but I figured it out; the Japlonese were about to get their butts kicked!

Later that afternoon, I ran down to Bobby Himmler's house to tell him what I heard. I knew that he would be interested because he once told me that some of his father's relatives had been 'locked up' by our government because they were Germans. At the time, I wondered why they had been 'locked up.' I reasoned that if men had germs, they should have been in the hospital, not in jail. I decided to ask Bobby about that. He would know more about it because Bobby was a lot older than me...and my daddy told me that the older you get, the smarter you get...and Bobby was much older than me. When anybody asked him how old he was, he held up all the fingers on one hand and a few more on the other hand. I could only hold up the fingers on one hand. I discovered Bobby way down in his backyard playing with two white ducks in their enclosure. He was very excited…not about seeing me, but about what he had achieved with the two ducks.

"Look at what I discovered!" he called out as I sidled up to him.

For a moment I did not understand, but then I noticed something very strange about the two ducks. They were joined by a piece of string, not in any conventional way, but joined beak to rear. Let me rephrase that…the ducks were standing one behind the other and the front duck had a long piece of string protruding from its beak and the other end of the string was…you guessed it…protruding from its rear end where eggs usually appeared. Now the interesting part…the second duck standing a foot behind the lead duck was joined to its companion by the same piece of string…and, wait for it…the second duck like the first had the end of the string hanging from its rear. On closer examination, there was a small piece of what resembled animal fat attached to the end of the string. I was flabbergasted!

"How did you do that Bobby?"

He replied, "Stinky Jones, my older cousin, told me that if you fed a duck a small piece of animal fat, the duck would pass it out in time because the duck cannot digest raw fat."

"What does it mean to digest?" I asked.

The older and smarter boy replied, "Digest means keep it in and 'cannot digest' means poop it out." That Bobby Himmler…he sure was smart.

He continued, "Well, I figured that if I tied a small piece of raw fat to the end of a string and fed it to a duck he would poop it out and he did, so I figured that if I fed that same piece of string with the fat attached to another duck he would also poop if out and he did. But it took the second duck much longer. I had to wait a long time, but it was worth it."

"What you gonna' do now, Bobby?"

"I'm going to hook up a few more."

"And then what, Bobby?"

"Then I'm going to take them for a walk. I will train them to follow me in a line wherever I go."

"Why would you want to train them to follow you, Bobby?"

"Then I can sell them to the circus when they come to town."

That Bobby Himmler…I told you he was smart.

Just then his mother appeared from the kitchen door and headed our way. Bobby got real nervous and I knew that something bad was about to happen, so now it was my turn to be smart…I took off!

I did not see Bobby again for a week and when I did he never told me what happened, so I never asked him because they were his ducks…I wondered where he got the animal fat. That bothered me some.

Other things were soon to bother me more. School! I had two older brothers who went off to school five days a week and, from what they told me,

I was convinced that it was like the place where they kept the Germans. My understanding was that once they entered the school premises someone somewhere rang a bell that immediately turned the children into mutes. Nobody spoke. Nobody, that is except a warden who was disguised like a teacher. His job was to herd the children into a hall and yell at them until everybody was so scared that they sat down in rows in front of a raised stage. Nobody was allowed to cry. Some peed their pants, but nobody cried. Then the headmaster who was actually the head warden read from the Bible. That was supposed to make the children feel better, but my brother Bob, who was also smart because he was older, told me that the real reason they read these Bible stories was to scare the hell out of the kids. Like the story of how 'millominions of 'Gypsies' who were chasing children from Israel in chariots drowned in the 'Ready Sea' because the tide came in. This was to warn us not to make fun of 'Gypsies' and also to be careful at the beach when the tide came in.

Well, I was soon to find out for myself. One morning after my brothers had left for school, my Mama took me by the hand and led me into her sewing room. I was relived that it was the sewing room because she never did anything brutal in her orderly sewing room unlike the bathroom, where she often led me by the hand to remove gravel from my ears. Once in the room beside her beloved Singer sewing machine, she produced a neatly made pair of serge shorts and a white shirt. I knew what this meant. School!

That's how all the kids dressed for school. Serge shorts and white shirts were the school uniforms of the day. As I stood mortified at the thought of being cast to the wolves, my Mama whisked off my play clothes (khaki shorts and vest), pulled on my new serge shorts over my underwear, and carefully buttoned a crisp white short-sleeve shirt that she had lovingly helped me into. My world would never be the same again!

I would have cried, but noting the pride in my Mama's eyes as she gently smoothed over the clothes that she had so professionally made, would have been a betrayal of everything that mothers represented. Then she said sweetly, "You look so grown up, my baby!" That did it! How could I be so grown up and still be called 'my baby'?

But, as I learnt in years to come, I was her youngest and last child and, therefore, I would always be 'her baby,'…but at the time, I had a picture in my mind depicting my mother handing me over to the head warden of the school and telling him to take care of her 'baby.' I decided then and there that I would not cry at school…but what if I peed my pants?

I remember my first day of school. It was nothing like I had expected…thanks to the distorted and chilling images that my two elder brothers had conveyed to me. I made a mental note to get even with them one day. It was, however, only one of many, many paybacks that I planned in the future.

Back to 'day one' at school…my mama walked me the short distance to the school and took me directly into a large reception room full of about thirty new recruits. Half were boys; all dressed exactly like me, except that some of the rich kids wore shoes. Half of the crowd was girls. Whose idea was that?

From my experience, all girls were good for was crying. So, why were so few of them crying? I guessed that somebody had promised them candy. So, where was my candy? I never got candy at home. My Daddy told me that there was no candy because of the war. That meant that whenever there was a war, the first thing that the government did was to stop making candy 'before' locking up the Germans.

Doting mothers were busy pacifying their young, some of whom were crying, but nobody had wet their pants. *Just wait until the head warden takes over*, I thought. *These guys were in for a shock!* Not so...I was the one in for a shock...or rather 'in for a surprise'...a very pleasant surprise. Turned out that we first-year kids were not going to attend that 'big school.' We were just there to be enrolled, after which we were all escorted on foot by our mothers and a few really nice lady teachers to an old concrete block building across the road. This well-constructed and ornate building had previously been a Masonic temple that had been donated to the town for a 'small school' for us little people. This made me very happy, but I feared that at some time in the future, I would have to attend 'big school'! I wondered about that and decided to ask Bobby Himmler, who had just started his first year at big school. I figured that if he could survive there, I could. I felt sure that if the school accepted someone who could join ducks together then someone like me, who had only once spat on Mr. Frack's new Buick as a dare, would also be accepted. Anyway, everybody knew that Mr. Frack was making lots of money by charging people for petrol (gasoline) to run their cars and trucks, and where did Mr. Frack get his petrol? From the ground under his petrol station. I wished that we had petrol under our ground.

The first day of school turned out much better than I had expected, despite the fact that we had to put up with girls. But, we soon learned that after two years of little school, we would move on to attend 'boys only' and 'girls only' schools. That was a relief, because girls got in the way of men things...like rough and tumble and marbles...and they could never be trusted to keep a secret. Like when Johnnie Little told Jane Fowler that before going to bed at night Mr. Barker used to remove his glass eye and soak it in a glass of special cleaner fluid. Not only did she tell the other girls about Mr. Barker's glass eye, but she added a fib by saying that even though Mr. Barker was asleep, his glass eye could see everything that was going on. I wondered about that some.

Johnnie got even with Jane. A few days later on his walk to school, he trapped a live bee in a hibiscus bloom and gave it to her at the school gate. When she took the flower, he let it open and the bee came rushing out, and scared the living daylights out of her. As can be expected, one of the other girls 'tattled' to the teacher, who told his mother, who told his daddy, who laughed about it. That made Johnnie's mama 'mad' and caused an argument in the Little home. It's true that girls can cause lots of trouble for no reason.

I soon discovered that kids actually *could* learn things at school not only from teachers, but also from other kids, some of whom were actually smarter than the teachers. Take Conrad Cooper. 'Coop' knew more about who and why so many people drowned in the Red (not 'Ready') Sea in the Bible, because he knew someone whose parents were there at the time. He explained that their neighbors were Jews who were really children of the 'children of Israel' who were the people being chased by Egyptians (not by Gypsies) when the tide came in and drowned the Egyptians. Coop said that when the children of Israel got to the other side of the Red Sea, they changed their names to Jews because they did not want anybody to know that they could swim so well, otherwise they would not be allowed into the 'Holy Limpic Games.' The head warder at the big school had it all wrong!

I met a lot of new kids at school who knew things that surprised me, but I don't think that all of them told the truth. Luckily for me, I was the kind of person who knew when they were not telling the truth. I would check things out myself. Like the time that Penny Potter said that her teenage sister was double jointed. I had seen her sister Maggie and looked her over carefully...she only had two arms and two legs. Penny could not fool me. But, on the other hand, I believed what Coop told me about Maggie...she had two boyfriends...but that was double-crossing...not double jointed.

So, not all learning took place in the classroom...some important stuff came from yard talk during our twenty-minute playtime outside. The yard area was enclosed by a four-foot high wire fence. This fence was to keep strangers from coming in and not to keep us from running away. Who would want to run away from a place that had indoor plumbing? Beats going at home in that hot wooden privy that was at least a one-minute walk from the house. A lot can happen to an over-anxious stomach during a one-minute walk! About the fence around the schoolhouse...Danny, the really tall skinny guy with the bulging eyes, said he could jump over the fence if he wanted to...but he did not want to. I was not sure if he just said that because he would not make the jump for the same reason as mine...except he had a stronger reason to stay at school because their privy at home was much farther away from their house...and he was scared of the dark, so he saved all his goings for daylight hours...except he peed through the window at night if he was caught short.

Something very interesting for your information...First Lady Barbara Bush, the delightful and forthcoming wife of President George H. W. Bush, mentioned in her book that at night her husband peed through the upstairs bedroom window of her parent's home to avoid flushing the noisy toilet, which had disturbed her mother. Nobody wants to disturb a sleeping mother-in law!

About the school fence...the thing that bothered me was that, if Danny could really jump over the fence, then what would stop a bandit from jumping over the fence and stealing our lunches? Which brings up my question about Mr. Tommy Tickle-Toes. Every last Friday of the month, Tommy Tickle-Toes would be waiting at the gate with a bag of candy when we went out for playtime. He then dispensed one piece at a time to each child, providing that they greeted him by saying, "Good morning, Mr. Tommy Tickle-Toes," to which he always replied, "And a good morning to you, my little friend."

Tommy Tickle-Toes was a mystery man to us, but not to the teachers who knew him personally as a generous and loving old man whose main pleasure was to bring joy to young children. In today's world, nobody would be trusted near a schoolyard, particularly a man handing out candy to eager little children. Oh, for those wonderful days of moonlight and roses…and free candy. Why did he do this regularly and where did he get the candy? Somebody said that he must have known the Prime Minister or somebody who owned a candy factory. I thought about it a lot, but never thought to ask the teachers. How unusual is that? Now, sixty-five years later, I wish I had asked someone about this kind and caring old gentleman. The mental picture of him is fading. He was tall, but to a six year old, everybody was tall. He had graying hair in a 'short back and sides' style, neatly combed and soft in the wind. He walked tall and proud, and had a military air about him. So I thought…yet he had a certain sadness in his pale blue eyes. He always dressed the same…khaki slacks and shirt open at the neck with short sleeves that exposed strong arms and weather beaten hands. Oh, if only I could remember more…if only. If only…just so that I could say thank you one more time and to tell him that through his actions, I can never turn away from a need. Thank you, Mr. Tommy Tickle-Toes.

WOW: A GOOD TIME TO KEEP YOUR MOUTH SHUT IS WHEN YOU'RE IN DEEP WATER.
QWB: HOW COME TARZAN HAS NO BEARD?

Like all the other kids in 1943, life went on…too young to understand the reality of the war that was raging 'overseas.' When England declared war on Germany in 1939, South Africa as a member of the British Commonwealth followed suit and, in short order, we were dispatching military personnel to 'the front.' Uncle George and some of my cousins enlisted and virtually disappeared for the duration of the war, after which we would be one man short in the family.

My father, who was considered 'too heavy' for military service, became a member of the Home Guard with particular emphasis on sea patrol. I was convinced that he had attained some form of rank because he received permission to mount a pair of military issued headlamps on the front bumper of his Hudson for night patrol during blackouts, which had been instituted as precautionary measures in the event of an air attack. The lamps were designed in such a way as to concentrate their beams directly onto the road surface immediately in front of the front bumper, so as not to allow a beam to shine ahead of the vehicles. In this manner, the enemy would not see and track the vehicles from a distance. The downside was that speed was severely restricted, as drivers could only see a few feet of road as they rushed off to protect the citizens. Those military 'bumper lamps' were a source of much discussion and, in some instances, much ribbing. The main reason for this was the fact that during blackout rehearsals when the alarm wailed across the town, only the Home Guard vehicles were allowed on the roads. On the first trial exercise, two of the Home Guard vehicles fitted with the bumper lamps collided head-on somewhere on Beach Road. As the vehicles were moving very slowly, the main damage was to the bumper lamps on both vehicles, which necessitated them to utilize the main headlights for the rest of the exercise. But in fairness to these dedicated townsmen, in time they got their act together and rendered excellent service in general emergencies.

The main concern was to detect enemy submarine presence along the Southern Coast of Africa. German U-boat attacks were taking place on the American East Coast and logic suggested this activity would be expanded along the African East Coast through which allied convoys passed.

It must be remembered that in 1942, German U-boats sent nearly 400 cargo vessels to the bottom of the ocean off the Eastern Seaboard of America and the Caribbean. In many circles, these losses are considered to have been a greater strategic setback for the combined Allied war efforts than the destruction suffered at Pearl Harbor. These successful U-boat attacks, unless curtailed or eradicated, could well have cut Britain's lifeline from America, not to mention the effect on the American war effort.

> WOW: ALWAYS DRINK UPSTREAM FROM THE HERD. (Southern wisdom)
> QWB: WHY DOES MY WIFE'S ROCK HUDSON LOOK-ALIKE GYNECOLOGIST MAKE HER UNDRESS BEHIND A SCREEN IF HE IS GOING TO LOOK ANYWAY?

For the record, during the last Panther game (no comments please), we were seated in the stadium when my wife's gynecologist and his fourth wife took a seat nearby. My wife was disappointed that he did not recognize her. Should I have tapped him on the shoulder and asked whether he remembered her? The question is: Would he have recognized her with her clothes on? Now that's the very question that his second wife, Freda, asked just before their divorce. Get it? If not, you may need further QWB practice.

Who's Who in the Zoo?

The school year was late in January through late November with the month of July off, which is opposite to the American school year. Why was that? Simple…South Africa is in the Southern Hemisphere and America in the Northern Hemisphere. Soooo? So, when you pull the plug to release water from a washbasin in Africa, the water spins the opposite way to the water being released in America. Okay, so that has nothing to do with anything, but did you know that? (?)

Back to the school year and me. Children had to be either seven years of age or would be turning seven in their first year at the small school. My mother either did not know this rule or she did not remember my date of birth…not surprising because she could not remember how to spell my name. That's a long and interesting story, but I will explain later. For the moment, I will stick to the facts. My mother sent me to school when I was five and turned six in May of that year. I have no idea how this came about, and I presume that whatever records were kept at the small school, nobody picked it up. My size must have featured in the scheme of things, because I was big for my age. No doubt influenced by the fact that my father stood at around six foot three and about two hundred and eighty pounds, and my mother who topped six foot in her high-heel shoes must have had some influence on my size. I was also very active and had a big mouth. Bottom line…I went to school too young…and paid dearly for it in later years.

I suppose that I should actually start at the beginning.

My father, Harry, was the youngest son of my immigrant grandparents. My grandfather was a British officer who with his regiment, the 'Inniskilling Dragoons' (no kidding!) was deployed in South Africa during the Boer War. He met and married my Scottish grandmother in South Africa. My father was the youngest of nine children. He was very young when his mother died around the time of the flu epidemic that devastated the world in the early 1900s.

My father (let's refer to him as Harry from here on) was, as I have already mentioned, a big man in every sense of the word. He was the strongest man

I have ever known. My mother (let's refer to her as Ella from here on) referred to Harry as 'disgustingly strong'! I recall how one morning in a used car showroom the salesman was telling him how fuel efficient the small French rear engine Renault was compared to bigger American cars and that Harry, despite his size, should consider buying one for puttering around in the city. Harry told the man that the car was built too light, which made him believe that its handling could be compromised in windy conditions. The salesman laughed and argued that the vehicle was not light. Without saying a word, Harry walked up to the front of the Renault, crouched down on bended knees, grabbed the front bumper with both hands, and lifted the front of the car about a foot off the ground. He held it for a few seconds and then let it go and when the wheels hit the ground, it bounced and the shock absorbers allowed it to wobble a few times. A week later, that salesman had hernia surgery. It was rumored that he almost burst his 'fuffy valve' trying to lift that Renault. He should have known better. Harry was a Hudson man!

My mother was tall for a woman. Although she was rather thin, this Afrikaans-speaking descendant of the Voortrekkers was made of 'concrete,' according to Harry, my father. At this juncture, I may need to clarify some of the last sentence. The 'Voortrekkers' were the Afrikaans-speaking settlers who set out from Cape Town in the 1830s to head inland to find their own place in the sun. This was very much the same as the pioneers in early America.

There are some similarities between these two groups on opposite continents. The American pioneers and the South African Voortrekkers were mostly immigrants from the same sources.

First: Both groups headed across land inhabited by fearlessly proud indigenous tribes. Early American pioneers encountered the Indian tribes, whereas the South African pioneers encountered African tribes. This is not intended as a history lesson, but history records the conflicts endured during these times.

Second: In later years, both America and South Africa fought the 'bloody' English! Fortunately for America the English were defeated. Not so in South Africa where, after the English had initially suffered several humiliating defeats at the hands of the Boers, the English prevailed, but only after establishing concentration camps.

I must apologize for digressing from the original course of this chapter. I started out covering my family, but sort of went off track when covering my mother's Afrikaans Voortrekker roots. I am surprised that I referred to British concentration camps because when I set out to write this book, I had planned to keep it light. But now, pondering on this subject, I feel compelled to tell it like it was. No history lesson was intended, but here are the facts.

In 1900, in South Africa, the British established the first concentration camps for civilians in recorded history. Some forty-four camps were built to incarcerate Boer woman and children, who had been taken prisoner after their homes/farms and crops were burnt to the ground during the absence of the men folk, who were away fighting the invaders…the invaders…the 'cream of the British Empire.' The Boer forces in South Africa were made up of similar farmer-like groups that fought against the British in America. The English word for 'Boer' is 'farmer.'

The concentration camps for civilians were ill equipped, disease ridden, and consequently 28,000 perished, the majority of who were children under the age of sixteen. At that time, my great-grandmother and her youngest daughter were, unfortunately, among those defenseless women who were incarcerated after the brave British soldiers had destroyed their two farms, crops, and livestock. Both my great-grandmother and her youngest daughter perished in one of those dreadful camps.

The tragic loss of civilian life in those camps forced the Boers to negotiate peace with the British in 1902.

On analyzing the Boer War (Anglo-Boer War) of 1899-1902, some interesting and tragic numbers are revealed. The British deployed 450,000 enlisted men of which 22,000 were killed. The Boers, on the other hand, deployed 88,000 men. All were 'unpaid' volunteers!

The Boers lost 7,000 men…however, when noting that 28,000, mainly women and children died in British concentration camps including my great-grandmother and her youngest daughter, Boer losses actually totaled 35,000! It must be mentioned that the British also erected sixty-six concentration camps for the Africans who were Boer sympathizers. The records reveal that 14,000 Africans perished in those camps.

The surviving Boers never forgave the British for their civilian losses…including my mother's family!

Besides being the first war to utilize concentration camps to incarcerate noncombatants, the Boer War led in other fields. It was the first war of the twentieth century where camouflage was introduced. Boers cleverly camouflaged trenches and 'themselves' to blend in with the landscapes.

For the first time, machine guns, automatic handguns, and magazine fed rifles were introduced.

During that conflict, the world's first propaganda films and news footage were produced.

There is a good reason why the Boer War is referred to as the Anglo-Boer War. For the first time, Canadian troops were dispatched overseas. Australia sent 20,000 men and New Zealand deployed more than 6,000 men and 8,000 horses. I often wonder how the New Zealanders felt about the horrific death rate of the British horses. The average life expectancy of those poor British horses was six weeks from their arrival in South Africa. It is recorded that over 300,000 horses were killed in battle. And, to make matters worse, the British soldiers resorted to slaughtering 'many' a horse for meat when their supplies were cut off by those 'pesky' camouflaged Boers.

For the record, the Irish were sympathetic with the Boers. In the late 1899s, 20,000 Irish citizens attended a rally in Dublin in support of the Boer cause. "UP THE IRISH!"

Details of the Boer War would not be complete without the reference to two of the world's greatest men who served in this shocking conflict. Winston Churchill, a twenty-something London journalist acted as a courier between Spioenkop and the British HQ for General Buller. Mahatma Gandhi was a stretcher-bearer for the British in that battle for Spioenkop. Both Churchill and Gandhi were fortunate to survive that encounter with the Boers who savaged General Buller's troops, killing 242 and wounding or capturing 1,250 men.

The world can be thankful that these two men survived the conflict. A scary thought. This is what Sir Winston Churchill wrote of the Boer soldiers:

"The individual Boer, mounted, in a suitable country, is worth four or five regular soldiers. The only way of treating them is to either get men of equal character and intelligence as riflemen, or failing that, huge masses of troops."

South African troops have always stepped up to the plate having served with valor in both World Wars, Korea, and the Terrorist war in South Africa.

Harry and Ella – My Soon-to-Be Redneck Parents

Having related the fact that my father, Harry, the English-speaking offspring of a British military officer who fought against the Boers and my mother, Ella, who was a direct descendant of the Afrikaans-speaking Voortrekkers who despised the English for their civilian losses in the concentration camps, one may well enquire, How on earth did they become man and wife? A good question…in fact, a very good question. It's a long story, but to cut to the chase…

At that time, at age twenty, Harry had qualified as a butcher and had been transplanted to manage a remote trading store in Zululand for a Swedish business friend of his father. The word 'remote' is an understatement! Extreme 'boondocks' is more appropriate. The clientele were all male, almost exclusively Zulu, except for the occasional white trader or farmer. The bottom line…Harry was very lonely!

On Saturdays when the store closed at noon, Harry took off on his Harley to ride far and wide to take in the scenery. On one such trip, he came across an Afrikaans family in a field picking cotton in the scorching sun. The family consisted of a father, three sons, and a tall skinny daughter wearing a long cotton dress with long sleeves and a wide-brimmed hat securely tied with a green ribbon…no shoes. She was no Esther Williams, but she was female. Harry stopped and propped his bike against a tree, sucked in his stomach and walked over to greet the group. Luckily for Harry, the father who was from Scottish stock spoke perfect English, despite the fact that he had adopted Afrikaans as his daily language when he married an Afrikaans woman 'before' the outbreak of the Boer War.

Despite the differences in their backgrounds, the family welcomed Harry and offered him some water as they took a break under the shade of a grove of trees. The three young boys exchanged conversation with him, asking him questions about the 'outside world.' Except for the eldest lad, the other two boys spoke broken-English relatively well. The daughter said nothing! That would change. The following Saturday, Harry was picking cotton! And several weeks later, he was walking the skinny woman home and met her mother!

The girl's mother normally never spoke English, but made an exception this time when she realized that Harry was of English extraction. Lashing out in a strong accent, she informed Harry that he was not welcome. "In fact, no 'Engalsman' was welcome in my home," she added.

This was the beginning of a clandestine courtship between Harry and Ella. That is, until my brother Douglas Walter George was conceived and all hell broke out. The couple eloped and started married life in the huge port city of Durban, where Harry returned to the butcher's block…in more ways than one!

A few years later, my brother Vivian William John was born, after which the family moved to Port Shepstone on the South Coast where I was born on May 24, 1937. Because that was Queen Victoria's birthday, it was declared a public holiday (Victoria Day). Consequently, I never attended school on my birthday. "Yep, me and Queen Victoria were tight."

Well, having dispensed with the subject of my heritage, I will now move on with the rest of the saga relating to the background of the average colonial lifestyle from which the majority of South African redneck immigrants emanate.

Who Are South Africans?

The history of South Africa and its present day mixture of races and cultures is most intriguing, but far too complex to be adequately covered in this book. It was never my intention to cover this vast subject; however, at the end of the book, I have included a few pages titled, "South African History Lesson" for those who are interested in my 'personal' understanding of the subject.

Very briefly:

Prior to the arrival of ninety white Dutch sailors who set up a permanent 'post' at the tip of the continent in 1652, all the inhabitants, in broad terms, were African consisting of many tribes. Not unlike the early settlement of white people in America, which at that time was inhabited by Indian tribes.

Why did the Dutch set up a post at the southern tip of the African Continent?

Answer: To provide their mariners with fresh vegetables, water, and meat to sustain them during their voyages between Holland and East India known as the "Spice Route." This post was established by a ship's surgeon Jan Van Riebeck for the Dutch East India Company.

To understand Colonial South African life, one must first take an 'in-depth look' at their roots, starting with the African continent.

This enormous land mass is comprised of many different countries, embracing vastly contrasting cultures within cultures, which include diverse religious beliefs and tribal customs. It is also a fact that although many religions and faiths are practiced, millions of its inhabitants had never heard 'the Word,' or any word at all. But, Africa has many faces and I intend introducing you to an Africa that is unlike anything 'generally' perceived by the majority of first world cultures.

What follows is intended to introduce the reader to the 'White Tribe' of South Africa... Caucasian people who migrated to South Africa. These people were drawn primarily from Europe and Britain, however, other people from many parts of the globe followed in similar fashion to the early American immigrants.

The history of the white peoples of Africa and, more specifically, of South Africa is fascinating and intriguing. It is, however, not possible for me to adequately cover this enormous subject in this book. Since these people are the central characters, it is imperative that I briefly cover their history for the reader.

South Africa has one of the most complex and diversified population mixes in the world, a rich mosaic of distinctive minorities, but without any 'cultural common denominator.' This is underscored by the fact that not one of the eleven official languages is spoken by the majority of all their people. South Africa is a microcosm of the whole world. Its peoples reflect both the ethnic diversity and the disparities in social and economic development of the globe. It can be said, therefore, that no other country mirrors the ethnic and development profile of the world so nearly reflected in South Africa. Unfortunately, due to this most complex and disparate population mix, this largely misunderstood society has no common "South African" identity with universally accepted cultural and political norms.

South African Rednecks 101

It is in this setting that I now move on with the lighter side of colonial life in South Africa. My earliest memories are from the final years of WW II (1939-1945) in Port Shepstone.

During July each year, the Indian Ocean beaches of this coastal town were prime locations for the 'sardine run.' Millions and I mean 'millions' of sardines, a small silver fish about seven inches long, moved in massive shoals along the coastline heading north up the east coast. Many times during this unusual phenomena, surges of sardines were washed ashore by the powerful waves that are so common on this part of the coast. When this phenomenon took place…school was out…not officially, but when the school principal and staff heard from the fishing grapevine that the call had gone out, "Sardines!"…Nobody even remotely considered going to school. In those wonderful years, experiencing the sardine run was more educational than arithmetic…and I mean 'more educational.' Where else could one see grown men and women rushing into the broiling surf with every imaginable container, scooping up slivering silver shining fish, and then running back and forth depositing these slippery critters onto their marked out territory on the beach.

It never failed to amaze me how orderly and civilized the crowds were as they worked feverishly to capture as many fish as possible. Families, in particular, worked a system where small children were in charge of their personal 'staked' area on the beach and their main task was to throw sand on the flipping and contorting little fish to prevent them from bouncing away. These were sights that would have to be seen, to be believed. Men and women of all shapes and sizes rushing waist-deep into the surf to haul in their catches, many bowled over by waves and usually retrieved by helping hands amid raucous laughter and friendly banter. I have seen men scooping sardine into their shirts and even women using their skirts to trap these fish and pull their slivering living loads of small fish onto their bosoms. Close your eyes and picture these scenes… 'real live education' for us schoolchildren.

I have this image of Mrs. Honeywell, Coop's teacher, running into the surf fully dressed, shoes and all, and scooping up a load of fish in her summer skirt and then rushing back up the beach to deposit her catch on the sand. Then she used her feet to kick up sand over the fish before heading back to the foray. Her pink shoes matched her pink underwear…but not her bra…that reminded me of a small 'musical' hammock…all swing and some bounce…. No kidding.

Sardine Fever

There was also some danger in this otherwise intriguing annual beach ritual. The sardine shoals attracted thousands of game fish, which followed them in a feeding frenzy…fish such as barracuda that were known to chomp off a leg muscle from swimmers and fishermen alike. A more sinister threat was, however, the presence of shark!

Now, here is a tale that I can relate and which was witnessed by many sardine catchers. My father, dressed in cut-off khaki military pants secured by a red bath robe cord and a gaff fitted with a short coil of light rope conveniently clipped to his side, was waist-deep in the surf helping to pull in a net full of fish onto the beach for his butcher business…when what he termed as 'a half-drowned shark' appeared nearby. He, not so calmly whipped off his hand-gaff, which he stupidly plunged into the shark. To everybody's surprise and our relief, there was no reaction from the shark. It had apparently 'drowned' after overfeeding on all the fish it had devoured. Now to clarify this statement…I have no idea if a shark can actually drown. Can a human drown from too much fresh air? All I know is that is what the press release stated the next day with a picture of my father with the dead shark lying on a counter in his butcher shop. A fair size shark about six foot long, when my father cut its stomach hundreds of fish, almost all sardines, poured out. All good for his business, which, after all, was called the Fresh Fish and Meat Company.

That Friday night, all the usual Friday night patrons at the Bedford Inn bar raised their glasses to toast Harry for his 'heroics,' which my mother referred to it as 'dumb' gaffing of a 'big' shark in the surf. The more they drank, the bigger the shark became…some even believed it was a great white. In all honesty, I have no way of knowing what species it was…but one thing I *do* know is that it was 'dead' when he gaffed it, otherwise Ella would have been looking for another husband. I wonder if that news report and picture still exists.

Speaking of 'The Bedford Inn,' although Port Shepstone had only one funeral home, it could boast of two major drinking holes…the Bedford Inn, as just mentioned, and their rival 'The Port Shepstone Hotel' bar affectionately referred to as the 'Sheppy.' It was the custom of working class men to congregate in bars on Friday nights and pour beer down while shooting the breeze, playing snooker, darts, cards, or 'push half penny.' All normal thinking wives hated this custom and many a beer-filled husband arriving home late for supper was treated to a menu of 'hot tongue and cold shoulder.' This worked well with young married men, especially those recently married…but for the battle-hardened, 'long in the tooth,' misunderstood, married men it was like water on a duck's back. They consoled themselves by accusing their womenfolk of jealousy, but never ever in public, and only in the hallowed confines of the 'men only' bars among their simple-minded compatriots.

Harry's Shark

My mother, Ella, warned that one day the bars would be opened to both men and women. When asked whether she would ever consider entering a bar she replied, "I will go in that hell-hole and drag Harry out by his ear!" Ella, like her mother…not her father…never drank and hated all things alcoholic. Fortunately for Harry, it took many years before 'enlightened' politicians altered the law to allow women in bars…and by then Harry, like most other men, lost the desire to drink in mixed company. After all is said and done, what red-blooded man would enjoy drinking in an establishment that had dress codes and codes of conduct, such as no more rough language. Men had to wear a shirt at all times. Now, not only did they insist on shoes, but also socks! "Men's drinking habits and pleasure will never be the same," Harry lamented. Never a truer word of wisdom was uttered.

Well, to Harry's drinking pals, he was considered somewhat of a wise man. Real men who had for years knocked down pint for pint with Harry, like 'Shorty' Thornton who stood at six foot eight and 'Curly' Gigson, who never had a hair on his head…also no eyebrows. They all attested to Harry's prowess as a hunter with a keen eye for the kill. They figured that any man who poached alone without being caught had to be smart. That was before Harry was finally charged with poaching…an interesting story for later…maybe.

Before leaving the Bedford Inn bar, there is one additional story that needs to be told. As previously mentioned, there was considerable rivalry between 'Harry's Bedford boys' and 'Clem Turton's Sheppy boys,' like who could hold his breath the longest immediately after downing a cold pint. This is how it 'went down.' A contestant, being carefully timed by three judges, would grab a bottle of cold beer already opened by Flash Henry, the barman, and pour it down his throat as quickly as he could swallow. Then to prove that the bottle had been drained, it would then be turned upside down by the contestant on his head and held there for ten seconds, called by the judges, to convince the audience…all bar flies in various stages of inebriation…that the beer had, in fact, been correctly consumed according to the written rules. All the while, the contestants were being closely observed by three judges from the opposition bar who, for the purposes of fair play, were invited to adjudicate after each had been provided free beer. The free beer was never considered a bribe…merely 'good manners.'

On with the contest. After the judges called this first part of the contest fair,' the shout would go out by the chief judge…then the contestants 'sank a pint,' took a deep breath and held it. Fortunately for Harry's boys, old 'Barnacle Bently' was on the team on Friday nights. He not only set a new record of one minute seventeen seconds, but he also accomplished this historic feat without throwing up. What a man! This record stood for years…until women were admitted. You may think that the admission of women in bars caused the demise of this wonderful manly contest…forget it. Sylvia Morton not only broke the record by twenty seconds…she *also* did not throw up, but she did spend most of the remaining evening in the 'men's room'…. That's not an error…just because women were allowed into previously 'men only' bars, not everything changed immediately. Somebody forgot to add a women's facilities, but not for long. However, until this situation was rectified, the 'good old boys' did the gentlemanly thing...they left the room when nature's call could no longer be ignored, despite the mixed company, and relieved themselves against that mighty old oak tree out of view behind the kitchen.

Not sure if it can be confirmed today...but the story goes that the following spring that old oak tree that had not produced much of a crop over the previous ten years...suddenly found new life and produced the heaviest and healthiest crop of extra large acorns ever seen. Everybody attested to that fact by the constant gun-shot-like sounds that interrupted drinking as those acorns, as hard as stone, bounced off the corrugated iron roof. Goes to confirm what my grandfather used to say, "Best thing for watering fruit trees...liquid hops filtered through the human system." They may not have been his exact words, but remember that he was a police sergeant...and policemen were smart...right?

Back to those 'men only' bathrooms...within a week of the new dispensation allowing women into the Bedford, a woman's committee was formed (What else?). They arranged a delegation (What else?) to confront Sir Arthur Moneypenny, the well-spoken middle-aged proprietor of the Bedford Inn. This 'good old chap' was, in fact, an ex-remittance man, 'financially assisted' out of England by his parents who feared for their reputation, which thus far had been severely tarnished by their wayward son, Arthur the third.

The delegation from the newly-formed 'Bedford Ladies Society' was headed by the rotund Ms. Glynnis Natrass, a freshly divorced, forty-something nicknamed, 'mattress' (no pun intended) by her second husband who ran off with a man. That says something for 'Women's Lib.' As could be expected from an Englishman and a gentleman, he entertained the ladies in the 'good old English' tradition by serving tea in the very best China and cream scones from a silver platter on an ornate silver tray. Dainty sugar lumps were also part of this typical 'high-brow' English custom, enhanced by the fact that the tea tray was delivered with much aplomb by the senior dining room waiter, Saleem, who was resplendent in English/Indian uniform complete with red sash and colonial Indian turban. Sir Arthur personally took care of pouring the 'afternoon tea' into those delicate cups after first carefully removing the teapot from under the tea cozy (warmer). He also served the scones, cream, and strawberry jam. It was rumored that after the meeting when three of the four ladies left at the conclusion of a most successful and productive meeting, Ms. Natress remained in the company of Sir Arthur to personally thank him for agreeing to have a ladies bathroom added to the bar facilities. She did an excellent job because the very next day, workmen started the project, prompting some bright spark to remark, "Ms. Natress must have laid down the law for Sir Arthur." After all, before you could say, 'pick your nose,' he provided soft bar stools, ashtrays, and frilly drapes...yes, that 'Ms. Mattress' sure was convincing.

It was no wonder the real men switched to drinking at home, not only because of the intrusion of women, but the thought of drinking a beer on a padded bar stool, while sitting next to a male wearing deodorant, was simply the end of the world…not to mention that the barman Flash now wore a white long sleeve shirt, black bow tie, and a black vest and was clean shaven like those darlings who worked the bars in France.

However, the worst was yet to come…in the form of 'barmaids!' The sky was falling except for that deodorant doused, clean fingernail crew who now drank martinis at sundown, while discussing new drapes with the ladies sitting on those soft barstools. This new breed of dandies had no idea what went on in the real world. Happy Harper said it right. "Somebody had told Ginger McClean, who in turn had told Flash, who had whispered it to Harry that the first time the ladies inspected the 'men's' bathroom they were most intrigued with the tall upright men's urinal." It was said that Mrs. Cotton shocked them all by stating that she would only use the urinal if nobody else were present. Nobody would have passed this information to the new 'sundowner' set. This was real men's stuff and never to be shared with anyone except the old crew; however, it did reach the Sheppy boys who were having their own problems with the women encroaching on their waterhole. Finally the Bedford boys and the Sheppy guys had a common cause. But little did they understand the strength of 'Women's Liberation.' Something that they underestimated at their peril

At this juncture, I simply can't leave the good old Bedford Inn without relating an incident concerning my mother's unexpected visit there one sunny afternoon. A visit, although at first seemingly incredulous…the fact that my mother, Ella, did pay that establishment of degradation a visit…but not by walking through those bat-wing doors that had since been repainted plum to match the new drapes. No, sir…she drove in! Allow me to 'splain. This episode had its beginnings a few months prior to this incident.

During the war, Ella decided to learn to drive. Some of her friends had the same notion…so it was 'on.' Harry's old Hudson, his pride and joy, was always carefully parked in a garage that he had personally constructed from old corrugated iron sheeting painted silver for aesthetics in his otherwise dreary neighborhood. Attached to the outside front wall was a fair sized 'fowl run' (a chicken coop fenced in with chicken netting).

On Sunday afternoons, as was his custom, Harry would take a nap. Ella decided to wash the Hudson. That was her story…and she stuck to it! She somehow drove the car out of the garage…not sure how. After washing the car…she really did…she jumped in, cranked that mighty straight six, and drove Harry's pride and joy into the garage, through the corrugated iron wall, and into the fowl run. Harry was not impressed, nor were the chickens…but at least many experienced freedom for the first time, and we had scrambled eggs for supper that night.

As the Hudson was fitted with an extremely solid front bumper, the car suffered almost no damage, but those two military headlamps fitted to the bumper were once again history. Harry had some 'splainin' to do to the Home Guard. So, now on with the Bedford Inn and Ella's visit.

Once Harry realized that Ella was determined to learn to drive, he arranged for his friend Johnnie Johnstone, an experienced driving instructor, to take on the awesome responsibility of teaching 'the little woman' to drive. I must remind one and all of the fact that Harry was a very large man who of necessity when loading himself into the car, had to position the heavy front bench seat of the Hudson in the fully extended position...so far back, in fact, that any passenger sitting directly behind him would have restricted foot room, hence my small feet. That is why my two older brothers always made me sit behind my father when we were allowed to take a ride with him, a rare pleasure curtailed by the wartime gasoline rationing.

The first time that Ella, the tall skinny 'little woman,' slipped in behind the wheel of the Hudson, her feet could not reach the driving pedals because Harry's driving position necessitated the front bench seat be set back as far as possible. From day one of Ella's driving lessons, the first order of the day was for old Johnnie Johnstone to reposition the driver's seat in a much more forward position, so that his student's feet could comfortably reach the three pedals necessary to control the stick-shift cars of those days. He achieved this by deploying the robust metal handle at the side of the seat just above the floor on the driver's side. Once the handle was pulled, the seat shot forward propelled by the return spring that had been compressed when the seat had been originally set back to accommodate Harry's large frame.

Initially, Ella's driving lessons went well until lesson number six...Ella's lucky number. The lesson was well into its final stages and, as the sun was setting, Ella with a now less nervous instructor suggested she take the next turn at the intersection where the Bedford Inn stood like a lighthouse to the throat of the parched men folk of the town. She gritted her teeth as she swung the heavy Hudson left to swing past the 'hell-hole' (remember?) situated on the corner of Bedford Road...and then fate took a nasty turn...or...I should rephrase that...the Hudson did *not* completely make the turn.

Apparently, the seat catch had not fully engaged when the seat was moved to the forward position to accommodate Ella. As the car moved into the sharp turn, the seat latch released and the strong return spring snapped the seat back. Ella was propelled backward and, in an effort to correct the problem, she did two things...both wrong! To avoid moving too far back from her driving position she grabbed at the steering wheel and, in so doing, she inadvertently turned the car off the road towards...you guessed it...the Bedford Inn Bar! The second thing she did was to hit the brake...so she thought...instead she stomped on the accelerator (gas pedal). As old Johnnie later told the news reporter in those days before seat belts, "The sudden turn combined with the surge of power threw me off balance, so that I was unable to take control of the vehicle as I would normally have done...but this was no normal situation." This was a quote that the press, bless their hearts, y'all published and which was responsible for my mother's only 'recorded' failure…and also responsible for the endless ribbing that her husband would endure for years to come.

When that Hudson hit the sidewalk curb, the momentum lifted the front wheels off the ground and when the rear wheels caught the curbing the power kicked in; remember that Ella had floored the gas pedal, launching the vehicle, 'like a big black monster with its mouth open' (referring to the wide chrome grill that was so prominent on the Hudson of that era).

This is how Chetty, the Indian chef, described the event. He was working at the kitchen sink that was situated in front of the window directly in the Hudson's path. He had run for his life when the big black Hudson flew across the sidewalk and slammed into the kitchen wall immediately below the large window. As the sedan tore into the wall, it caught the bottom of the window, causing the wooden window's frame and glass to explode into the kitchen. Did I mention that Chef Chetty…and a few others…had run for their lives? At that point, the car stalled with its nose protruding into the kitchen of the Bedford Inn.

Later jokes included the one that Ella had aimed for the bar, but missed the 'hellhole,' by providence.

For a few weeks while the Hudson was under repair and builders affected the necessary repairs to the kitchen wall at the Bedford Inn, Harry commandeered his work vehicle from George, the regular driver. This rusting 1936 Plymouth panel van was used daily to transport fresh fish for his butchery business. Sea air and salt from the fish was a recipe for rust that ate away at the Plymouth. Being cooped up in this vehicle during the prevailing summer heat (remember…no A/C those days) forced some changes to his domestic schedule and activities; e.g., those Friday nights after riding in his fishy Plymouth, he would have to bathe a second time before heading to the Bedford. Not just bathe, but he also used Ella's shampoo on his hair…twice! Did he use baby powder, too? He needed to be sure that he 'smelled good' before being given a ride by Leslie Wilson, his neighbor who operated a funeral home adjacent to our home.

Now Leslie was no ordinary undertaker…besides his normal business activities, he ran a Poker School the last Saturday of every month in the 'stock room' beside the showroom where a variety of caskets were on view for the bereaved. The Poker School had very strict rules, including 'men only' and other rules that were necessary to maintain a high standard…no kidding…this was according to the book. Although the location may have been 'viewed'…excuse the pun…as bizarre by some because there were usually a few customers languishing in those massive fridges, as well as in the fridges in the stock room, it was ideal for keeping out wives and female friends…and even the law, or so he thought. I shall not expand on that. I do not want to risk offending any of the descendants of a certain poker loving law enforcement officer who shall remain nameless, particularly in view of the fact that my cousin Jack married his daughter, Miss Felicity Stevens.

Oh…I forgot to mention that Leslie had an unusual sense of humor. He insisted on driving Harry over to the Bedford in his shining black Pontiac Hearse, the same one that he used when courting his future wife during those moonlit evenings parked on lover's lane in the cemetery. The Bedford boys cheered and raised glasses as Harry stepped out of the hearse and took his usual seat at the south end of the bar. That evening, after several beers, Kenny Hale leaned over and asked Harry in a whisper, "Are you wearing deodorant? You smell like baby powder." Harry bought him a few beers until Kenny lost his sense of smell. Beer can do that to some people…especially if they have more than seven pints.

Once the Hudson had been repaired, Harry proudly drove it to the Bedford that Friday evening. Unfortunately, the appearance of the Hudson brought out renewed teasing relating to Ella's accident. Finally, when Peter Peters made a second 'not too tasty' remark, Harry cut him short and all drinking paused. To a man, everybody knew when 'enough was enough'…and they also knew that it took a long time to rile their big butcher friend, but they also knew not to push him too far. Memories of his demolition of opponents in the boxing ring before retiring were still fresh in the minds of all real men. To make a 'big point,' Harry was about to relate a story that became a classic and was handed down through generations for posterity…and repeated in that facility for many years.

This is what Harry told Peters as all listened between gulps; nobody ordered and Speedy the barman took advantage of the lull to dry glasses:

"Peter, my friend, let me tell you a story. In 1888 in Texas, there was this young cowboy who wanted to be the best gunfighter in the West. He spent all his spare money buying bullets, so that he could practice drawing his pistol and shooting at targets he set along a fence. In time, he moved so fast and shot so accurately that he became expert. However, never satisfied, he felt the need to get expert advice to improve his draw, so he sought out someone who had a reputation for the fastest draw to ask his advice. He rode into Dry Gulch and walked over to the Silver Slipper Saloon, where he heard that the famous retired Marshal Henry Cooper spent time at sundown having a drink. He stood outside for a moment and looked through a window. He scanned the room and noted a well-dressed man playing the piano. The musician had a nice touch and the music was typical old western." Harry took a breath and continued with his tale.

"The young cowboy scanned the four corners of the room and noted Marshal Cooper sitting alone at a table on the far side of the room. He seemed to be pre-occupied with the pianist and his music. Our boy slipped through the swinging doors, removed his hat, and moved carefully over to where the marshal was sitting. He greeted the man, introduced himself, and received a pleasant smile and a friendly, 'Howdee, what's on your mind, young fella?' The young man was delighted and went to lengths to relate how fast and accurate he was with his six-shooter, and then explained that he was hoping the marshal would give him some tips to improve his speed and style."

By this time, the Bedford boys were desperately in need of another drink...but like the atmosphere in the Silver Salon, nobody stirred...except the piano player who kept the tempo irrespective of what might go down. Returning to Harry's story, Harry continued, "The young cowboy then asked Mr. Cooper directly, 'Would you mind sharing some tips with me?' The older man looked him over from 'boot to shoot' and nodding his head in agreement and told him to tilt his holster slightly to drop the six-shooter an inch. The boy made the adjustment and his tutor asked how it felt. Without a word the young man, anxious to impress everybody drew his pistol in a flash, fired one shot across the room, so accurately that he shot the cigar out the piano player's mouth. Everybody was in shock except the piano player who, while playing with one hand, slipped another cigar in his mouth and started chewing on it...never missing a note on the ivories.

"The boy told the marshal that his tip had increased the speed of his draw and enquired whether he had any further suggestions. The man looked him over carefully once more, and suggested that he tighten his gun belt a notch. The young man did as was suggested and then once again, without warning, he fired a second shot across the room and, as before, he shot the cigar out the musician's mouth. Once again, the cigar was replaced without missing a beat. Everybody in the place froze. Finally, the marshal gave the young man some advice without being asked. He told the young guy to go outside, take some axle grease from the axle of the wagon that was parked there, and smear the grease all over his shiny six-shooter before replacing it in his holster. The boy seemed reluctant and stood thinking about this latest tip from the experienced marshal.

"After some hesitation he asked, 'Will the axle grease improve my speed?'

"The older man replied, 'No, boy, but when Wyatt Earp over there stops playing the piano, he is going to shove your six-shooter where the sun don't shine...and you will want it to go in real easy.'"

As Harry concluded his story, the whole bar erupted in laughter and then someone asked Harry the point of the cowboy story.

"Simple," he said...then with a wry grin he turned to face Peter Peters as he spoke very pointedly, "Now the moral is that Wyatt Earp gave that boy two chances, but the third time he had had enough...now Peter, you have had your two chances. I don't play the piano, but more importantly, I have nothing with which to grease this pint bottle."

Harry had made his point! The subject was closed and would never be brought up again.

When Harry was leaving later that evening, Plotty Glover walked out with him and as Harry reached his car the man asked him, "Say, Harry, did Wyatt Earp really play the piano?" The real question is, Could Plotty have been a redneck?

In fairness to Harry, there was also a serious side to his life. As Deputy Mayor his duties included unveiling a stone monument to Dick King, who like 'Paul Revere' in American history in 1775 made an epic horseback ride for the sake of his countrymen. But, Paul Revere rode that night to warn, "The British are coming." In 1842, Dick King rode 600 miles in ten days from Durban to a British Garrison located in the Cape to get the British to send relief to oppose the Boers in Durban. Unlike the American situation where Paul Revere's efforts were a factor in the defeat of the English (British), Dick King's ride contributed to the defeat of the Boers by the British.

"Never in the field of human conflict," (with due respect to Sir Winston Churchill) "had one horse 'dung' so much for so many Brits." One horse, ridden 600 miles, including evading African warriors, wild animals, and crossing 100 (?) rivers according, to the history books. So, what was this horse? It was a bay without any long distance conditioning and stood fifteen hands. Its name was Somerset. Bless its heart, y'all. What if it had tripped! Or, ended up as a supper for the lions! One horsemeat meal could have altered the course of history! Without delving into the historic details, it would be remiss of me not to mention two very important facts regarding Harry's officially unveiling of the monument to Dick King:

Fact 1: Harry bought and wore a suit for the occasion; and
Fact 2: A guy named 'Dick,' (Dick for 'dork' in Boer talk) also later nicknamed 'numb ass' helped the British to defeat the Boers by riding a horse named Somerset for 600 miles and all he had to show for it was a stone marker in Port Shepstone! What about Somerset? No stone statue of him…not even a mention of its name. Just goes to show…you can ride a horse through water, but you can't make it a hero. You may want to think about that for a moment or three.

But, the really big question is, Can you name Paul Revere's horse? Welcome to a learning experience.

I have related two stories about men's bravery, but both were only made possible by the horses they rode. History reveals the names of those horses. As an animal lover and a descendent of true equestrians and equestriennes, I am unable to resist including the following true and documented account of the bravery of a rider and his horse that saved the lives of fourteen men in early South Africa.

Unlike the two previous mentioned horses, this is about 'a horse *with* a statue.'

This is the account recorded at the time…

In 1773, there was a particularly bad storm in Table Bay. There were five ships of the Dutch East India Company lying in the bay. None of the vessels should have been in the bay, instead, they should have sought anchorage at Simon's Bay, as this was considered to be a safer winter anchorage. It was the Company's ruling not to anchor in Table Bay after May 15, due to the unpredictable weather. For several days the ships had been ready to put to sea, but a northwesterly gale had been blowing hard and had prevented them from sailing. On May 31, 1773, the gale had reached its full height and each of the ships had dropped additional anchors in an effort to hold them steady. Soon the hawsers holding the anchors began to snap under the pressure of the storm. Worst placed of all the merchantmen was the *De Jonge Thomas*, carrying 207 men and captained by Barend Lameren. At five o'clock in the morning of June 1, 1773, she was straining at her last anchor. Rather than be caught unprepared and be driven ashore at the mercy of the storm, Lameren decided to beach the vessel whilst he could still choose the spot. Accordingly, the anchor rope was cut, and with the light sails set, the ship bore down on the beach. The captain had chosen the level stretch north of Salt River mouth to run ashore; unfortunately, he was unaware that the Salt River had burst its banks and was emptying into the sea near the spot he had chosen. Even more unfortunately, at the moment of impact, *De Jonge Thomas* swung broadside to the beach. In less than two minutes of pounding, the gigantic waves broke the ship's back and she parted in two at the mainmast, which crashed overboard.

This was the sight that met the eyes of Governor Van Plettenberg at dawn, when he scanned the bay anxiously. His first reaction, no doubt, was to breathe a prayer of thanks that the eighteen money chests, which the *De Jonge Thomas* was carrying from Holland, were still ashore in the castle for safekeeping. Then he sent thirty soldiers down to the beach. Normally this procedure was of little avail to the unfortunates wrecked out in the bay, but that day it was to save lives.

The first military step, as usual, was the erection of a gibbet on the beach to hang any trespassers. Then the soldiers commenced collecting salvaged goods, periodically casting a sorrowful glance out to sea, where pitiful cries could be heard from those survivors still clinging to the wreck.

Amongst the soldiers was Corporal Christiaan Woltemade; in the course of the day his father, Wolraad Woltemade, rode up on horseback, bringing him a bottle of wine and a loaf of bread. Wolraad Woltemade was no youngster. As a soldier, he had been stationed at Muizenberg as early as 1752, and by 1770, he was in command of that post. He must have retired after that, though there is some confusion as to his occupation in 1773. Thunberg says that he was the keeper of the menagerie (at the top of the Company's garden), whilst the *Dagregister* refers to him as a dairyman.

Filled with pity for the luckless sailors aboard the wreck, Woltemade mounted his horse, Fleur, and urged the animal into the sea, determined to save some of those in peril. Why he did not carry a line to the wreck is not clear, but the fact is that he rode into the sea without a rope. The horse was a fine swimmer and fought its way gamely through the surf. As they approached the wreck, Woltemade turned the horse and called for two men from the ship to jump into the sea and grasp the horse's tail. After a moment's hesitation, two men threw themselves into the water and did so, whereupon Woltemade urged the horse forward and dragged them to shore. Not satisfied with this feat, Woltemade returned immediately and rescued another two men. He repeated this again and again, until he had drawn fourteen men to safety. By this time, instead of hesitation there was competition amongst the sailors for the next place; as for the horse, it was staggering with exhaustion. Woltemade dismounted to rest the poor animal, whereupon a great cry of despair went up from the wreck. Despite the entreaties of his son, Woltemade mounted the horse again and rode back into the water. Realizing this was probably the last trip, the men onboard lost all restraint. As the laboring animal neared the ship, half a dozen men jumped into the water and grasped the horse; one stupid fool caught it by the bridle, dragging the horse's head under. It was all over in a moment…horse, rider, and sailors disappeared beneath the waves. No further attempt was made to rescue those aboard the wreck.

As night fell, they watched the beach empty as the soldiers returned to their barracks, and the officials to their warm firesides. Through the night, they clung to the wreck in sodden misery; gradually the weather cleared. On the morning of June 2, the sea was still rough, but Jan Jacobs, the junior mate, and twenty-four men waded ashore from the wreck. In all, forty-seven men had survived, of whom fourteen owed their lives to Woltemade. That day the shore was littered with bodies; amongst them were the captain, and Wolraad Woltemade.

The captain was given an official funeral, but there was nothing so grand for Woltemade. The general opinion at the castle seems to have been that he was an officious fool who had lost his life unnecessarily. In the first report to Holland, his name is not even mentioned…though considerable space is devoted to the eighteen boxes of money providentially saved. However, Karl Thunberg, who had witnessed the event, did not forget Woltemade, nor did the former countryman, Anders Sparrman, when he wrote his famous book, *A Voyage to the Cape of Good Hope* in 1775.

And so, the story of the incredible rescue spread. The company named one of its ships the *Held Woltemade*, and Woltemade had become a legend. Ironically, the ship *Held Woltemade*, surrendered ignominiously to the English in 1781, without firing a shot, and passed into history. Few people indeed, will be able to tell you the name of the *De Jonge Thomas*, compared with those who know Woltemade's name…yet, ironically, none knew the name of the real hero…the horse.

Woltemade's widow and sons living in Batavia were compensated. A statue of him was created in later years by the sculptor J. Mitford Barberton and erected in the grounds of the Old Mutual Assurance Society in Pinelands, which grew on the grazing fields of the dairy Woltemade had ostensibly managed. A railway station was named after him on the old dairy farm grounds and this serves the mourners coming to visit the Woltemade Cemetery. The highest South African decoration for bravery was also named after him, the Woltemade Medal.

This historic event was included in the educational curriculum and taught to every South African child at a young and impressionable age. Wolraad Woltemade's bravery was an example of how an ordinary man could 'step into the breach' for his fellow man. Just as relevant is the fact that without the horse named Fleur (on record), this rescue would not have been possible.

It is 'past' time that our children are taught who the real hero's were that shaped the destiny of this great republic to give them the comfortable lifestyle that they enjoy today in America. How is it that our children hero-worship someone who does fancy things with balls 'big or small' for huge financial rewards, yet are oblivious of the sacrifices made by the likes of Audie Murphy and thousands of others…oh, and their parents who have willingly sacrificed with love to give their children the security that they enjoy. Just last week, my son e-mailed me: "You are my hero."

The other day, a pilot made an emergency 'landing' of a passenger plane carrying a full load of passengers into a river without the loss of a single life! Ask your child to name him if you can get his/her attention away from some technological device. What's the bet that your offspring could tell you who did what in sports, movies, or entertainment in a heartbeat…and these youngsters will soon *vote*.

As a young boy, I recall how both of my grandfathers loved and cared for their horses. Both men had served their fellowmen, fighting for what they cherished, both mounted on horses that they trusted with their lives.

When I was nine years old, my 'Oupa Pringle' entrusted me to 'Kaptein' (Captain) his big Chestnut stallion after telling him, "*Op-pas vir my kind.*" In English, "Take care with my child." That mighty animal did exactly what he was told…he took care of 'Oupa's child.' As that proud animal took me around that farmyard, both man and horse experienced something that money can't buy.

This one is for you, 'Kaptein.'

The Bridge to Nowhere

Returning to Port Shepstone, Harry and the city council will be best remembered for what transpired during a fiery private council meeting when Harry had introduced a motion to consider replacing the antiquated bridge that fed traffic from the north across the Umzimkulu River and into the town. To understand the subject of the council meeting, it would be of interest to describe this 'old lady from the past.'

This bridge that was situated several miles north of the town was unique because it was designed to serve both automobile and railroad traffic on the same narrow one lane…not at the same time! A guard equipped with a red flag was posted at each end of the bridge and stopped all automobile traffic whenever a train approached. This bridge also had a narrow (about five foot wide) pedestrian section 'hanging' on one side of the upper structure for pedestrian traffic. However, pedestrian traffic was not permitted when a train crossed because the whole structure rattled, shook, moaned, and groaned as those massive locomotives and coaches moved slowly across the bridge.

At that time, my two older brothers were the two founding members of a juvenile secret society whose initiation into membership required that they sneak onto the pedestrian crossing just before a train approached and lay down while the train passed nearby. They tried unsuccessfully to recruit new members and, finally, it came down to which of the two only members would become 'The Supreme Secret Wizard of Umzimkulu.' My eldest brother Douglas claimed this high office by jumping off the bridge into the swiftly flowing river and, finally, emerging at the old boat house where a man operated a rowboat crossing about a hundred yards down river from the bridge. Two old-timers were sitting on the dock at the time and, when my brother emerged from the fast flowing river, the older of the two, older and wiser… remember, asked him whether he had swum across the river. He replied that he had jumped from the bridge and floated down to the boathouse. The younger of the two thought for a spell and said, with wisdom, "Lucky that the train was not crossing the bridge at the time…could have scared the daylights out of you."

Not to be outdone, several days later my other brother Bob, now the junior member of their secret society, jumped off the bridge with our dog Pincher in his arms as the Senior Secret Wizard of Umzimkulu looked on in shock. In this way he achieved two things:

First: He became the Vice Supreme Secret Wizard of Umzimkulu because he was the second-highest-ranking member.

Second: By 'persuading' Pincher to jump with him, he had increased the membership by one, even though Pincher was a dog. No ordinary dog…he could now claim the title of Secret Wizard, but nobody knew, because he was sworn to secrecy. Did I mention that Pincher made the shore in record time? Oh, and my brother Bob overshot the boathouse by some fifty yards. Those two old timers were not sitting on the dock this time, but Stokky the Zulu fisherman had to move his line to avoid snagging the biggest catch of his life.

For the record, several months later, the whole family including Pincher were on a hike, which included crossing the bridge and that crazy dog jumped off into the river below. My parents were horrified, but some time later he reappeared wet and excited to rejoin the hike. My mother exclaimed, "I don't want any of you boys or Pincher on this bridge again. What if one of you fell in trying to stop the dog from jumping off?" I never could figure why that dog jumped from the bridge. He was already a Secret Wizard. This was no ordinary family! Dare I say, "A redneck family?"

Back to the council meeting, Harry came home with a bruised cheek, the mayor sported a black eye, the treasurer had a cut lip, and a broken chair had to be replaced at the expense of the members. Many years later when revisiting the town with my wife, I had the pleasure of driving over a new bridge that brought automobile traffic directly into the town over the mouth of the impressive Umzimkulu River, a concrete monster without any charm or character…it's called modern. A darn shame…I was happy that the old girl up the river could not see her replacement…would have broken her heart.

However, I can never erase the memory of that return visit to Port Shepstone, accompanied by my wife. We entered the town crossing the new concrete bridge spanning the mighty Umzimkulu River mouth as its powerful rush slammed into the Indian Ocean, but the huge brown stain of the river's water was not to be repelled by the sea. It held back the blue of the sea for miles, as the brown blended more and more into the distance until finally fading into obscurity. It was just as I remembered as a boy…and as I write, I still have that glorious image imprinted in my memory. On entering the town that day, I headed the car along the familiar narrow river road leading to the old wooden bridge that I loved, as only the young at heart can understand. We drove in silence. My wife, ever conscious of my nervous and expectant demeanor, graciously allowed me my private space as we drove.

Then, as we were rounding the final bend in the road, the old lady slowly revealed herself. There she stood in all her glory. Maybe not as glamorous as in bygone years, as time had not been kind to her…but in my eyes, she was beautiful. Love at first sight all over again. After the initial euphoria, other more sinister and crude adornments caught my attention. The entrance of the bridge had been crudely cordoned off with heavy wire. Signs proclaimed the fact that trespassers would be prosecuted and that the condition of the bridge made it dangerous to cross. I smiled to myself and thought, *too dangerous, my eye*! Then my wife's voice brought me back to reality. She remarked, "That bridge must be over fifty-feet high. Did anybody ever fall off it?"

I sucked in a breath and answered, carefully choosing the words, "Nobody ever 'fell' off it. Who could be that stupid?" I was not about to mention anything about a crazy dog jumping off. Not even a redneck would get into that.

With that…it is time to bid farewell to Port Shepstone.

TIME OUT!

We are taking a break. Why? Well, if the Panthers and other NFL teams can take a time out, so can we. Ever wonder what they discuss during those annoying breaks in play? During one of these breaks at a NC State home game the great Charles S. explained, "I can go to my left or right, I am amphibious."

Sometimes an athlete who is not under any pressure will do even better during a press conference. A Chicago outfielder, on being interviewed as a role model, offered this WOW. "I wan' all dem kids to do what I do, to look up to me. I wan' all the kids to copulate me."

And, not to be biased, this WOW from the NASCAR pits articulated a driver who had just won a race, "It was a blast! You know. I want to like thank Coke, Butterball, Toys 'R' Us, and all the others like *The Charlotte Observer*. Like, I had a blast out there. You know…like I was having so much fun. You know. I'm sorry that I wrecked the number 666…like I like him. You know…but he should have given me like more room at that point in time, you know. I want to thank all the guys in the shop. Like, you know, like the engine guys, chassis guys, the pit crew, my crew chief, Durango Martindale…like, all the guys who at this point in time have made this, you know, win possible. I must also thank my main sponsor, Viagra, because like, you know, that without their help, I would not be here today."

Aaaand, what about this medical warning?

"The makers of Viagra warn that guys having eyesight problems while taking their product should see a doctor if there is no improvement after four hour. Did I mix up the problem with some other side effect?"

It must be very hard for a driver to concentrate while dealing with that four-hour problem while driving a six hundred-mile race. No wonder there are so many accidents. Also makes one think about why many drivers decline interviews after climbing out their cars and rush straight to their comfortable RVs after a race.

END TIME OUT…for now.

Country Rednecks Meet City Rednecks, or Vice Versa

Shortly after celebrating VE Day (Victory in Europe) after my seventh birthday in 1944, my family, motivated by my mother, moved to Pietermaritzburg. Now there's a mouthful! And in the interest of saving ink, that name will be shortened to 'PMB.'

Harry sold his business, sold the house, most of the furniture, resigned as Deputy Mayor, bid farewell to the Bedford gang (What a party!), and even paid his last respects to the Sheppy boys (What a party!). The Sheppy boys had mixed feelings about Harry's departure. Who were they going to blame for all the 'men things' that the wives had been told were instigated by Harry? It was a real dilemma, not only for the Sheppy boys, but also for most the Bedford gang.

The whole family…Harry, Ella, my brothers Douglas and Bobby, and our dog Pincher…traveled in the old Hudson with the A/C on full (all four windows rolled down) to combat the searing December heat and arrived in PMB just before Christmas 1944. We moved into an old dilapidated house on the wrong side of the 'wrong side' of town…first mistake!

In this typically colonial city, the educational center of the province, our arrival caused many an eyebrow to be raised. There were many factors that contributed to this…I'll 'splain. Word around town spoke of the fact that someone from 'out of town' with an Afrikaans wife and a brood of kamikaze kids had slipped into town and purchased the very popular Anne's Confectionary without anybody realizing that it was for sale. They were not the only ones surprised! We three young boys grew up thinking our father was a butcher, and now he was a baker? What was next, a candlestick maker? This was my father's style. Many a surprise would follow in years to come.

Something else very troubling surfaced soon afterward. Some of the fine folk of that city spread the word underground that they suspected that Harry was connected to the 'out of town' community who were fast becoming central players in all facets of the business community. What was that all about? One must take into consideration the fact that PMB was considered, 'the last outpost of the British Empire"…meaning, for one thing that none of us had a hope of ever becoming a member of the aristocratic 'men only' Victoria Club, where the black ball had, and always would, ensure that only the descendants of true Colonials would walk through those hallowed doors. We had news for them!

Harry was a very practical man in every sense of the word. He was very decisive and had no patience with time wasted. For example, he worked out the quickest, least expensive, and most convenient way to acclimate the family and make us all familiar with this new very large city…his solution…he collected brochures of the city, which covered all aspects, including local history. He then took the family to the local municipal bus depot, where he purchased inexpensive 'round trip' tickets that covered individual city routes from its origin back to the bus depot. Then, the interesting part, Harry had learnt that at the conclusion of each route, those same buses went on a different route every time that they returned to the bus terminal. Soooo, Harry had worked out that if we remained on the bus at the end of the first route, we could stay on the bus and take a different route and we did not have to purchase additional tickets. That Harry was one smart redneck! We' all rode that rattletrap all day! Did I mention that my mother prepared a lunch basket?

The bus took alternate routes, each ending at the depot from where it started. We all simply remained on the bus…in the rear seat that stretched across the full width of the vehicle and rode the additional routes at the tax payer's expense, until Harry was satisfied that we had covered most of the city…but not before his butt had fainted from the long ride. I must mention the fact that we were the most entertaining troupe ever encountered on a municipal bus. At every stop, people jumped on and off that old Leyland, and I swear that several of them duplicated their ride to stare at the strange family, which not only rode the bus all day, but also tucked into a picnic lunch on the ride between the city dump and the sewer plant. Someone even asked the bus driver whether the city had included a local tour guide after listening to Harry cover the various aspects of the areas that the bus traveled.

> WOW: DON'T LOOK A GIFT HORSE IN THE MOUTH. How bizarre is that? Speaking of horses, see QWB below.
> QWB: IF MEN ARE SMARTER THAN WOMEN, HOW COME WE DON'T RIDE 'SIDESADDLE?' Are they the same guys who listen to the *William Tell Overture* and think of the Lone Ranger?

Enough about horses, already!

Sleepy Hollow

We need to talk some about Pietermaritzburg. What is the origin of such an unusual city name?

To find the answer, we need to look at the history of its foundation and this is what history records going back to the 'Voortrekkers'...remember them? Well, it goes like this...Pietermaritzburg was founded late in 1838 by the Voortrekkers, who had migrated earlier from the Cape, and was named after Pieter Retief and Gert Maritz, its two Boer leaders. Remember them? They combined the Christian name of the first man with the surname of the second, and added 'burg' which is Afrikaans for 'city or town.' Good thinking when considering the first proposal of 'Pieterretiefgertmaritzburg.' Those old timers would have been in a quandary if the names of the two leaders were Ben Daniels and Steven Down. Or, how about Fuller Jones and Daniel Crabbs?

Returning to Pietermaritzburg...thankfully and much to the relief of the advertising industry, the name has been shortened to 'PMB' in an effort to save our precious environment. Look at it this way...by reducing the name to PMB colloquially, we effect great savings. We save black ink made from fluid containing water, a precious commodity, absolutely necessary to sustain life. We also save some of the viscous material mixed with the fluid, thus reducing mining operations and all those chemical procedures necessary, including thermal heat and cooling with water to finally produce the black ink.

But, a word of caution when making this case against the production of black ink, the members of the 'Brotherhood of Fairness to Reptiles and Spiders' (BOFTERS) are watching. They are always watching. They go back to the Roman times when black ink was called 'zool,' which was the black defensive secretion of the Cephalopod. And, how did those kindhearted ancient Romans 'extract' that secretion? You guessed it. Picture the scene...an ancient Roman scribe ready to write removes the Cephalopod from his aquarium, dries it off with a silk hanky delicately woven by slave labor in India, and then by applying pressure (squeezing) to the poor defenseless Cephalopod until the poor creature 'poops' (oops...secretes) its black fluid until it is on 'empty.' (There were no gauges in those times to alert the squeezer that its tank was empty.) For a refill, the scribe simply returned the exhausted and pooped out Cephalopod to the aquarium, carefully selected another suitably overweight Cephalopod, and repeated the squeezing process until…you guessed it…the next one ran dry. This was all good and well while there was an abundance of Cephalopods, but as civilization progressed or maybe regressed (depending on your personal point of view) there was an ever-increasing need for ink to satisfy man's desire to write…take, for instance, the works of Shakespeare. It would have taken most of the world's supply of Cephalopods to extract sufficient Zool to write those manuscripts. Imagine the foreword on the first page of Julius Caesar. "Many thanks to those poor Cephalopods in making these volumes possible." Or possibly, "The publishers and printers would like to take this opportunity to personally thank all those hardworking Cephalopods. Without your co-operation, these works would have been denied to the world"

I'm thinking, *some loss!* You mean not having to study *Romeo and Juliet* in high school would constitute a loss…not if they substituted *Little House on the Prairie*…or my previous book, which shall remain nameless lest I am accused of trying to promote it? In all the above we, that is, I, almost forgot the serious side of PMB. After all, referring to the capital of a province (Limey equivalent of a state) as *Sleepy Hollow* needs to be seriously 'addressed'…love that word (addressed)…means everything except 'answer.'

Speaking of the use of certain unusual words out of context, or sayings, metaphors, or clichés by those who are of the opinion that by doing so, they will somehow sound smart…necessitates a separate chapter. One that may 'enlighten' us…remember that in the course of reading this book we will 'address' (closely examine) the 'origins' of many things, e.g., origins of the redneck, origins of sayings, origins of words, etc., etc.

Stay tuned, y'all.

Say What?

Returning to the word 'address'...as frequently used (misused) by politicians when confronted with a question, e.g., a member or the press core asking the question, "Sir, how are you going to pay for this new legislation?"

Answer: "We are going to 'address' that issue in committee," which in everyday language really means, "We will tax the crap out of y'all!" You may be a redneck if you don't understand that!

Another example...in answer to the question, "Sir, why are you using tax money to fund a student environmental study group, which is conducting a survey on how humpback whales can reproduce in frigid water temperatures?"

Answer: "The results will help us understand why humans can't do it while taking a cold shower." (JOKING!) If you don't think so, then you may be a redneck. After learning that elephants only do it when they are wet...those humpback whales must never stop to eat! So, what was the real answer provided? "We need this information to protect the humpback whales while they are 'doing their thing.' We must prevent whaling activities while this process is taking place." Whoa! Back up the wagon. Would that not be the most opportune and cost effective moment to kill two birds, uh fish, uh mammals, uh animals with one stone...uh harpoon? Now that would be some savings. Harpoons and their attached explosive charge come at a high cost.

Another thought...can you imagine the size of the smile on the dead male whale when they drag his ass on deck? But wait, because I have not included the rest of the answer, which went like this, "The more we encourage the reproduction of whales, the more whale fat the Japanese will have to produce those age reducing facial creams that women use to make them look younger." Yeah, right...like that works! Ever look around Congress. Good luck with that. Forgive me...I am digressing...because the statement went further by saying, "Don't be so critical. You can't have your cake and eat it." Wow! Does anybody really know what that means? But then follows those most famous of words of wisdom that are supposed to shut your pie trap. "You must ask yourself the question," here it comes, "Is your cup half full or half empty?" Now, I could once more go into a long discussion to understand the true meaning of this wise statement, but one sentence should set the record straight. Here it is, "It all depends on what is in the cup. If it's honey, that's good and well…but if it's sewage…say what?"

Which leads to the next smartest saying, which was a favorite before the aforementioned became the hot one, "My boy," as my wise daddy was commenting when he heard that I was going to immigrate to America, "the grass is not always greener on the other side of the fence." Was he right? Sometimes when you step over that fence onto that lovely soft green plush grass…you discover that you are standing on a septic tank! Well, I told my daddy that it is better than standing on quicksand! How the heck could someone standing in quicksand jump a fence? Think about it. If you can't work that out, you may not be a redneck.

Comment: Did you pick up the connection to these two quotes? As I wrote earlier…it will challenge your intellect…and make you smarter.

I must concede that not all quotations are misleading, especially when espoused by none other than Confucius. A particular one comes to mind now that we have dispensed with the previous two. How about this 'irrefutable' (big word like marmalade) wisdom…Confucius say, "Man and woman lying on lovely soft green plush grass, have piece on Earth."

What about this? "The higher you climb, the harder the fall." There are several problems with this statement; first, it presupposes that you will fall, and second, it may be that you land on something very soft like a patch of soft, green, plush grass. Better still…wear a parachute.

Most quotations are used by the 'so-called' informed 'smart folk' to inform the less informed in a manner that makes the less informed seem more informed. If you understand that, you may have a redneck relative. However, there are times when straight honest advice is more relevant than quotations. There are times when we all appreciate sound advice, and this often involves sports advice, especially in the game of golf.

Allow me to give an example. During a break in the PGA practice sessions at Augusta, I was talking to some of the lads in the bar and decided to ask for some professional advice regarding my game. I turned to Arnie and asked, "What advice can you give me about my game?"

He caught his breath for a moment. (Old golfers do this a lot.) Speaking very slowly (Old golfers do this a lot, too.), he said kindly (Old golfers don't do this often.), "I've been out of the game too long, so why don't you ask Tiger?" Now that was good advice! So, I turned to ask Tiger, only to realize that he had overheard Arnie and was making a hasty retreat. Younger golfers do this a lot. Then when I swiveled back on my green upholstered bar stool, Arnie had vanished.

Sitting alone at the bar I realized that Pedro, the friendly undocumented immigrant barman, had been listening to our conversation. Listening is not the same as eavesdropping. He smiled at me and I smiled back, which normally means that I need a drink. However, before I could order, he came over, looked me straight in the eye, my good eye, and asked, "Would you mind if I gave you some advice?"

"Not in the least," I answered nervously, thinking that he was probably going to advise me to drink less or drink non-alcoholic beverages. But, without flinching, he offered this golfing advice, "You need to add loft to your back swing and release the blade through the ball." Can't beat that, so I thought, *Well, if that don't beat cockfighting!* I decided then and there to take up golf.

It is no coincidence that the golfing story appears at this juncture...no, sir. This gives us the opportunity to pause for a moment to reflect on what we have learnt at this 'point in time,' a brutally over-utilized saying that we will also 'address' at another 'point in time,' after having had our intellect increased at this 'point in time.' You must have now noticed, at this 'point in time,' that through the enlightenment gained at this 'point in time,' you would have developed a third sense, namely a sense of discernment.

To illustrate this newfound talent, we discover some interesting and hidden truths in the golfing story:

First: Old golfers never lie. They simply circumvent the truth when confronted by the 'less informed' where golfing is concerned. Less informed is a copout for 'idiots.'

Second: Never ask for advice in a bar. The barman is always listening...not, eavesdropping.

Third: Barmen know more about any subject than their patrons. That is because they are not allowed to drink while on duty. You must confess that we have learnt a lot at this 'point in time.' For example, I have personally used Pedro's golfing words of wisdom to help others in the golfing fraternity. After I gave my cousin Lonny this advice just before the NASCAR golfing charity tournament, he went on to tie for forty-second place with the blind driver, Johnnie Dark. The fact that there was not a full field of forty-three competitors had some bearing on the outcome...I think.

This chapter 'by and large' (another saying that could draw us into a 'splaination or three) concerns popular sayings that have spilt out from taverns and bars. Why is that? To be brutally honest, most truly memorable sayings originate in bars. While absorbing this new revelation, it must be pointed out that the tunes of many favorite hymns found in Christian hymnals today also had their origins in bars (British pubs), however, with vastly improved lyrics! Could it be that your hymnal includes any? Heaven forbid! Easy there, Gertrude! Just asking.

You may be forgiven if you are wondering what bars and bar scenes have to do with anything at this juncture, not 'point in time,' but in later chapters this subject may have to be revisited because the simple truth is that no redneck history is complete without including this subject. Remember that somebody had to 'see the light' to transpose those bar ditties to hymns. Sooo, stay tuned.

And, before we move on, let's take a look at another subject…

The Origins of Sayings…
or 'Say What' Once More

Have you ever considered or wondered how some of the most well known sayings originated? e.g., "Getting your own back."

Corky Pointpekker Vl told it this way. His great-great-grandfather Stopper Pointpekker Sr. had successfully climbed the second highest mountain in the world, Mt. Fiddlewood, adjacent to Mt. Everest in the Himalayas. He was the first American to reach the summit and he was so overcome with pride that he decided to record his first words as an historic saying to be shared with his family for posterity.

Unfortunately, he was in serious need of a pee, so before uttering his historic expression he stepped to the brink of the summit, undid himself, took careful aim, and fired his all across the divide to see if he could reach Mt. Everest. Unfortunately, Stopper was facing east, the very direction from which the mighty East Wind kicked up at times without any warning. This was such a time. It was then that his Sherpa guide exclaimed, "Pek-Kh-longlooo-puterringa wherr u squuurta notta gooda."

Which was interpreted as, "Getting your own back!"

I readily concede that this first attempt at 'splaining the origin of this first saying that I tackled is no great shakes, but in my defense, I did not think that the reader was yet fully prepared for the big one.

Now having eased into this theme, I feel more confident that y'all are ready for the big one…he really big one! The only saying that can be considered to be is 'out of this world' because it was first uttered in outer space.

What were those words spoken by Neil Armstrong when he became the first man to set foot on the lunar surface? History records that Neil Armstrong uttered these now famous words, "One small step for man. One giant leap for mankind." But, were they Neil Armstrong's first words on the moon?

"Yeah, right!" spluttered Jimmy Crankhouse, who was watching the moon landing on TV at the lodging house on 20 Oak Road, Sober City, Tennessee. We shall return to Jimmy later. HOLD THAT THOUGHT!

This is when the reader must 'muster' (you like that?) every alert brain cell from wherever they languish to assist in separating truth from hearsay. And, let's return to Neil Armstrong's first words spoken, not uttered, when he stepped onto the lunar surface, and bring in Jimmy Crankhouse, as mentioned above.

What was their connection? Well, it all has to do with the fact that Neil Armstrong and our boy Jimmy Crankhouse, years before the lunar landing, were both student roommates at the lodging house on 20 Oak Road, Sober City, Tennessee.

A very thin wall separated their living area from a neighbor's bedroom on the other side of the wall. That bedroom was occupied by a neat, middle-aged spinster named Marlene Finklestein, who had never dated a man. That is, not until one 'historic' (a lot of history coming up) Friday night when Stumpy Dillinger came over to court her with a bottle of wine in hand. While her next door neighbors Jimmy and Neil listened, not to be confused with eavesdropping, with their ears glued to the woman's bedroom wall, they heard Ms. Finkelstein ask Stumpy, "You want me to do 'what' with what?" Then after a moment of silence, they heard her exclaim loudly hurting their eardrums, "A man will walk on the moon before you get me to do that!"

What did old Stumpy want her to do? She was obviously referring to Stumpy wanting her to do something that she had never considered before. Indulge in wine. Right?

Anyway, to cut to the chase, what follows were the first words spoken by Neil Armstrong under his breath when he stepped on the lunar surface, "Go for it, Ms. Finklestein!" (No kidding!) So much for all that stuff about, "One small step, etc., etc."

Unfortunately for Neil, everything said was recorded by mission control; but, fortunately, they had a ten-second delay on everything live. This may be why Andy Applewish the well-known spokesman for the Flat Earth Society suspected that the whole lunar landing thing was a 'big fat lie' (his words). He demanded to hear the taped recordings of the landing and when mission control refused obviously because of what Neil Armstrong had first said, Andy convinced Silvester Hornby, the other member of his society, that the lunar landing was a hoax.

The unanswered question is, Did Ms. Finklestein ever take one small step for woman or a giant step for womankind?

WOW: HOW IS IT THAT WE CAN PUT A MAN ON THE MOON BEFORE WE FIGURED OUT IT WOULD REALLY BE A GOOD IDEA TO PUT WHEELS ON LUGGAGE?

Who...What...When...
Where...How...Why... "Say What?"

In the case of the lunar walk story, the most pertinent question was, "SAY WHAT?" That then 'opened up a can of worms,' so that the other questions could wrap things up. Well, the two examples of the origins of a saying covered all those questions, so that we could arrive at the true facts. Good. Now we can move on, but first...

To test that theory, let's look at the origin of another well-known saying, "Don't play with fire or it will burn you." My mama said that in 1943 after my brother Bob had accidentally burnt down hundreds of acres of sugar cane when he made a fire to cook a bird that he had shot. An absolute true story, which is recorded in a charge sheet at the Port Shepstone Police Department at a time when our father was serving as Deputy Mayor. Oops! Is the term redneck appropriate? So in that circumstance, my mother had used that age-old term to warn us of the perils of playing with fire. I wrote 'age-old' deliberately because this saying was 'originally' recorded before there was a 'written word.' "How is that possible?" you may well ask. In fact, you must now ask HOW? Those other important questions will follow. This is what went down...

A gazillion years ago in Iraq, before any written word was penned or chiseled, a Neanderthal by the name of Lucky had just killed a Rhinosoreass (a rhino with a bad attitude). He dragged its sorry three thousand-pound ass into his cave for supper. As he contemplated the best way to prepare his meal, his buddy Dingus fell into the cave with some exciting news. He told Lucky that his sister Mary-Inloo had discovered a better way to prepare a meal. She had worked out how to make a fire and then burned the raw meat to make it hot and taste better. She carefully explained how she took a small amount of dried grass and, by striking a flint stone on another flint stone, a spark flew off into the dry grass and set it on fire.

Later, after Dingus had tripped out of the cave to return to his more modern and tastefully decorated cave around the other side of mountain, Lucky set about building his very own fire. In his haste, he never considered cutting his kill into small pieces to expedite cooking. He decided to make a big fire to cook the whole beast at once…a 'big' mistake! But, Lucky was not very bright. He flunked the 'Ride a Rhinosoreass 101' course. How do I know that? Hang loose.

Rhinosoreass Riding 101

Well, Lucky made a 'big' fire and it got bigger…much bigger! You guessed it. That thing took off and incinerated the whole planet. All living creatures either died of asphyxiation or were burnt to a cinder.

This historic event has been confirmed. During the Iraq War, a detail of American soldiers who were searching for Saddam Hussein came across a cave with crude paintings on the walls. Anthropologists were called in and they deciphered the drawings. There were two well-preserved examples. The first picture clearly showed a rider falling off the back of a rhinoceros. The other painting depicted someone trapped in a massive fire. The anthropologists all agreed it depicted the same idiot. They also disclosed that the artist had signed his work. It was signed by a figure holding up a middle finger at the idiot who was in the fire. The deciphered hieroglyphics read, "Don't play with fire or it will burn you. Signed: 'Dingus.'" Thus, the origins of some well-known sayings have been revealed to us because someone 'asked' some of those smart questions that I have pointed out.

It is also clear that the first BBQ was responsible for the end of life for the dinosaurs, the cave men, and the first recorded idiots who roamed the earth. What I don't understand is how did the earth later take care of all that manmade pollution and turn it into he Garden of Eden before Al Gore showed up…and before he invented the Internet?

When 'Hopalong Cashamgee,' my Indian friend with the limp, heard about this he opposed my argument about who was the first real redneck. Do you think that after all the evidence has been presented that he really suspects that Albert is the first real live 'politician' redneck? Nah…Hoppy thinks that just because his son Nancy won the spelling bee in Chicago, he is also filled with wisdom. No chance, pal.

TIME OUT to check out a few relevant "what ifs." I'll explain…WHAT IF a mute person needs to buy a toothbrush?

Answer: He walks up to Pepe, the shop assistant who can't understand English (American) anyway. By flashing his sparkling white teeth and imitating the action of brushing, he is finally able to successfully express himself, and eventually a purchase is made. I deliberately chose the words 'finally' and 'eventually' because it did not go too well from the get-go. I am not sure what Pepe understood from the demonstration of teeth cleaning, because after nodding his head in reply, he first handed the patron a harmonica, then a picture of Jimmy Carter. But, he got it right on the third time around.

WHAT IF a blind man is the next patron and he wants to buy a pair of sunglasses (shades)? We know that because of his blindness, he could not have 'seen' how the unfortunate mute customer gesticulated in a manner so as to illustrate his request. So, the question is: How does the blind guy indicate what he wants?

This is 'show time!' Your answer to this question will reveal the extent of the knowledge you have gained thus far, having absorbed the secret powers of discernment that have been transmitted through my writing. Indulge me. Keep posted at this juncture, no train station intended; you may well be uncomfortable due to the fact that I have mentioned certain people with certain impediments. You may be surprised to learn that these individuals have a keener sense of humor than the average person.

TIME OUT!

Here's a story about a man with several disabilities, who had a real sense of humor…it's a 'Pirate' tale. Way back Bandy, an 'old salt,' was slowly making his way up a street from the docks where his ship had just berthed. He walked with a limp caused by his 'wooden' left leg and he kept his head tilted to the right because of the patch over his right eye. He was missing an ear and he had a terrible scar across his deeply pockmarked and scarred face. In place of a right hand, he had a hook attached to his severed wrist.

He had been at sea most of his life and he always looked forward to some fun between voyages. As he passed by the first house of 'ill repute' located close to the docks, as a half dressed damsel leaned out of a top story window and called out to him, "Hey, mate, come on up and I will give you something that you have never had before!"

The old salt stopped and looking her over, he called back, "Holy cow! Must be leprosy!"

Back to Business

I want to discuss another less serious (a matter of opinion) affliction, Dyslexia. In modern times, parents and doctors have become able to recognize the symptoms at an early stage and through various modes of therapy and other medical procedures and lots of love, those with this issue have been able to adjust and cope in all walks of life.

South African rednecks were aware of this medical problem long before the Americans. Not only were they ahead of the game, but they also came up with a solution with regard to spelling problems in their writing. Allow me to 'splain…American rednecks refer to their parents as 'Daddy' and 'Mama,' but their much smarter (?) South African counterparts refer to their parents as 'Dad' and 'Mom.' So, what's my point? The point is that American children with dyslexia had a heck of a time writing even the simplest of notes to their parents, e.g., Little John in Raleigh intended to sign his first Christmas card to his parents so he 'wrote, "To Daddy and Mama." However, due to his affliction, he wrote, "Ot YddaD dna amaM." (Zero out of three.)

Whereas, little Sparky in South Africa wrote, "Dad, Mom" (three out of three) 'cause 'Dad' and 'Mom' spelt backwards is still 'Dad' and 'Mom.'

It worked for me, too. I remember how I wrote my first Christmas card to my parents. It read: "Dad, Mom. YPPAH SAMTSIRHC. EVOL, ZEL"

Did I mention there's a new sheriff in town?

For the record…my elder brother's name is not really Bob…it is Vivian. My parents changed it to be sure he did not spell it backwards.

You may well wonder how someone who can't spell can write a manuscript. After all I would have to write more words than just Dad and Mom. Dead Right! It has taken me three months to reach this point, and I am not even left-handed. Here is how it works. After the completion of a manuscript, I mail a copy to my publisher. He immediately forwards it to China where Mereed, his Chinese editing expert slave who is proficient in Mandarin, looks it over. Remember, all Mandarin is written in reverse, meaning that they start a book on the last page and write until it ends on the first page. (?) No wonder those Chinese kids read so fast and win most the spelling bees in America, except the one that 'Nancy-boy' cracked. Luckily, we don't write our school text books in reverse, because our kids will simply only read the first page and then go and switch on their Chinese TV. Okay, back to how I get my books published…

Mereed does the original editing. He simply reverses the pages, after which he sends the manuscript to Red Spirit Springs in Nevada where a group of Navaho Indians decode and correct all the spelling and return it to my American publisher, who deletes any unsavory details and poor English (American). I am fortunate to have Harry my other brother correct my spelling in all my personal correspondence, since I once made a disastrous spelling mistake when writing to my wife when I was interviewing her new female gynecologist while away conducting research for my first book. I left the 'e' out of a word… I wrote, "The weather is lovely. Your gynecologist is most obliging… Wish you were her!" (I left the 'e' out of gynecologist!)

I had intended to end this chapter with the 'big daddy' of all the origins of sayings uttered on terra firma, but my gut feeling tells me that y'all are more interested in how the blind guy ordered dark glasses. Bless your hearts. How did he indicate what he wanted? He simply opened his mouth and asked for a pair.

Speaking of dark glasses…

Several years ago I drove across the South African border in my orange Beetle into Bophutatswana to attend a live performance of Kenny Rogers, a favorite singer of mine. For those who don't know Bophutatswana, 'Bop' for short, was an independent state. You may also be unaware of the fact that the Bophutatswanans built a massive casino complex 'slap dab' in the middle of the bush complete with an incredible golf course at the tourist Mecca named 'Sun City'…sound familiar? (As in Native American Reservations.) For those in the golfing world in the know, the very first golfing 'million dollar' prize tournament…American dollars…took place on that golf course. One of the holes is adjacent to a manmade pond, which contains a few live crocodiles. No kidding! They have been photographed waddling around on the 13th green. That is why nobody tries to retrieve misshit (Er…miss-hit) golf balls from the water. There is a rumor that a caddy disappeared on that green one evening, but sources at CNN who investigated the 'alleged' incident suspect that he had run off with one of the belly dancers from the Kenny Rogers Show. The next time I play a round of golf with Kenny, I will bring up the subject and report back.

However, when my wife and I visited that facility last year, I planned to ask the barman what went down. Remember, a barman hears everything. Note that listening to drunks is not the same as eavesdropping. I planned my sleuthing strategy down to the last detail and I even dressed appropriately for the part. I wore my PGA look-alike purple blazer and strolled into the bar with an English pipe between my teeth at just the correct angle. As I stepped into the bar area, an enormous guy in a tuxedo stepped up to me with a warm and friendly smile and said, "Excuse me, Sir." I was flattered that somebody ten thousand and sixteen miles from my American home had actually recognized me. Then he said in a low tone, "This is a non-smoking area, sir." I had forgotten about the pipe and replied innocently without thinking (I do that often), "That's fine by me because I don't smoke." I shall not repeat what he told me to do with the pipe, but he also suggested that I take a stroll and smoke it next to the 13th green."

The following evening I gave the 'Golf Bar' a miss and headed for the 'Safari Bar.' This time I dressed casually in Khaki shorts and shirt, boots, and a pith helmet. I wanted to blend in with those wealthy American tourists who were on various safaris. I have seen them with my own eyes dressed this way…and *they* vote. From the moment I stepped inside the Safari Bar, I realized that I was the only one dressed appropriately, except for the 'bar person.' That term is suggested for reasons of political correctness. This 'individual' serving behind the bar was wearing a wooden mask and, as the bar counter was four foot high and the bar person was only about four foot six, I was not able to see how he or she was dressed. So, I took a shot and greeted him/her like this, "If you don't mind, I need some information."

"Do you want to buy an AK-47?" he/she responded.

I'm not sure if it was smiling because of the wooden mask, so I left without even buying a drink…there's always a first time. Now that I have set the scene, I can move on with the other shady 'shades' story.

As I headed toward the Kenny Rogers Show, I passed the movie house that shows those naughty movies. Some refer to them as X-rated movies. My wife, who raised chickens for a living, calls them something completely different without actually using 'fowl' language. That is a rare talent. Anyway my attention, my total attention, was directed at the 'coming attractions' layout adjacent to the entrance of the theater. I was staring with both eyeballs in 3-D mode at the billboard advertising the movie currently being shown. The display consisted of a huge picture of a thankfully 'almost' naked woman and thankfully several smaller photographs of couples, thankfully men and women, doing what looked like Jujitsu. I noted the title of the movie, *Three Little Words, Yes! Yes! Yes!* and I had always thought that movie was called, "*Three Little Words, I Love You.*"

I must have spent longer than I thought taking a quick look at the poster because about thirty minutes later, the exit doors opened wide and patrons exited in mass. The extraordinary thing about the patrons was that they were all male and all dressed exactly alike, complete with long heavy jackets with collars turned up and wearing various types of headgear. All Dick Tracy look-alikes, but they had not been watching any 'who-dunnit' movie. No, siree, they had been watching a 'somebody-dunnit' movie. In addition, it was over 100 degrees Fahrenheit in that place. No wonder they all stooped as they walked. But here's the most incredible thing about those men…they all wore large dark glasses (shades). It must have been a movie for blind men. Bless their hearts. I must add that they sell more shades in Bophuthatswana than in the rest of Africa. Wonder how many toothbrushes they sell?

Twenty minutes later, I joined my wife at the Kenny Rogers Show. She arrived after I did. She mentioned being almost run over by a large group of blind men as they dispersed into the main casino. "There must be a convention for the blind," she said.

"Not so blind as those who didn't want to be seen," I said. She corrected the saying, but I was not about to risk my life, as the overture to the Kenny Roger's Show started. And, what a show!

Kenny was on top of his game completely overshadowing his guest host, the tall Susan Anton…and the emphasis is on 'tall.' I could not figure out why a relatively short guy like Kenny would host such a tall woman, and the fact that she wore a pair of those popular extra high heel shoes made matters much worse. She looked about five feet sixteen inches tall and standing beside her, poor old Kenny reminded me of the scene in the movie *An American in Paris*, where Gene Kelly (also not the tallest of guys) was standing looking up at the Eiffel Tower.

While watching the two interact on the stage, I could not help wondering about that Hollywood divorce between Susan Anton and her former actor husband 'Rocky Rambo Stallone.' I created a mental picture of the two by substituting the Rocky Rambo image with that of Kenny on the stage. It only took one look to convince me of the fact that Susan and Rocky Rambo were not compatible. Picture them together, as I did. There's this sexy, tall, very tall, slender, eloquently groomed blonde standing next to this character who although much wider than Kenny, is even shorter and is left-handed. (?) Whatever their conversation, one can't help sympathizing with Susan about the fact that his replies were mainly, "Yho." Or "Yho, baby!" This dialogue was a 'put-on' because, in reality, Sly is brilliant at his career, which has made him a very wealthy man. Did Susan somehow miss this? So, who is the smart one in the chicken coop?

All this must not detract from the fact that Kenny Rogers was fantastic! He had the audience eating out his hand. He is not left-handed. Right. I recall that early in his show he asked the audience for song requests. The lady beside me sitting in the aisle shouted out, "LADY!"

He called back, "If I sing my current hit *Lady*, everybody will think that the show is over and go home." Somebody convinced the woman not to slit her wrists and the show moved on.

I must mention that 'many' years later, I went to see Kenny Rogers perform at Myrtle Beach. Although older, he seemed taller without Susan Anton. He had replaced her with a young male piano player as a host. On reflection, I would rather have replaced the piano player with Rocky Rambo or, even better, with his brother Frank. Think about that. But, in fairness to the piano player, he never mixed up the white and black notes.

During Kenny's Myrtle Beach show, he did something very unusual between singing breaks in the show. He would randomly ask any of the audience to stand and he would throw a Frisbee across the auditorium so accurately that the person would not have to move to catch it. He did this many times and no matter where people stood, he was right on target. How do you do that, Kenny? If you tell me, I will send you the words of a song.

The following day on our return to Johannesburg, I took a short detour to show my wife the site of the nuclear facility at Pelindaba. It amazes me that so few ordinary people outside of South Africa know of its existence northwest of Johannesburg.

Shortly after World War II, the Atomic Energy Board built a uranium enrichment plant at Pelindaba. South Africa, at the time, was recognized as a powerful fighting nation with arms capacity as advanced as any in the world. Because of South Africa's isolation from the international community, their nuclear program was shrouded in secrecy. The question was, Did South Africa possess nuclear weapons? In late 1977, it was rumored that a secret nuclear test was to take place underground in the Kalahari Desert in the Northern Cape. When confronted, the Atomic Energy Officials conceded that a cold test 'without' uranium was planned. You think? However, the Western and Soviet governments warned that preparations were being planned for a full-scale nuclear test.

In late September of 1979, US satellites detected a double flash typical of a nuclear explosion over the Indian Ocean. Fresh rumors abounded, linking collaboration between South Africa and Israel; however, this has never been officially confirmed. For years, South Africa denied possession of nuclear weapons. That is until 1991 when President F. W. de Klerk terminated the nuclear program (not Mandela as is often mistakenly thought).

The Atomic Energy Corporation has since been renamed NECSA and supplies high technology products to markets worldwide. Many are considered to be 'very innovative' earning millions in foreign revenue. The reactor SAFARI-1 in Pelindaba is the most commercialized nuclear reactor in the world. So 'light your pipe and smoke it.'

South African Nuclear Facilities

Facilities at Valindaba and later at Pelindaba successfully enriched uranium for the Koeberg Nuclear Power Station located on the west coast of the Atlantic Ocean 30 km north of Cape Town. Construction on the Koeberg facility began in 1976 and Unit 1 came online early in 1984. Unit 2 hooked up in August 1985.

During construction in 1982, the facility was attacked and damaged by bombs planted by an activist, Rodney Wilkinson, which caused an 18-month delay with a price tag of R500 million. In 2002, six Greenpeace activists scaled the walls with anti-nuclear banners. In 2005, a technical fault caused the reactor to switch into 'safety mode' and caused serious power disruptions for four weeks.

In December 2005 during routine maintenance, a loose bolt inside the generator of Unit 1 caused serious damage, which shut it down for five months.

'Controlled' shutdowns caused power failures for twelve months in 2006-2007.

In September 2010, Cobalt-58 dust contaminated over ninety staff members.

Pelindaba

In 2007, four armed men breached the 10,000-volt security fence, eluded security cameras, and attacked the two staff members in the control room. One was shot and wounded and the other badly beaten before a security detail appeared and the intruders made a hasty retreat. What were they after?

Pelindaba holds enough weapons grade uranium to build a dozen atomic bombs! Scary!

SUGGESTION: Research 'Koeberg' and 'Pelindaba'.... Your hair will fall out!

SOOOOOO:

1. All enriched uranium in South Africa has been accounted for. (HOPEFULLY!)
2. The I.A.E.I. keeps an eye on present nuclear activity in South Africa. You think?

Big Daddy of All Origins of Stories

I have covered the origins of a few well-known sayings, all in 'good' or, at least, 'reasonable' taste. But what of those that are considered to be not so squeaky clean? This is a big challenge, but I figured that it would be even a bigger challenge if I could find an acceptable way to explain the origin of one of those that are never spoken in mixed company. I am referring to one of those that contain a bad word or two. It is common knowledge that there are other undesirable words that begin with letters other than letter '#6' in the alphabet. Consider letter #19 for example. There is a word starting with 'S' that should never be used in mixed company. The only exception that comes to mind is what happened when a famous hypnotist accidentally dropped his expensive pocket watch and destroyed it during a private performance at a retirement facility. If you have not heard that one, please stand by. But for now, back to the challenge of covering the origin of a very often-expressed saying that includes the 'S' word. And, remember, it must be done without actually using the 'S' word. You are to be forgiven if you think that this is an impossible task, but what you are about to discover is that this can only be achieved by a dyslexic and remember that…"I ma eno!"

The giB yddaD…

Many years ago, the Shah of Iran and his beautiful actress wife and family spent the occasional vacation in South Africa. That is a fact. No (?) is necessary. Well, this story has absolutely nothing to do with them, but it has to do with another royal family from a similar part of the world.

This particular Shah and his ordinary (not to be confused with ugly) wife and family were the guests of the head of state of a country, which shall remain nameless for the sake of Italian security. They were wined and dined in a modern villa near the capital of that unnamed country and were provided with the most competent personal bodyguards ever trained by the Vatican and the Mafia. This particular Shah and his plain (sounds more respectful) wife had a young teenage son who, because he was the son of a Shah, protocol demanded that he always be referred to as the 'Shan.' I repeat, that in that culture the son of a Shah was always called the 'Shan.' The son Philippe who was about thirteen years old, unfortunately, was prone to seizures. This was an additional concern for the security detail that could never let the youngster out of their sights, particularly around the private swimming pool that was double the size of Saddam's swimming pool in Baghdad.

One balmy warm afternoon, the personal guard Tony who had been selected to protect young Philippe had his own lapse. Allow me to rephrase that…Tony had dropped his guard and some items of his clothing (remember the hot balmy conditions)…while distracted by the voluptuous housemaid Stella Maria. That's all it took to set up a most unfortunate security lapse. Just one 'short' (Tony was shorter than Kenny or Sly) lapse with Stella Marie under the apple tree. I think there is a song about sitting under the apple tree. By the time Tony had composed himself Philippe had drowned! It was a tragic story, indeed. So what happened?

When Felix, the head of the unnamed country's security, was called in from his Rome headquarters to investigate the unfortunate tragic drowning of the Shan, he immediately called in Tony, the security guard who had had a lapse (remember the apple tree and Eve). Felix asked Tony this question, "Where were you when the fit hit the Shan?"

I tser ym esac!

I simply cannot leave y'all wondering about the origin of the 'S' word. Most 'old golfers' think it originated on the golf links of Scotland, but this is simply not true. Just as the bagpipes never originated in Scotland, the "S" word never originated there either.

The origin of the 'S' word…this is the truth (?)…

In the sixteenth and seventeenth centuries before the invention of commercial fertilizers, manure (the 'original' stuff) was transported in large quantities by sea on huge ocean-going ships. Only 'dried stuff' was shipped to reduce the weight because 'dried stuff' weighed much less than 'wet stuff.' Despite this cargo being stored below deck, some sea water splashed on it from time to time and, not only did the cargo become heavier, but the process of fermentation began once more producing 'methane gas.'

As the 'stuff' below deck produced large quantities of methane gas, you can imagine what happened when some unsuspecting sailor went below deck with a lantern…BOOOOOM!

Several ships were destroyed in this manner before it was determined what was happening.

After that, the bundles of 'stuff' were stamped with the instruction: STOW HIGH IN TRANSIT. This instructed the sailors to stow it high enough off the lower decks so that any water that came into the hold would not touch this volatile cargo and start the production of methane, And this is used to this very day. So, it is from the 'acronymized' stamped instructions, 'Ship High In Transit' that the "S" word originated.

If only the stamped instructions were, "Ship High and Neatly," then whenever a golfer missed a putt or hooked a drive, he would have exclaimed, "SHAN!"

QWB: WHOSE IDEA WAS IT TO PUT AN 'S' IN THE WORD 'LISP'? Thoundth thupid to me.
WOW: GENERALLY SPEAKING, YOU AREN'T LEARNING MUCH WHEN YOUR LISPS ARE MOVING.
Epilogue to fertilizer boat demise...

Two Irish sailors who had miraculously escaped a fertilizer boat explosion were adrift in a lifeboat. While rummaging through the boats provisions, one of them stumbled across an old lamp. Secretly hoping that it would produce a genie, he rubbed the lamp vigorously and, to the amazement of the castaways, a genie appeared. This particular genie, however, could only deliver one wish...not the standard three wishes.

Without giving much thought to the matter (remember we are speaking of the Irish here), O'Malley blurted out, "Make the entire ocean into beer!"

The genie clapped his hands with a deafening crash, and immediately the entire sea turned into the finest brew ever sampled by mortals. Simultaneously, the genie vanished. Only the gentle lopping of beer on the hull broke the stillness as the two Irishmen considered their circumstances. After a long tension-filled moment, Hannity finally spoke. "Nice going, O'Malley, you idiot! Now we have to pee in the boat!"

Okay. I know that y'all are far more interested in the origin of the bag-pipes, right?

How about this...

The bagpipes were invented by a couple of jokers in India. The Indian population saw the joke and introduced them to Ireland. The Irish, after two centuries, saw the joke and sent them to Scotland. The Scots have not seen the joke, yet.

P.S. My family in Scotland sent me a box of laxatives for Christmas. Bless their pipes, y'all.

Soooo, what about letter '#6' in the alphabet? That dreaded 'F' word! Am I crazy!...or what? ... Am I really going there? Sure I am!

But, please, stay calm! Like the 'S' word, I believe that the 'F' word can also be discretely disclosed in acronymic form without the book being burnt by that group in Florida...or, my mother appearing from the grave.

NOTE: Car guys will catch on 'quicker' than the rest of y'all. In particular, car guys of the fifties whose knowledge of tires will make understanding what follows a breeze ('breeze' as in 'tornado').

Here goes...

Remember how Kelly Tires advertised on the radio? An enthusiastic announcer belted out: 'K.T.A.T....K.T.A.T....KELLY TIRES ARE TOUGH!"

So, some bright spark came up with: "F.A.R.T....F.A.R.T....FIRE-STONES ARE 'REALLY' TOUGH!"

That was the 'F' word that y'all were thinking of...RIGHT!

Dyslexic Trivia...and Restaurants

Did you know that the word 'racecar' spelled backwards still spells 'racecar?' But, not if you spell it 'ecar rac.' And...that 'eat' is the only word that if you take the first letter and move it to the last, it spells its past tense 'ate.'

Talk about 'ate'...at this 'point in time'...'like' I mean the point when I start to think of food 'like' I mean, 'Man cannot live by unpublished words alone.' I joined a dinner group of sixteen fellow pheasant hunters who, for privacy, had booked a private room for seventeen at the rear of a Mexican restaurant. My wife and I were the first to arrive and were greeted by a very friendly guy wearing an oversize Mexican sombrero. That convinced me that we were at the correct venue. The man under the hat said, "Welcome, table for two?"

"We are part of a group who booked a private room for seventeen people," I replied. He smiled and replied, "Have a nice day," and immediately led us to an intimate table for two. I suspected that he had misunderstood me, so I politely said, "I think there is some mistake. We are part of a group that booked a private room for seventeen guests." He smiled, handed us two menus, repeated, "Have a nice day," and he and his sombrero disappeared. As we stood around in a daze, another guy wearing a bigger Mexican sombrero and an even bigger smile appeared out of nowhere and, after a few anxious moments, sorted out the seating arrangements and escorted us to a private room with a large table for *seventy* people. Then he also disappeared!

In time, the guests arrived and, after rearranging the whole cotton-pickin' seating arrangements, we all hugged one another as is the custom of the pheasant killing club members before loading our AK-47s.

I was apprehensive about how to order Mexican food, as I am not fluent in Portuguese. My previous visit to a Mexican restaurant had not gone so well. On that occasion, I had ordered something that sounded familiar, but I ended up getting a well-done Echidnas, the long-snout variety. He/she was served with a golf ball in its mouth. They were out of harmonicas.

With this image still freshly etched in my memory, I decided to ask our best shot, my friend Hawk-Eye who was seated beside me to interpret the menu. To my acute embarrassment, he pointed out that every item on the menu was numbered so that on selecting a particular dish, all a patron needed to do was read the number listed beside the various dishes and call it out to the server. This simplified the whole ordering process by eliminating English (American). That had come about because some idiot had mistakenly ordered a well-done Echidnas at some other Mexican restaurant and they were nearly closed down for serving endangered species.

We were warned, however, to call the dish number out clearly to the server and not order by giving the server the finger. Seems that there had been a mix-up earlier when Chips Revera, the wood machinist with two middle fingers missing on his right hand, had received dish number two instead of number four because he had ordered by fingers instead of by calling out the number. His order of the rice dish special with beans turned up as the soup of the day with a double helping of angry-looking red beans.

Ordering dishes by number certainly made matters easier, except for when ordering a side order. There was no number listed beside the house salad because there was simply no choice and you were served it whether you were a vegetarian or not, but you had the choice of different dressings. My wife was very clear when asking Carlos for honey mustard dressing. He brought 'ranch.' When she mentioned the error he said, "Have a nice day," smiled, and disappeared. All seventeen in our party also got 'ranch." Now to be fair, most of us do enjoy 'ranch,' but as it comes in those heat sealed aluminum sachets that are impossible to tear open, we all ate our salad naked.

I can't leave this subject on that note without including the fact that every single meal on the menu included beans. Not Mexican jumping beans because they are only grown in China, but those angry-looking red and brown beans that the dieticians advise us to include in our diet for roughage. I made the mistake of ordering number 66 from the menu, not realizing that number 66 included a 'double' helping of rumble beans. My poor old stomach rebelled and built up enough gas to launch Ms. Finklestein and Stumpy to the moon without a rocket. Wonder what those two would get up to on the moon...provided Stumpy took a bottle of wine with them. No doubt they would have uttered some famous 'couple' words like, "One small sip from man, one giant slip for woman."

Lest my rendition of the Mexican restaurant experience be construed as being unkind with respect to cultural differences, I must confess that as an English/American speaker, I 'myself' have been on the other end of the totem pole many times. You may be surprised to learn about the problems I have encountered because of my different accent. Ordering a 'half' cup of coffee in a Southern grill is probably the most difficult order any of the servers have ever encountered. You may well ask, Why is it so difficult to understand that I only want half a cup? I like my coffee very hot and consumed with my meal. As my parents never allowed us to drink anything with our meals, I could not wait to leave home and be able to wash my food down like the cowboys did in those old movies. My parents believed that any liquid consumed with a meal had the effect of diluting the stomach acids, which would lead to stomach problems. That's why frogs never suffer from stomach ulcers.

I mentioned the fact that I like my coffee hot. Well, from my experience, the server often brings a clean cup directly out of the refrigerator then pours in the hot coffee, where it cools in a hurry. So, to overcome this problem I order a half-cup, which helps heat the cold cup, and I drink it quickly before ordering further half cups until the meal is concluded. This sometimes confuses the servers and I have overheard them express unkind remarks like, "That Limey don't know spit from snow." That hurt. How would you like to be called a Limey? I have learnt never to upset the servers at any cost because it's as I mentioned previously, "I would rather have a 'half-empty' cup of coffee than a 'half-full' cup of sewerage."

It's much worse in non-English speaking countries. In France at the Eiffel Tower Restaurant, I ordered a steak. The waiter returned thirty minutes later with a bowl of chopped liver. An Australian friend of mine told me that the French dislike anybody who speaks American or English. I can't imagine why because without the Americans and the English, they would be speaking German. Speaking of German, the next time I ordered at a Paris restaurant I avoided speaking American and ordered in German. The waiter returned forty-five minutes later in a sweat and served me a Volkswagen carburetor. I hate to think what I would have got if I had ordered a 'half' cup of coffee.

I have the solution in American restaurants. Whenever the server takes my order, I simply tell my wife to order in American. It works like this: My wife orders unsweetened cold tea for herself (Ugh!) then politely tells the waiter person to serve me a 'half' cup of hot coffee. Nine times out of ten, the server overfills my cup. Why do the restaurants not provide saucers? That way I could sip the overflow from the saucer like my 'Oupa' taught me after my ride on Kaptein.

Once, in a mountain grill on a really cold morning, my wife asked the waitress to warm my coffee cup before adding the coffee. She replied, "We don't have any way of heating the cup." My wife suggested she use the microwave. That was in the winter of 2002, and I swear that cup is still cooking.

Question: Have you ever heard of 'bald' peanuts? They bald them in really hot water.

WOW: A BUMBLEBEE IS CONSIDERED FASTER THAN A JOHN DEERE TRACTOR.

Southern Advice: According to Jeb Pitt, "Your fences need to be horse-high, pig-tight, and bull-strong."

That's why my plumber July August advised, "Don't ever take a fence down before you know the reason why it was put up." He should know 'cause he moved in next to the alligator farm.

The King and I

When we last referred to my South African redneck family, they, including 'yours truly' had transplanted to PMB, the 'big' capital city of the Province of Natal, since renamed 'KWA-Zulu.' PMB was considered the educational capital of the province because it boasted the highly regarded Teachers Training College, the most schools, all categories, Nurses Training Home, and the most popular feeding ground for dates, museums, cultural centers, etc., etc., offering the very best of opportunities for all members of my family to grow in culture and widen our horizons for the future…yeah, right!

To be fair, PMB was a bustling city rich in colonial history, gracefully situated in a valley in the foothills of the Drakensberg Mountain range. And, to add to its appeal, it was the capital of the Province of Natal. These factors must have influenced the British Royal Family to include Pietermaritzburg as a stopover during their 1947 Royal tour of South Africa. Did I mention the fact that I had met the British Royal Family? Sure did! The whole bloody family…King George VI, his Queen Elizabeth, Princess Elizabeth (currently Queen of England), and Princess Margaret. How on earth did this redneck meet the cream of the British Commonwealth? Allow me to 'splain…

The Royal tour of South Africa took place during February and March of 1947, and as I mentioned, one of their visits included our city of Pietermaritzburg. This was at a time when as a youngster of eleven, I was on top of the world and bursting with energy.

The Royal Family attended a huge open-air gathering at the oval situated in the heart of the beautiful 162-acre Alexandra Park. This venue included facilities for all sports including soccer, cricket, athletics, and cycling—all situated on the banks of a strong flowing river. The organizers chose this site as it conveniently included a magnificent Victorian pavilion in front of which the royal visitors would be seated on a dais where they would receive many dignitaries, including the Zulu king.

Arrangements had been made for school children to attend, all dressed alike and provided with British flags, the Union Jack, which they were instructed to wave vigorously during this occasion. I was included in a group on the far right fringes of this massive crowd, far removed from the action. Like the others, we were all dressed alike—black shoes, gray socks, blue serge shorts, and white short-sleeved shirts with the appropriate school tie knotted around our necks. It was the ties that differentiated one school from another, in that they were mainly of a different color and design and, in my case, the tie was very colorful. Unfortunately, in my haste that morning, I had clumsily knotted my tie causing its length to extend much lower than the belly button regulation. During the proceedings, we were under the control of teachers who would not permit us to leave our designated areas, except to visit the many temporary toilets that had been specially provided for the Royal occasion.

During one of these visits, instead of returning to my group, I slowly worked my way closer to the front, sometimes pushing through the throng. It was my intention to get as close to the dais as possible, so that I could take a good look at the King of England and the Royal Family. Finally, at a point when the crowd was cheering and waving their flags, I sneaked into the front row. There I discovered two small groups of little first-year schoolchildren—a group of four little girls on one side and a group of four little boys on the other. They were positioned directly in front of the dais only a short distance from the Royal Family. These cute little children were all shined up and nervously standing under the supervision of two chaperones—one for the girls and the other for the boys. I suspected that they were there for a special reason...maybe to sing, I surmised. I just had to know. Just then, the proceedings seemed to me to be coming to a close and everybody was once again jumping up and down, enthusiastically waving their flags. I took my opportunity. In a flash, I was next to the boys' group and at that precise moment, the chaperones ushered the two groups onto the dais, including me. There we were, four little girls and four little boys, plus me. My sudden appearance had taken the boys' chaperone by surprise, but before she could react, the Queen stepped forward and started greeting the little girls on our left. The chaperone dared not make a move...she simply glared at me.

After a cursory glance at the other boys, I quickly pulled up my socks, but was not able to adjust the length of my tie. The Queen was followed by the King and the two Princesses, politely greeting the children beside me. I noticed that the little girls curtsied and I wondered what the boys would do. I watched closely and was relieved to note that the boys, unlike the girls, bowed when approached. It was obvious to me that both teams had been strictly coached, as they all repeated the exact same greeting, which was, "How do you do?" Then it was finally my turn. The chaperone beside me was mortified! The poor woman was between a rock and a hard place as she kept smiling, but not moving a muscle. The Queen took my hand and said, "How doo-yoo–doo?" I heard myself reply, "How dooo-yooo-dooo?" The chaperone nearly fainted. The Queen then asked my name and I quickly replied Pete...I was acting really smart, I knew better than to give my real name. The Queen, still holding my hand, then graciously remarked, "I like your tie." I quickly responded saying, "Thank you, Your Majesty." That seemed to surprise the chaperone. The King was next. He gripped my hand firmly as we exchanged the prescribed greetings, and looking me over remarked, "Na-na, na-na, nice tie." As he moved off, I replied "Thank you, Your Majesty." The chaperone approved. Then Princess Elizabeth very elegantly appeared and took me by the hand. We swapped the identical greetings. She was very friendly and remarked that we all looked cool in our shorts. As I smiled in reply, she then added, "Your tie is so pretty." This is when I noted that the chaperone was very nervous, but when I replied, "Thank you, Your Royal Highness," she seemed impressed. Finally, it was Princess Margaret's turn. What a breath of fresh air. She was a bubbling teenager who spoke to everyone in the line, kidding and laughing, despite the stern glances from the King. The Queen, on the other hand, was not concerned and smiled graciously, as always. With that, Princess Margaret took my hand and instead of the expected greeting she remarked, "You must be older than the others…you are so much bigger." The chaperone was watching wide eyed as I replied, "No, Your Royal Highness, I'm just a fast grower." This seemed to tickle her and she replied with a loud giggle, "Your tie must be fast growing, too." The King caught that remark and gave his daughter a disapproving look, the Queen, on the other hand, remained composed, as always.

The Royal group then moved further across the dais where they were to repeat this process with a group of well-disciplined African children. At this point, two organizers came over to us with a pretty box containing little pin-on medals, which they proceeded to attach to our shirts on the left breast. They commenced with the girls at the opposite end, working their way quickly one-by-one as they pinned the medals on their shirts. When my turn came, they seemed to be one medal short. Was my worst nightmare about to happen? However, as the chaperone moved toward me to clarify matters, the organizer intervened, and to my surprise apologized to me. He then cheerfully removed his own medal from his shirt and pinned it to my pocket. I could see the red-faced chaperone preparing to pounce on me at the first opportunity. She would, however, be denied this certain pleasure.

At that instant, the military band close by struck up a patriotic march, which motivated the huge crowd to react with cheering and the rehearsed waving of the flags…and I was out of there in a flash! You could not see my ass for dust! As I headed for home, I noted that the ceremony was coming to an end and the royal group climbed into their huge specially built Daimler.

Arriving home, I quickly unpinned the medal and slipped it into my pocket. I was going to surprise my family at the dinner table by producing it at the end of the meal when, as the house rules dictated, we children were then allowed to speak…always providing that we had eaten all the food dished up for us. I was so excited that I could hardly wait for the dinner bell. Finally, at the end of dinner, the conversation turned to the royal visit. My parents, aware that I had attended the proceedings, asked me what had happened. Despite the fact that I was bursting to tell them of my experience, I deliberately, coolly replied, "Oh, nothing happened…except I met the King of England!" Nobody took me seriously…however, my parents, but not my brother Douglas thought

I was very funny. I then continued saying, "I not only met the King, but also the whole Royal Family." As expected, my brother commented first saying, "Yeah, right." Then my moment of glory! I retrieved my medal from my pocket and laid it on the table. My father's expression shocked me and I very quickly added that I had not stolen it. Speaking even faster, I went into the details of the day. They were all stunned, but somehow not surprised. The important thing is that they believed me.

The medal resembles a silver coin, a littler larger than a quarter. On one side, it is stamped with the profile of the King and Queen surrounded by the inscription, KING GEORGE VI AND QUEEN ELIZABETH. The other side is also stamped, VISIT OF THEIR MAJESTIES - 1947. The medal is suspended from a small red, white, and blue ribbon patch similar to military medals. I still have mine as an important memory. After all, how many people have shaken the hand of two successive reigning British Monarchs? In my instance, King George VI and also the reigning Queen Elizabeth of England. Oh, and for the record, did I mention that I also share my birthday with Queen Victoria? You remembered!

I often reflect what if anything, was said by the Royal Family that night as they relaxed in their 'White Train.' Could the conversation possibly have included something like this? Perhaps the King had remarked,

"Who was the ka-ka, ka-ka, kid in that necktie?" (King George VI stuttered...keep posted.)

Maybe one day I could ask one of their Majesties, but time is running out...unless I mail them an autographed copy of this book. It could become a bedside reader while Her Majesty waits for the next whacko to evade the Buckingham Palace security and sit on the royal bed. Maybe she could hit him on the head with my hard cover edition. Talk about being brained...er bashed! What do you think?

If you were surprised to learn that King George VI had a speech impediment, I feel that it is only fair to cover his stuttering in a 'fair and balanced 'manner.

The poor man struggled with trying to overcome this health issue all his life. From his earliest childhood, he was tutored for hours by speech therapists and as an adult, he took great pains to overcome his affliction. He achieved success for most words except those starting with the letters 'K' and 'F'... Well, 'K' words like 'kid' were hard to avoid, but on the 'udder' hand, he struggled to avoid the 'F' word. He managed to avoid words starting with 'F,' except on one occasion...

Some background history is appropriate to fully illustrate the point. During WW II when the Commonwealth pilots saved England in the air 'Battle of Britain,' many pilots received medals for their achievements. The word 'Commonwealth' is used deliberately as many pilots were from countries other than Britain, (including those from South Africa) about which Sir Winston Churchill remarked, "Never in the field of human conflict was so much owed by so many to so few." ('The Few')

As mentioned, many pilots received medals during this conflict and what better way to honor these brave guys, than to have the King of England personally decorate them. At the very first medal awarding ceremony, two famous pilots Rogers and Smith were presented to His Majesty, who was provided with written citations from which he would read the details of the awards. Pilot Smith came forward first, smartly saluted His Majesty, and proudly stood to attention in front of his King. The King then proceeded to read the citation. He read…er misread…

"Pilot Smith, I present you with this medal for shooting down six Uh, Fa-Fa-Fa-Fokkkker, Uh, Fokka…Focke-Wolves."

Wing Commander Jones who stood beside the King ready to hand him the medals for presentation whispered discretely in the King's ear, "Begging your pardon, your Majesty, he shot down seven Focke-Wolves." The King grimaced and reluctantly corrected the citation…

"Excuse me, Pilot Smith, I believe it was seven Uh, Fa-Fa-Fa Fokkkker, Uh, Focke-Wolves." He then proceeded to pin the medal on Smith's chest. The proud pilot beamed, saluted his King, and marched off the stage. The second pilot, Rogers, then smartly appeared before the King, saluted in respect, and stood to attention. The King then read the second citation…

"Pilot Rogers, I present you with this medal for shooting down three Uh, Fa-Fa-Fa Fokkkker, Uh, Fokka…Focke-Wolves." To the King's dismay, Wing Commando Jones once again leaned over and whispered, not so discreetly in his ear, "Begging your pardon, your Majesty, it was four Focke-Wolves." The King realizing that changing the number of enemy planes to 'four' presented him with another 'F' word…so, he turned to Jones and said in muted anger, "There may be Uh, Fo-Fo-Fo-Fo-For-Four…Uh, Fa-Fa-Fa Fokkkker, Uh, Fokka…Focke-Wolves, but there is only one Uh, Fa-Fa, Fa-Fa, Fa-Fa, Frikken medal!"

QWB: COULD KING GEORGE VI HAVE BEEN A 'ROYAL REDNECK'? The highest-ranking redneck ever?

Can you imagine how difficult it would have been for His Majesty to ask his valet to buy a 'Family Photo Frame From Fritch and Fritch?'

As mentioned, many South African pilots served with distinction in the Battle of Britain. In fact, during a certain period in those battles, one of the South African pilots by the name of 'Sailor Malan' was accredited with the highest number of enemy aircraft shot down and was awarded the DFC and DSO. On the field of battle, several South Africans were awarded the VC (the Victoria Cross), the highest British medal awarded for bravery. Quinton Smythe, a local farmer and relative of one of my in-laws received the Victoria Cross.

Returning to the 1947 Royal visit…

Speaking of the royal 'White Train,' it was magnificent, built specially to accommodate the Royal Family for their six-week visit to South Africa, as well as Northern Rhodesia (now Zambia) and Southern Rhodesia (now Zimbabwe), situated on the northern border of South Africa. The train was a shade over one-third of a mile long, painted white with gold and ivory trim. Brightly painted royal crests adorned to the sides of all the carriages. Within its coaches were housed a post office and telephone exchange, as well as repair facilities for any unexpected emergencies. As the Royal Family was to spend six weeks on rail, nothing was spared to meet their accommodation needs. Each family member had a private bedroom with bathroom. The King was provided with a study and his quarters also included a separate sitting room. A full dining room was provided, as was a large drawing room for movie shows and card games, etc. One of the coaches was specially designed to accommodate the huge Daimler, which was available for any road travel.

The train was parked for a few nights at a siding adjoining the main railway station. As expected, military personnel closely guarded it around the clock. An interesting story made the rounds during this time. Apparently, on the first night, the King startled a patrolling serviceman when he stuck his head out of the window and loudly complained about the incessant noise that was produced by the military boots on the gravel surface. The response was immediate. All patrolling security personnel were immediately issued with white sand shoes made from canvas with soft rubber soles. The security personnel were not impressed, as they looked ridiculous in military attire with dainty white shoes on their feet. However, the problem was solved.

In the mornings, the train was repositioned at the main platform. At the exact prescribed time, the family would emerge to a red carpet treatment. Ironically, as history painfully reveals, the red carpet was at the very place where, in May of 1893, Mohandas (Mahatma) Gandhi had been unceremoniously thrown off a train by railway police because he insisted on using a carriage reserved for whites only. I must remind the reader that this unfortunate incident occurred at the time of British rule in South Africa…long before the 'A' word gained prominence. This was a shameful and disturbing event in South African history and one that would come back to haunt the South African Legislature in future years. So, put that in your British smoke and pipe it.

Allow me to reflect on other activities that took place at this majestic Victorian railway station. In this instance, I'm not referring to famous dignitaries that passed through, but for the purposes of this publication, I have taken the liberty to include the comings and goings of some of my earlier (redneck?) family.

In the late 1800s, my police sergeant grandfather (my father's father), had been called upon to carry out various duties at this vibrant location. On one such occasion, a man who had taken a woman hostage in a carriage delayed a train. Apparently, she was leaving him and leaving town. In the process of arresting the man, he unexpectedly produced a firearm and in the events that followed, he fired a shot at my grandfather in close quarters in the railway carriage. The shot somehow missed its target, but unfortunately, it splintered through the wooden compartment wall and sliced off the earlobe of a passenger in the adjoining compartment. My grandfather forcibly removed the offending man from the train suitably handcuffed. The amazing part of this whole incident is that the damsel in distress decided not to leave after all, but the poor guy who lost an earlobe would never be able to wear a 'pair' of earrings again.

As could be expected, some lighter moments also took place at that station. Enter my father...at age twelve. Allow me to set the scene. Every night at 6:00 P.M., the overnight train bound for Johannesburg from Durban stopped thirty minutes to collect mail and packages. This was its only stop during the journey, which would end at 6:00 A.M. the following morning. This train included a saloon coach with full bar. Despite the fact that this included bathroom facilities, nobody was permitted to use them while the train was parked at the station. Flushing while the train was parked at the station was not allowed...for obvious reasons. During this regular stop, businessmen routinely hopped off the train to buy cigarettes, candy, and the evening paper, etc....but more importantly, to use the public bathroom.

During such rush periods, a separate men's communal toilet was brought onto line to accommodate additional patronage. A strong flow of water was released through a large porcelain trough over which separate wooden cubicles were strategically situated, in which patrons sat to take care of business. In this manner, the swift running water would carry away all deposits.

During one such rush period, my father took a wad of cotton waste, which he saturated with kerosene. He then set it on fire and dropped it into the water as it entered the pipe. He then took off! Most of the soggy missile would be submerged...but, unfortunately, not enough. Pandemonium broke out! There were screams and shouts as men came pouring out of the building...many with pants down! Fortunately, nobody was seriously injured, but some were singed. However, nobody requested medical attention. This incident, however, caused the train to be delayed as those involved insisted that the stationmaster find the culprit. The stationmaster was furious, but was unable to satisfy their demand. There were two problems—one was that nobody really knew how the prank had been achieved. Added to this, was that the perpetrator was obviously a lone ranger. Nobody had any idea who the prankster was. I must mention, however, that during the train's long journey further up the line, there was many a story about guys trying to run with their pants around their ankles.

During the course of writing, I have compared and, in certain instances, linked American and South African situations because there is a connection between those 'so-called' American rednecks and their South African counterparts. Continuing in this vein, I will now relate an incredible connection between American and South African servicemen. Surprisingly, this connection does not take place in America or in South Africa...but, of all places...in Korea during those years of conflict. Even more incredible, is the fact that these courageous men from opposite sides of the world were, in this instance, connected by a 'privy in a paddy.'

However, before we go there, please allow me to set the scene, because as I had mentioned previously, it would be necessary to include some details of the more serious world events when tying up the American/South African connections and, in this instance, I am referring to the Korean conflict. Before relating the 'inter-continental' sequel to the station bathroom prank, I will need to connect the dots with regard to the Korean War. Please indulge me.

During the 1950-1953 Korean conflict, the South African government placed a fighter squadron at the disposal of the United Nations. This was '2 Squadron SAAF,' which incidentally included some of our valiant WW II Spitfire pilots. They initially flew prop-driven Cheetahs, but later converted to Saber jets. During operations, thirty-four South African pilots were lost, due mainly to accurate ground fire from the enemy. However, only one South African pilot and aircraft was lost in actual air-to-air combat. As in WW II, the SA pilots once again proved their superior flying skills…on this occasion, against superior Russian-built MIG-15 jets. These young pilots were recognized for their contribution in that conflict and were the recipients of many American combat medals: 55 DFCs (Distinguished Flying Crosses), 1 Cluster to DFC, 40 Bronze Stars, 176 Air Medals, 104 Clusters to Air Medals, 1 Soldier's Medal, 2 Silver Stars, and 3 Legions of Merit.

Number 2 Squadron of South Africa was also awarded presidential citations by the President of the United States of America. These airmen also received a basketful of honors and awards from the Republic of Korea, the United Nations, the Commonwealth, and the South African Government.

Sadly, a total of eight servicemen from all branches of the military were taken prisoner and the Roll of Honor numbered 34 pilots and 2 ground crew. They will be remembered.

It was in this setting on that far away continent that this sequel takes root.

Privy in a Paddy

A large camp housing US and SA pilots was established somewhere in that foreign land. The Americans had built the camp, which included a communal latrine similar to that of the railway station…except, in this instance, there were no separate cubicles. The men sat shoulder to shoulder while doing their thing. The ingenious Americans had diverted flowing water used to flush out the nearby Korean toilets to pass through their facility and then return once again through the Korean toilets. The forty-seat monster was referred to as 'the thunder box.' Once again, the scene was set. A mischievous member of the SA contingent constructed a small wooden float on which he placed kerosene soaked newspaper, which was set on fire. The little vessel was then launched upstream from the thunder box. Same reaction! Chaos reigned! Men came rushing out of the facility, many tripping over their pants. Despite concerted efforts, the Yanks never discovered the identify of the 'lone ranger.'

In an amazing coincidence, many years later, this incident would be related to me by a neighbor, Ted, who had actively served in that group. He, in fact, recorded the incident in a subsequent publication of the Korean conflict. To my surprise, he related that the prankster in Korea had gotten the idea from an incident, which took place many years before in South Africa. Ted's father was one of a group of businessmen on a train bound for Johannesburg on that fateful day. As can be imagined, this coincidence was extraordinary. You can only imagine his surprise when I was able to confide in him that it was my father, Harry, who had caused such chaos that day many years ago. At that point (not in time), Ted and I were the only two people in the world who knew the identity of the original station prankster and also the Korean prankster. 'Someone' had copied the idea from his father's experience on that fateful night at the PMB railway station. Now y'all know, too. Just as well that in today's modern world, we no longer have outside privies. Can you imagine our grand kids busy while playing with their blackberries in one of those wooden thunder boxes?

The thunder box tale and old time privies remind me of the American President's private bathroom and what took place there during President

Clinton's time, and I hasten to add that it has absolutely nothing to do with any interns...no, sir, this involves the then Vice President Al Gore. Maybe I should re-phrase that...

One evening during a late session in the Oval Office, Al Gore asked to excuse himself to take a bathroom break. Before he could leave the room, President Clinton suggested that Al use his private bathroom. Al was shocked because protocol did not allow it under any circumstances, but the hour was late and both men needed to join their wives ASAP. Speaking of which, that night Al bragged to Tipper about his Presidential bathroom visit, "You should see the opulence of the fittings," he told her. "And you won't believe the unusually shaped upright urinal! It's made of gold...no kidding! And I am the only person other than the President to use it!"

Late that night, Hillary asked Bill why he was so grouchy?

He replied, "You won't believe me, but some idiot peed into my saxophone!"

Redneck Family Moving on Despite Personal Setbacks

Shortly after the Royal visit I suffered a severe health problem, but I was not the only one; polio interrupted many a young life in South Africa and in our city in 1947. For some unknown crazy reason, the epidemic struck children under the ages of sixteen and that is when my luck ran out…but not for long…I'll 'splain…

It has always been my contention that no matter what the circumstances, the normal everyday 'Joe' and 'Jane' somehow summon the strength and the will to overcome. It is that tenacity in endurance that has made America the greatest country in the world. These virtues were the same in the South Africa of old. You gotta 'make your own luck.'

It is not my intention to labor on the unpleasant side of my polio experiences. Others fared far worse than I. We can dispose of those stories of hourly penicillin shots, lumbar punches, and physical therapy and move on to how all of us can turn our luck around. The best examples are those of our brave wounded vets…those men and women who have put country first and, in so doing, kept us safe. Please continue to remember them.

Before moving on, let's talk about 'luck' and 'making our own luck.' One of the most famous golfers, during an interview after winning a green jacket, listened as an interviewer (some are dumber than others) remarked, "Well, Gary, you were very lucky to make that put on the last green."

Gary grimaced (old golfers do that when confronted by an idiot) and replied, "Yeah, the harder I practice, the luckier I get."

The moral: Perseverance pays and there is no better example of perseverance than that of those indisposed in hospitals. It is in these circumstances that bonds are formed that will be set in concrete. From my own experiences during hospital confinements, another factor comes into play to help with recovery…humor…no kidding.

How Doctors and Nursing Staff Survive

While we all appreciate the care and healing received in hospitals, nobody wants to stay there a moment longer than necessary. Tell me about it. During my personal polio hospitalization, there came a time when I wanted 'outta there!'

After several months in isolation wards followed by weeks in general therapy, I was personally ready for release, except for that darn wheelchair, a temporary situation until my legs cooperated fully. Nevertheless, having to use my arms to propel and maneuver that rickety contraption did two important things for me: First, it strengthened my arms. Second, it made my brain work. The combination of the two meant only one thing—a wheelchair race! Think about it. All those other kids in wheelchairs were about to take part in the first NASCAR race (National Association of Serious Children Anthropomorphously Racing).

Back to the hospital race scene…I needed the help of an older and wiser kid, so I recruited Wing Nut Peterson. Who else? He was the oldest guy in a wheelchair and he could control that baby. It was rumored that he could actually spin the wheels. I tried this once and burnt the skin off my palms, so I figured that he would probably win the first race.

It took several days to put the 'secret' race plans together and it was finally agreed at the 'secret' driver's meeting that the big race would take place in the Talladega courtyard during the usual afternoon lull in the hospital activities. In due time, all the race-fit competitors, twelve in number, lined up at the edge of the courtyard and on the command from Sledge Collins (whose wheelchair was in for repairs and rode passenger with Willie Sneedon), the race was called, "Gentlemen, warm your tires!" followed by "Go…" and they went!

'Man-to-man,' the race was 'on' but, unfortunately, on the very first turn, the youngest competitor lost control when Jet Roberts bump-drafted him into a laundry cart and, remember, there were no safety barriers. Others crashed into the out-of-control vehicles and guys were flipping out of their chairs all over the track. This was before safety belts. It was a mess! Nurses and laundry staff appeared out of nowhere even before our own 'first responders' were able to limp to the crash site. I am happy to report that other than Skinny Potter, nobody was injured. Skinny skinned his funny bone. That is why he can't help laughing about it to this day. As for me…after the enquiry in the red trailer, I was grounded. My wheelchair was confiscated, but it was returned the following day for humanitarian reasons.

Post race: 'Jimmy the Cricket' (Jimmy Crocker) was declared the winner because he was the only driver to complete one lap. When interviewed he said, "I had a blast…like, you know…at this point in time, this was like my first…you know, race…like in my career, at this point in time…" and all future NASCAR drivers took note. Oh, I almost forgot to mention, Porky Wales was disqualified for driving with new tires when all the rest of us were on slicks. Some guys start their criminal careers early.

Several weeks later, boredom reared its ugly face and the guys became restless. As all wheelchair races were banned, we all turned our attention to promoting a different kind of race. We selected two teams of competitors—three on one team recovering from having their appendix removed, and three patients who had endured hernia surgery. As you can imagine, these were not the fastest guys on the block, so stopwatches were not necessary to arrive at a winner.

After careful planning, one afternoon after visiting hours when the nurses were pre-occupied, we lined up the six competitors at one end of their ward. It was agreed that the winner's prize would be that he could eat the desserts of the losers over the next six days…'cause losers are losers…right! The distance of the course was dictated by the length of the ward, about fifty feet.

On the count of three, Billy 'Rooster' Watson made the sound of a rooster crowing and the race was 'on.' The race took forever! All the competitors wobbled along clutching their stitches moving like human crabs as they agonizingly made their way to the finish line. Tony 'the spick' Florentino won easily by walking backward. There was an official complaint from Teddy Dangfort, which was rejected, as the rules never specified how the contestants could run (er…walk). On reflection, I was glad that nobody ran (er…drove) backward during our infamous wheelchair race. That could have caused problems. You think?

Butcher…Baker…Candlestick Maker…Whatever

I had previously mentioned that Harry and Ella had bought a well-established confectionary business. After several years of hard work, the family coffers were starting to overflow. This was not just a case of our cup being half full…I mean full of the good stuff…better than honey…'dough' (pun intended). The bubble of success burst when Harry bought a racehorse. He also acquired a few other vises! Bottom line, within six short months, Harry was forced to sell the business and our home…and the two Hudsons disappeared. The word 'disappeared' will be 'addressed' later. We rented a house, not to be confused with a home, on the outer limits of the 'other side' of the tracks! 'The wrong side of the tracks' comes to mind. Ella took in lodgers and 'belt tightening' took on a whole new meaning! In later years when Harry recounted what had caused his downfall, he offered, "Strong drink, fast women, and slow racehorses!"

HARRY, ... with his "Biggest Birthday Cake in The World!" 1952.

Made and presented to Catherine Higgens, Miss South Africa 1952 Who was place in top ten in Miss Universe held in Long Beach CA.

Hudson, Hudson, Wherefore Art Thou?

I mentioned that during Harry's financial calamity, his two beloved Hudsons had 'disappeared.' Well, not exactly! Within a few months, Harry was in the taxi business…with two Hudsons, both recently resprayed in matching 'bronze.' Seems that when Harry had realized that he was about to hit the wall, he transferred the two cars to somebody living out of town! When you are a redneck…blood is thicker than water. On reflection, I wondered what Harry was up to because he spent many a day in the country with 'Cousin Johnnie.' I recall Ella complaining about the bronze paint stains on his overalls. You could be a redneck if you are able, not only to hide two huge new model Hudsons, but to make both of them magically reappear in bronze with BUNNY'S TAXI signs boldly displayed on the fronts doors. This new phase might be thought of as a tacit declaration of the emancipation of the Bromfield siblings! Hold your horses! It simply meant that Harry's sons were no longer 'under age' and underpaid confectionary workers. Further, we were soon to be 'under age' and underpaid (not if I could help it) taxi drivers on those busy Friday and Saturday nights. Within six months, Harry's Hudson fleet grew to five bronze cars. Many more bronze paint-stained overalls in the wash. It was the weekend increase in fares that dictated the need to increase the size of the fleet. During the week, threes cars were more than sufficient for Harry and his one full-time driver, Lefty Williams, whose right hand had been lunch for a shark in his youth. I wondered what his nickname would have been if he had lost his left hand. But thinking about it…I don't suppose that it would have made any difference.

Who in the world would have called him 'Righty'?…Right?

I mentioned that Harry's sons would soon become under age taxi drivers on Friday and Saturday nights. I must 'splain. All taxi drivers had to obtain a 'public service' license, which involved a more comprehensive and stricter driver's test. A further restriction was a minimum age limit. Only adults over twenty-one years of age were allowed to apply for this category of license. All other citizens applied for normal licenses at age eighteen…unlike in America, where the driving age is sixteen.

Over time, my two older brothers obtained legal status as taxi drivers, but in my case, I had to wait...not until my twenty-first birthday, but once I turned eighteen and passed the normal driving requirements, Harry 'used' me illegally during the busy weekends, mostly the late night/early morning periods. At this stage, Bunny's Taxi operated from an old house that Harry had converted into a taxi depot. Beside bathroom facilities, it had comfortable old easy chairs and bunks for the driver's use between fares. At the time, I was working Monday through Friday at a local factory and driving taxis on alternate weekends...dating considered, became a 'lucrative' and 'interesting' hobby. More 'splaining'...

'Lucrative,' because Harry paid in cash a percentage of the fares collected...unlike the small change he begrudgingly paid his sons in the confectionary business, and I preferred driving to making pies and icing cakes. Do not tell my wife that I can bake pies and ice cakes! She already has me shoveling compost on her garden to produce them greens that resemble weeds and end up on my dinner plate. Some of these greens have exotic names like 'mustard greens, collard greens' and one named after 'Ohpra.'

Back to 'interesting,' with regard to taxi driving ...when you are eighteen and wired like the spring of a tall grandfather clock, you think you know it all. Sound familiar?

Some more 'interesting' taxi work...well, I soon realized that I did not know it all...even at eighteen. Hard to believe in 'this day and age.' Another much abused term. However, take for instance the fact that some people are transformed when night falls; something 'like' human metamorphosis.

For instance, take Betty, my doctor's attractive young assistant, the one with the big Dolly Parton eyes that distracted male patients while Dr. Doolittlegood prepared one of those flu mule shots. On Friday nights, she would transform herself from the seriously concerned nurse dressed in a starched white uniform, to an overdressed but a very, very sexy number in an outfit that revealed cleavage right out of Heaven. Remember, I was just eighteen!

She used Bunny's Taxis every Friday night, despite the fact that she owned a cute Triumph TR3 sports car, which she could afford because her employer paid her well! In fact, she was considered to be the best-paid doctor's assistant in town. Lefty told me that.

As I worked the late shift most Friday nights, I would often take the call to pick her up at the Plough Hotel parking lot around eleven P.M. and drive her back to her cozy apartment downtown. I really liked her and she must have liked me, because she tipped generously. However she always added, "Don't ask...don't tell." Darn...for that kind of tip she could become invisible!"

I did wonder when and how she got to the Plough Hotel. All I had to do was ask Lefty. He filled me in. She used Kelly's Cab Service, our main competition; I asked Lefty how he knew that and he told me that his brother Lucas worked for Kelly. I later met Lucas and I noticed that he walked with a slight limp. I wondered whether he had been swimming with Lefty when the shark came to lunch.

I must mention that it was common knowledge, according to Lefty, that Dr. Doolitttegood's wife, Mable, was also a public-spirited person like her husband. She chaired the regular Friday night 'Women's Auxiliary,' working long and hard every Friday evening until late, helping the less fortunate and needy women to learn the art of sewing on the latest Singer sewing machines. I got the impression that on those same Friday nights, her husband was also working long and hard.

Did I mention that taxi driving was very interesting? I could write a tell-it-all that would challenge Peyton Place, but I did not really want to hurt anybody. So, why did I mention the doctor and Betty, his cute little assistant? Well, the truth is that Betty is not her real name and Dr. Doolittlegood is not the doctor's real name. You guessed that? AND the doctor's wife's name was not Mable. You never thought of that because you were too focused on the other 'pair'...a new learning experience for y'all.

The truth is that the whole affair fell apart when the doctor's young assistant skipped town with Lucas when he won the lottery. Then, within a month, the doctor's wife divorced her husband and married the Singer sewing machine agent. It's all in the record book now, so there is nothing to hide. I can't quite make up my mind whether I should reveal the truth about the circumstances of the loss of Lefty's right hand. That could top anything in Peyton Place.

Since I have included some taxi driving history that involved others, I feel that it is only fair that I should cover some of the escapades involving myself and, in some instances, others in my redneck family.

Confession time...

I mentioned that Harry paid the drivers a fair percentage of the fares. He also covered any out-of-pocket expenses, such as they were. Here's an example: Harry had a strict rule that immediately after drivers had dropped off their passengers, they were to call from the nearest phone booth...no CB radios or cell phones in those days. In this manner, drivers were diverted to new locations to collect passengers without first driving back to base. This was both a gas saver and a time saver. The only problem was that it cost a 'tickey,' a diminutive three-penny coin. It worked like this:

After dropping a fare, we would then drive to the nearest phone booth. We knew the exact location of every one in and around the city. We would remove the handset and dial the base number and, if we did not drop a coin in the box, a recording would inform us that we would only be connected once a coin had passed through the system making a loud clicking sound before connection was made. ENTER MY ELDEST BROTHER DOUGLAS! Allow me to digress. This is good stuff! My big brother, and I mean 'big,' he was six foot two at fourteen and grew bigger and stronger for several years thereafter, and nobody messed with him! Nobody!

Well, Douglas was one really smart dude. After high school, he joined the government telephone company where, after completing a five-year apprenticeship, he qualified as an electric technician. He then completed night courses in electrical engineering and, finally, at a young age he became the chief 'something or other' and he was given a corner office with a fantastic view. He knew more about telecommunications than Hitler's Goebbels.

So, back to the phone booth, this is what Douglas taught me. Bless his heart y'all. He showed how to use the public phone system without using coins. Really! He took me to a public phone booth and squeezed me in beside him…and I mean 'squeezed!' Those colonial phone booths were made for skinny Pommies…not for a monster and his little (not so little) brother. Question: Do you think it was possible for a couple to make out in one of those booths? I will relate an interesting story about that later. Maybe…maybe not.

Back to Douglas and I in that tight booth in the mid-summer heat! Once comfortable (kidding), Douglas removed a pin from his collar. Did you know that is where we all secreted the odd sewing pin? Handy for digging out splinters we regularly received when squirming around on those hard old church benches. This was, however, no ordinary sewing pin. It was twice the length of the average pin. He then took hold of the phone cord and carefully forced the pin into the outer cable and through one of the wires until the sharp end of the steel pin protruded out the other side. Once satisfied with his handy work, he grunted with satisfaction. Remember, the confined space. He then said, "Take note, little brother." I took note. He picked up the receiver, dialed his girlfriend (one of many), and when she answered, he scratched the sharp point of the protruding metal pin against the metal coin receiving box and, to my utter amazement, the familiar sound, like that of a coin being dropped in the box, came through loud and clear. He talked 'lovey-dovey' talk to the girl and made a date before replacing the receiver. JD: JOB DONE!

From that time on, I saved many coins, but I still claimed a 'tickey' from my father for every call that I made to base. Did I mention being underpaid? Every dime counts in this life. It's the same as the CEO of my bank who gets all those freebies, except his take is much bigger. Why am I confessing this at this time in my life? Well, to be honest, nobody can hurt Douglas now. He hurt enough in his final hours…and for me…frankly, my dear, after all that happened in Africa, "I don't give a Shan!"

For the moment, I will leave the taxi scene despite the many interesting, amusing, and sometimes sad incidents that roam around in my aging brain. However, I will consider bringing out the odd one if and when the opportunity presents itself. Stay tuned.

Newsflash – November 16, 2009

Fox News has just reported that a 911 call was received, wherein it was reported that a motorist had collided with an elephant...TRUE! I was taking a break from the stress of writing all this heavy stuff and sub-consciously, not to be confused with unconsciously, clicked on the TV news channel and listened with both ears. That's the best way to listen. As the young female reporter excitedly brought the conscious world details of the extraordinary Buick/elephant wreck, a thought flashed into my mind...well, maybe not exactly 'flashed,' but a little quicker than 'crept.' You guessed it! "Could this be the same elephant as the one who had spoiled Donny Mango's day at the Ashville Zoo?" I immediately called the zoo, but a recorded message informed me that due to unforeseen circumstances, all calls would be returned in the order in which they were received and that I should leave a message that included my telephone number. I left this message:

"This is Mr. G. Raff. Have you misplaced an elephant lately?"

Speaking of elephants, this is the second story involving an elephant, but not the last one. I have news for you. In later pages, I will relate an amazing and true incident of a young elephant and Harry...who else?

> REDNECK ADVICE: ALWAYS DRINK UPSTREAM FROM THE HERD!
> ANUDDER: "DON'T INTERFERE WITH SOMETHIN' THAT AIN'T BOTHERING YOU NONE, like a bumblebee.
> QWB: IS SANTA A SEX MANIAC? All I ever hear him say is, "Ho-Ho-Ho...Ho-Ho-Ho...Ho-Ho-Ho." Makes me see red whenever I lay eyes on him!

Did you ever wonder if there is any difference between a typical American Santa and the South African Santa? Are you kidding me? This is a good time to test the newly acquired wisdom that you should have acquired from all the brain food that you have ingested thus far. For those who have not advanced from the 'G-Plus' realm, I will paint a picture. In America, the Christmas season arrives in cold winter weather with white Christmases in many states. In South Africa, Christmas falls in hot summer weather and in some areas temperatures can exceed 100 degrees Fahrenheit. So, picture this Christmas scene in a rural town in the heart of Zululand, basking in the heat of the midday sun.

My old Zulu friend Shezi, seventy years old, two hundred and eighty pounds, and as hairy as an ostrich egg is wrapped up in a bright red Santa costume complete with elf hat and artificial snow white hair and beard, matching his two pearl white teeth. He wears steel toe safety boots to combat the heat of the sidewalk where he is strategically positioned in the blazing African sun to entice shoppers with small children into the department store that offers everything from eucalyptus oil to crocodile teeth necklaces. Talk about sweat! Get the message? Or, more to the point, do you get the difference between the typical cuddly American Santa and his microwave South African counterpart? The only similarity is the fact that their vocabulary is the same: "Ho-Ho-Ho, Ho-Ho-Ho, Ho-Ho-Ho." No comment!

SANTA UPDATE: The South African Union of Santas has negotiated a deal with all retailers, wherein it is agreed that all Santas would be accommodated inside stores and that a large comfortable chair would be provided for comfort. This new arrangement brings the South African Santas in line with the American Santa Union laws to encourage children to sit on Santa's lap and ask him to deliver certain gifts on Christmas Eve. It is these requests that are monitored closely by attentive parents who somehow get Santa to deliver these gifts via their fireplaces without being singed. Unfortunately, South African children are deprived of this delivery procedure because the large majority of South African homes do not have built-in fireplaces. Who needs to artificially heat a home that is already too uncomfortable at temperatures above 100 degrees F. over Christmas? Albert Gore should be asked to 'address' that issue at the 'global warming' chat sometime in the future.

ANUDDER SANTA UPDATE: Both the American and South African Santa Unions have added an important clause. All children not yet potty trained must wear diapers when handed to Santa for gift requesting sessions and those photo shoots…makes sense.

LAST, BUT NOT LEAST: Santas worldwide have been warned not to agree with any gift requests that may endanger the children. That came about because of the increased requests for AK-47s.

Musicians, Music, and the Unusual

Having briefly covered the origins of songs and lyrics in pubs, I felt the urge to draw your attention to the less-known facts regarding the dangers faced by musicians during public performances. Once again, you may be forgiven if you never realized that in some situations, there are those musicians who have actually been injured, or worse, while entertaining audiences. You are probably thinking, "Wow! Maybe some unsuspecting tenor was killed when the fat lady accidentally fell on him." Or the tenor, or the fat lady, or both fell into the orchestra pit. If you have followed the 'Arts Review' section in the Sunday newspapers, you will know that although on occasions, the odd artist has been injured, the most famous of all was Jacko Jackson whose hair was set on fire during a live concert. On the 'udder' hand, there is no record of a tenor being injured or accidentally killed by the 'fat lady.' However, there *is* 'on record' the fact that during a performance of *Porky and Bess* in London, a certain 'porky' soprano slipped and fell headlong into that small prompter's compartment in the front of the stage of the opera house. In her haste to extract her voluminous 'porky' body, she once more lost her footing and stepped into midair off the stage, landing on Gilberto, the skinny piccolo player, who has since given up playing. During the post fiasco press interview, the conductor, Adolf Sroudleheimer summed up the situation thus: "It was messy!" I have to conclude that he was referring to the 'messy soprano.' Definitely, no pun intended.

Which now brings me back to the subject of the dangers faced by certain musicians while plying their trade. Never far from my thoughts is my schoolboy friend Brian Shaw, whose violin string, the one that he used to create that high pitched screeching note that made his dog howl like a moonstruck coyote, snapped and curled back slicing a neat laceration on his left cheek. I am personally pleased to report that the injury was not life threatening; however, he was left with a thin scar around his left cheek, which became less and less noticeable as he aged. As his closest friend, I never mentioned the scar, but my cousin Lonny was known to refer to Brian as 'Scarface.' I thought that was very unkind, but then it was better than calling him lefty.

The two incidents just mentioned are a prelude to what can only be described as the "big one" with respect to musical calamities, a calamity in which I was directly involved one way or another. The setting is 1947 in PMB, where else? This is a true 'slightly' embellished account combining religion, music, humor, and dented egos.

After supper, one hot summer's evening when I was twelve years old, I went for a lengthy cycle ride. Although daylight savings time was not practiced in Africa, the summer evenings provided additional daylight. As I left, my mother called out to me to remind me to be back before dark, emphasizing that my father was still dragging his feet about buying me a light for the bicycle. I promised her that I would be back before dark. During my ride, the daylight seemed to be fading sooner than normal and I consequently decided to cut my ride short. This decision was to take me on a quicker route, but included a steep hill, which I would have to carefully negotiate. At the bottom of the hill, on the corner stood an old pub, which was the local watering hole for the middle class society who lived in the area. To gain entry to the pub, patrons were required to climb about a dozen concrete stairs to the two large swinging bar doors. Although alcoholic beverages were not permitted outside the building, it was not unusual on hot summer evenings to find several imbibers languishing on the front steps watching the world go by. In speaking of watching the world go by, every third Friday night, a local Salvation Army group would congregate on the grass verge diagonally across from the pub. As was the custom, this group who were all dressed in military-style uniforms with matching hats, would gather together beside their banner for church. The proceedings commenced with a suitable prayer followed by music by the band under the control of a music director. This would be followed by a salvation sermon from one of their number. The object of the music was to draw the attention of pedestrians and on this occasion those who sat on the steps outside the noisy bar.

The scene was set. I was 'flying' down the hill on my racing bike, head down and ass in the air. Halfway down the hill, I became aware of the band music in the distance. The band was in full swing and I recognized the Salvation Army style. I was picking up more and more speed down the incline and the thought crossed my mind that I should scoot close by the musicians and ring my bell to add a sparkle to the music. When within about one hundred yards of the group, I was startled by a pack of older professional cyclists returning from their training session. They were traveling at twice (embellishment) my speed, and noisily passed by on both sides of me. Their sudden and unexpected appearance scared the daylights out of me. That was no doubt their intention. For a terrifying moment, I almost lost control. That scared the 'shan' out of me!

Then very unexpectedly, a light delivery van reversed out of a driveway directly in the path of the cyclists as they passed me and none of us had lights. I presumed that the van driver had not seen us...it was almost dark. All the riders were forced to take drastic evasive action to avoid colliding with the vehicle, including me. The front riders swerved around the vehicle just missing it, but in so doing, they cut off the riders directly behind them, including me. To my horror, I realized that several of the riders were heading straight for the musicians, including me. Those poor musicians were so engrossed in their music and singing that they never noticed the approaching human missiles. The riders heading for them were out of control, including me. However, unlike the riders ahead of me, I was slowing down considerably. In this way, I was perfectly positioned for a bird's –eye view of the chaos that would follow.

    The music director, a small man, took a direct hit! His cap stayed, but he disappeared in a tangled mess of arms, legs, and bicycles. At that point, the trumpeter, trombone player, and tuba player went off key as a second cyclist took out the trombone player. He was felled like a tree! He went down with a thump as the rider flew into the air and completed an all points landing on the verge where he lay motionless. The third rider simultaneously collected the trumpeter, lifting him into the air, not unlike a matador on the wrong end of a bull. The trumpet flew through the air as the two men and machine landed heavily, just missing the trombone player who at this point was still in motion. The drummer was a central target. He was a big man with an enormous drum strapped to his chest. Fortunately, the rider who collided with him missed the drum. However, the big man took a broadside hit on one shoulder, spinning him around as the rider fell to the ground like a dead chicken. The drummer, a heavy man, somehow stayed on his feet, but in spinning around, his cumbersome instrument slammed across the body of the petite young banner bearer who was consequently sent stumbling across the verge. Poor Miss Anna, in a desperate attempt to retain her balance, she released her banner and as it flew out of her hands, it headed directly for the trombone player. This unfortunate musician was picking himself up, half-dazed from his encounter with a human cannonball, when the heavy wooden staff cracked him across his temple and left eye. He went down again! Meanwhile, Miss Anna missed her footing, and almost drunkenly stumbled and fell very un-lady-like on top of the trumpet player. Although she was appropriately dressed in a long skirt, I noticed a fine pair of nylon wrapped legs exposed as she rolled onto the ground. Her uniform would survive the encounter, however, her nylons were destroyed.

    The only musician not yet struck was the tuba player, who had been sitting on a folding chair at the time, watching the carnage in disbelief. He seemed mesmerized as he slowly stood up lovingly clutching his instrument to his chest. Then I hit him! He never saw me. He must have thought that the main onslaught was over. He never considered that a slower biker slightly behind the main bunch would appear out of nowhere. Well, whatever went through his mind, something much more mind-boggling was about to go through his underwear. I hit him in the rear, dead center! Not on the left…not on the right…but, right in the groove! At that point of impact, my bell rang! Despite the fact that I was slowing down when I hit him, the impact sent him stumbling forward and he crashed headlong into the already 'shell shocked' Miss Anna. They both went down! I fell off the bike on the grass verge with hardly a scrape, thanks to my reduced speed. I instinctively jumped up, picked up my bike, and leaned it lovingly against a nearby fence. I then returned to lend a hand. What a sight! It was chaotic! The only man standing was the music director, who was limping around calling out to the others. I could not help noticing his baldhead shining in the glow of the streetlight. People were appearing in droves, many from their homes, including a wave of humanity pouring through those heavy swinging doors of the pub, many of who were unfortunately still drink-in-hand, as they noisily converged on the scene. This was no Saturday Night Revival!

Most of the victims suffered bruises and cuts, but, fortunately, no broken limbs. Miss Anna was in shock and in tears; nevertheless she was doing her best to console the others. She was a sight! She was completely disheveled; one shoe missing and a gaping tear in her long skirt revealing a shapely leg through torn hose. The biggest concern seemed to be the condition of the trombone player. He was sitting up with a dazed look as his bruised face started to discolor. The music director, who on that evening was acting as the pastor, was gently questioning the bewildered musician as he sat staring into space. He finally responded by saying very audibly, "What the hell happened?" The pastor quickly calmed the man down…he needed counseling! Then the dazed musician added, "Some idiot hit me with a baseball bat!" With that, poor Miss Anna burst into tears. Then to make matters worse, one of the patrons of the nearby bar appeared, glass of beer in hand, wearing the music director's hat at a ridiculous angle and with a proud gesture offered Miss Anna his drink. Miss Anna, a true trooper, simply declined the offer and in turn politely invited the surprised man to join them at their next regular Sunday service. With that, she gently removed the hat from his head, thanking him for returning it. The man was flabbergasted and quickly left the scene. (I often wonder whether he has taken her up on her invitation.)

It was now dark and I realized that I would have to get home as quickly as possible. I pushed my way through the crowd quickly retrieving my bike and slowly wheeled it away. The last comment that I heard from the crowd as I prepared to leave was from someone who had obviously witnessed the events from a vantage point on the concrete stairs. I heard him remark, "I saw the music director flying ass over kettle!" I needed to get home before curfew!

A word about the Salvation Army folk…. Who are they? What motivates them?… Etc., etc.….

In South Africa, these were Christian believers whose dedication to their beliefs and their service to mankind bonded them in reaching out to one and all as they spread the word of salvation. Their love for their fellow man/women has been demonstrated by the many facilities that feed the hungry, clothe the poor, and provide overnight facilities to those in need…all done to glorify God…no strings attached. Their attire resembled uniforms similar to many military uniforms of times past. No different to our American members and those active Salvation Army members all over this world.

This tidbit of information is intended to enlighten the reader of the fact that those poor souls that were mowed down by the cyclists were no different to those in similar circumstances worldwide, except that they were in the wrong place at the wrong time! Like asking the 'wrong' question at the 'wrong' time. How's your memory y'all?

Time Out?

Further examples of being in the wrong place at the wrong time…

Something like someone (redneck…maybe) jaywalking down a railroad track happily playing a 'mouth organ'…same as a 'harmonica,' but aptly named in this instance, as 'mouth' is the operative word in this incident. Our boy Henry happily playing away wandered into a tunnel just as the Silver Bullet entered from the other side. The mortician was faced with the difficult task of extricating the instrument that was wedged between the teeth and the tonsils of the departed. Dr. Quincy later related to the gang at the Pig in the Poke watering hole, "You guys won't believe this, but I had to remove a musical instrument from a stiff this morning." A fellow patron chirped in, "That does not surprise me in the least. I once saw a man grab a musician and try to shove his banjo where the sun don't shine."

There is a difference between removing a harmonica from a guy's pie trap as opposed to removing a banjo from where the sun don't shine. You think?

When I was a kid, I saw an old movie with a comedy scene of a musician playing the smallest harmonica in the world, which he played without using his hands. He somehow kept the tiny instrument between his lips and played away. At the end of his performance, a well wisher slapped him on the back and he swallowed the darn thing. From that moment, whenever he tried to speak, the harmonica played. How do you like that? Can you imagine someone walking up behind Satchmo and slapping him on the back while playing the trumpet?

You also gotta be careful not to criticize musicians. Cletty Fowler sidled up to Quincy one night after a 'few belts' and said quietly and confidentially, "I was in a Vegas bar one night when a drunk made a derogatory remark about the quality of the live music and the poor guy ended up in an alley with broken eardrums." No telling how much loud music damages the eardrums. I noticed that my neighbor's teenage daughter has the look of someone who has been ten rounds with Ali when she removes those earphones after several hours of listening to her modern music. Oh…and for several minutes she is unsteady on her feet. This condition is similar to the effects of riding a merry-go-round too many times.

Bottom line is music does not only bring pleasure, but also much pain. (More on this subject 'somewhere' in this book.) So, if you are musically inclined, resist playing any instrument in the shower. You may step on the soap! I must confess that I love 'big band' music. My all-time favorite piece is Glen Miller's rendition of *In the Nude*. I have no idea what my wife's favorite musical piece is and I think it best that I don't ask her. On the other hand, my neighbor and ex-drinking partner found out his wife's favorite after she left him. It was *So Long; It's Been Good to Know You*. He was sort of surprised because she had previously told him that there was nothing good about him. Makes one think...don't it?

>REDNECK WOW: "Life is simpler when you plow around the stump." (If you have a John Deere.)
>REDNECK WOW: "Timing has a lot to do with the outcome of a Rain Dance."

Those Who Teach

Writing about the dangers of musicians at work, brought something to mind. Not a speeding cyclist bearing down on me out of control; no, I was thinking about the teaching profession. From my personal experience, I have concluded that the teaching profession is one fraught with danger. I hasten to add (Oops! Must try not to repeat myself at this 'point in time.') I am not referring to present day students who carry AK-47s to school in those Wal-Mart backpacks. I am referring to those who taught the likes of me in the good old days when Wally-World did not exist…nor did backpacks. We carried our weapons of self-destruction in miniature suitcases, important things like 'smokes and matches,' marbles…and cough drops. Also, a small Jack Daniels bottle…lovingly filled with milk by Mama for her baby! Also, the odd turkey sandwich for washing down with milk during the morning recess. Did you ever wonder how a bottle of milk and a turkey sandwich 'went down' after languishing in an old small battered suitcase in the African summer months? It is sixty years since my last turkey sandwich and the same applies to 'warmed' milk!

So, it is that we now move into the more serious side of teaching in the good old days. Did you ever fall in love with a teacher? That's a good question, huh? Falls into the QWB category, big time! I am assuming that this question is directed at guys…after all, what right-minded (including left-handed), normal thinking gal would read this book? I am also assuming that all guys in those days were taught by females at one time or other…because most men worked at trades in them days. Any able-bodied male reading this that never had a female teacher is excluded from answering this question, right? Think about that, Stanley!

My response to the question is: Are you kidding me? In my day, falling in love with a teacher was included in the curriculum…refer to 'Teacher Love 101.' Why do you think that nature made the apple tree? Not to tempt Eve, but to tempt all female teachers. How many apples do you think were secreted in those small battered suitcases? Any self-respecting guy with a hidden apple would do all in his power to be kept 'after class.' But, it had to be done discreetly, not the way Archibald Arsolein did it! He figured that he could accomplish two things at once—get detention, but at the same time impress the new young and very sexy female teacher with his intellect. Not easy when he could not even spell 'intellect.' It was "Teacher Love 101" at first sight. This is how it went down…

The Principal Mr. Bingle introduced Miss Bell, a new teacher, to our class. As she taught English, she suggested that the pupils introduce themselves to her by stating their full names aloud. She further stated it would be interesting and beneficial for each student to syllabize his/her name, particularly since her subject was English.

The first student stood up and said, "My name is Tom Taylor. T, O, M…Tom ; there's your Tom. T, A, Y…Tay ; there's your Tay. There's your Tom Tay. L, O, R…Lor; there's your Lor. There's your TAY-LOR. There's your TOM TAYLOR."

Then our boy Archie stood up and said, "My name is Archibald Arsolein. A, R, C, H…Arch;, there's your Arch. I; there's your I. There's your Arch-I. B, A, L, D…Bald; there's your Bald. There's your I-Bald. There's your Arch-I-bald.

A, R, S…Ars; there's your…

"WHOA," intervened the Principal. "That's good enough for now, my boy."

Poor old Archie…not asked to stay after class with Miss Bell…instead, had his Arsolein posterior warmed by Mr. Bingle. But, he did get to eat his apple on the walk home.

QUESTION: CAN YOU COMPLETE THE SYLLABIZING OF Archibald Arsolein's name? THE 'FIRST' READER TO SUCCESSFULLY ACCOMPLISH THIS CAN WIN $100 (A HUNDRED).

Well, Archie was not the first student to fall in love with a teacher…and he won't be the last. But, in Archie's case, he was not seriously injured. A little warmed up, maybe, and pretty Miss Bell survived to teach another day. But for me, my 'Teacher Love 101' turned out real bad for the teachers.

Take Miss Miles, for instance. She was my English teacher when I turned fourteen. Unlike with Archie who fell in love with Miss Bell at first sight, my affections took longer…three days. She was not many years older than me, I thought, and the height difference did not bother me because I was a fast grower. If it were not for the fact that I was not yet in line for my elder brother's shoes, I would probably have been only about three inches shorter than her. But, as I said, I was a fast grower. Miss Miles, a real beauty, was on her first assignment at our school.

Fresh for the picking…so to speak…I knew from the very first week that she liked me and I had already been in love with her for two days. She must have felt it. Why else would she pick me to read the part of Julius Caesar in class oral reading? Considering that Julius Caesar was the main character throughout the book, right? Let's drop that thought and cut to the chase.

Two months later, the love of my life was tragically killed in a small plane crash with her boyfriend Glen. How about that? She never mentioned that she was going steady. That's woman for you. Fickle to the core! Not that it was any consolation for me…stuck playing Julius Caesar. But, at least there was some consolation in the fact that I would have plenty of spare time eating apples while jerks like Charley Dangerfield made a mess of Mark Anthony.

A few years later at age sixteen, I fell in love with another English teacher, Miss Powell. I'm not sure why exactly because she was much older than me…but I figured that once I started to shave the age difference would not be so obvious…and once I got my driver's license, she would not be able to resist me. After graduating with straight Gs for 'Good,' I planned to date her once I started to shave. Unfortunately, by the time I needed a shave, she was in a retirement home.

And, finally, once I got my driver's license, she was in the funeral home. It's as I said right at the start of this paragraph, teaching is a dangerous profession for women. On the 'udder' hand, some of those dudes teaching are not bad looking either. Which brings 'Archibald Arsolein' to mind and my $100…no kidding!

Never Judge a Book by Its Cover

Never has a truer word been spoken. Never judge someone on how they dress. The same applies to someone's accent. Some examples...

A lady sitting beside me in a bus overheard me talking to my wife. That's not like eavesdropping, right? She interrupted me. That's worse than eavesdropping, and she asked, "You're from Australia?"

"No, Ma'am, I'm from South Africa," I answered grimly.

With that, the guy sitting on the other side of her, who was listening (but not eavesdropping) asked her, "Where did he say he's from?"

She answered him with a question, "Were you eavesdropping?"

"No, Ma'am, I just happened to overhear your question. That's not the same as eavesdropping. So, where did he say he was from?"

"From Australia," she answered.

Two friends were sunning themselves on a park bench in Albemarle, North Carolina. One was a plumber dressed in a brown coverall, heavy Red Wing boots, wearing a ball cap advertising liquid manure. He needed a shave. The other fellow sported a pair of emerald green slacks, a yellow shirt, greenish woolen vest, and wearing a pair of steel capped safety shoes. His green Vegas ball cap struggled to keep his ginger hair away from his ears. His matching ginger full beard had recently been groomed (not too recently). Like the plumber sitting beside him, this septic tank refurbishing consultant was out of work. All this important information I gleaned while sitting on an adjacent bench listening to their conversation. This is commonly referred to as 'eavesdropping.' One guy's name was Tom and the other guy's name was Tom. They had been discussing Tom's daughter.

Tom said, "Dr. Brady thinks that Alice has A.D.D., but I believe that her condition stems from Strep Throat."

Tom nodded in support and replied, "I think that you are on to something, Tom, because you told me last time that she was recovering from a serious sneezing attack. I suspect that as she had sneezed every few minutes for a month she obviously suffered from Pediatric Autoimmune Neuropsychiatric Disorder, which is associated with Streptococcus Panda."

Tom agreed, "You are absolutely correct, Tom, I know that the Panda condition occurs following Streptococcus infection, which is Strep Throat."

"Yeah, I concur, Tom, and symptoms of Panda also include Cognitive Inflexibility and, in most cases, Obsessive or Compulsive Argumentative Behaviors, including Tourette's Syndrome, which leads to A.D.D. And, if that ain't so, Tom...my name ain't Tom!"

"That's right, Tom. Alice is one sorry argumentative little girly."

"Catch you next Saturday, Tom."

"See you round like a doughnut, Tom."

I wondered if they were investment bankers. What do you think?

When I heard that Willy Nelson was booked at the Cabarrus County Arena, I invited two of my 'obvious' (in my judgment), redneck pals to join me for the last Saturday evening performance. I figured that I should dress appropriately, as I wanted to blend in with the expected crowd. "Who wants to stand out in a crowd?" I reasoned, so I got a tattoo for my right bicep...the one with a red heart with a dagger embedded in its left ventricle above those famous words, DEATH BEFORE DISHONOR.

I skipped shaving that week and forewent my end of week shower, dressed in torn jeans, a faded plaid shirt, and soiled running shoes and headed out in my vintage Thunderbird to meet the guys at the arena entrance. The parking lot was absolutely packed...with the most colorful arrangement of pickup trucks that I had ever seen. Many were flying the Confederate flag and NASCAR stickers were prominent, as were bumper stickers advertising the fact that they had voted for the wrong guy to live in the White House. I noticed gun racks in rear windows, but was relieved that no hunting rifles or AK-47s were on display. I would not have any trouble locating my little white two-seater in this setting...if it was still there after the show. But, the friendly police presence was very comforting. I joined the throng of humanity crushed together heading for the entrance. Let me clarify that statement...the crowd heading for the bathrooms deposited me at the front door where my two buddies waited wide-eyed in the foyer. They stood out like sunshine on a hookers face cream. Like all the other patrons in the expensive seats, they were very neatly and tastefully dressed. I was the only one dressed appropriately. At least I blended in with those other guys from the buddy section dressed like me who were peeing in the wash-hand basins, while all those nerds dressed like Lord Muck lined up waiting for their turn at the urinals. Just goes to show...when in Vegas, dress like Willy.

The Nifty Fifties…or…The Niffy Fifties

Growing up in the fifties as a teenager was incredible, except for soap and school. Television did not exist in South Africa. So, to amuse ourselves, we invented games such as 'spit and duck,' which was played in this manner. Two guys would lie down head-to-head on a suitable patch of soft, green, plush grass and they would each take a turn at spitting up into the air…the object being to see how much spit would land on the other guy, if he did not duck quickly enough. The rules did not permit anyone with a bad cold to participate. Girls were welcome, but never participated.

Another game pitted two guys, dressed only in their Jockey briefs against each other to see who could walk the greatest distance on their hands. Most testosterone-loaded teenagers can walk on their hands. Right! It's just that many have never thought to try it. The more adventurous older and bolder guys decided to take their show to the main intersection of Main and Church Streets. The winner of this competition was the guy who could walk diagonally across the intersection on his hands in the shortest time. Timing was of the utmost importance, not to mention it minimized the danger. High noon on Sunday was chosen because the majority of the citizens in my hometown were still in church at that time. Those who did attend church, and others who were on the golf links or still in the sack, kept traffic to a minimum. Unfortunately, during the summer, the Episcopalians and the Dutch Reformers set their worship time forward an hour and almost ruined the hand-walking competition. The interruptions of the Episcopalians were not as bad as those of the Dutch Reformed Church that caused the worst problem. Most the Episcopalian Church attendees had their own cars or car-pooled on the Sabbath and, although many crossed the intersection of Church and Main, the first of the competitors managed to dodge the traffic. But, after the Dutch Reformers passed through that intersection in their horse drawn buggies, Amish-style, the remaining competitors were not all able to dodge what the horses had deposited, although Bully Walton tried. Talk about being at the wrong place at the wrong time. He would have made it, except that the odor of the 'horse power' made him dizzy (his excuse) and he took a tumble right in the middle of…of the intersection. I bet you thought he fell in 'the middle of the diddle.'

There is a wonderful and beautiful sequel to this episode. Years later, Bully and Hester Brokenshaw hooked up, fell in love, and married in the Episcopalian Church. She confessed that it was love at first sight. She never forgot the sight of Bully in his underwear bouncing across Church and Main…could anybody? The loving couple is happily married and, despite his matured years, Bully can still walk on his hands across a basketball court, as he proved at their high school reunion last year. On that occasion, only one Dutch Reformer attended and he arrived in a Rolls Royce that bragged 280 horsepower. Good thing that those horses of old only boasted five pounds of horsepower per drop, otherwise poor old Bully would have remained single. Talk about the niffy fifties!

Flying Handstand
Author supported by Bunny "Strongman" Digue

Dirt Track "Special" (Citroen)
(Note "Beetle" crash helmet!)

Bush Series

"Every man for himself" (Demolition Racer)

Look Ma. No wheels!

Wall of Fire!
(Note "almost" naked roof passenger's leg protruding)

Pit Crew

"Happy landing"
From Ramp Launch

Funny and True

Over the years since my immigration to America, I have had to answer a myriad of questions regarding life in South Africa, but the one question that interests many is, What was your most scary or memorable or interesting wild animal experience? I have experienced all of the above, but I am reluctant to relate the few scary experiences because they took place at a time when even the new generation of young South Africans will doubt their authenticity. Yes, indeed, as a teenager in 1952, I had to run for my life from a rhino

That's when my buddies and I became expert tree climbers…and, yes, I suppose it is true that we could also be referred to as 'tree huggers.' Snake encounters were also part of those experiences. I even had to unwind a snake from my cat's neck in our front yard. Monkeys still roam freely in my old Umhlanga neighborhood to this day, and I have memories of chasing a troop of monkeys away from our 'paw-paw' trees by squirting a hose at them. My son Sean on his first visit back to South Africa during his university days in America had a close call when he was cornered by a group of adult monkeys while taking photographs of them in our yard in 1988. In his haste to escape, he threw his camera at the leader of the pack and made a run for it back to the safety of the house. The memory is still alive and well in his mind.

But, for me, my most memorable recollection is also the most interesting because, unlike wild animal incidents that unfold in the 'wild,' this particular wild animal experience took place in the middle of a bustling city. Yep, in good ol' PMB. Remember, Pietermaritzburg?

One afternoon as I entered the main road into the city from the north, I pulled up at an intersection as the light changed to red. When I stopped, a Lincoln Continental, four-door convertible, left-hand drive pulled beside me with the top down. Remember that South Africa is a right-hand drive nation. The Lincoln floated in and rocked to a stop. The monster resembled a boat, but she was a beauty. I noted the driver; he was a heavyset, red-faced, jowly man in a tailored white long-sleeved shirt. An expensive gold topped Parker ink pen protruded from his initialed shirt pocket. He was 'the man.' He smiled at me and I was about to compliment him on his wheels when a motorcycle squeezed in between us.

The rider Freddy was well known to one and all, mainly for the fact that he was an absolute motorcycle daredevil on the racetrack. He and his sidecar partner Kip had been South Africa's dirt track champions for years. On this occasion, Freddy had a very different passenger behind him on the duel seat. The passenger with his hairy arms around Freddy's waist was none other than Walter Mitty, his full-grown pet baboon. Both riders were helmet less, but both wore those large hideous WW II flying glasses. They were a sight astride Freddy's Triumph twin 650cc that he ran on pure 'dope' for extra power.

Their sudden appearance between the Lincoln and me was so unexpected that it took me a moment to believe my eyes. I had seen the pair on previous occasions from a distance as they cruised the highways, but this was the first time that I had seen Walter Mitty at such close quarters. He made me think of those kamikaze pilots, except that he was naked other than the hair that covered his body and those ridiculous flying glasses. On the other hand, the driver of the Lincoln could not believe his eyes as he looked in disbelief directly at the animal. The baboon, noting his stare, returned the compliment and his newfound admirer broke into a wide grin. Walter Mitty kept on staring intently at the driver and I wondered why. Without warning, the baboon shot a hairy hand out and, in the same movement, he snatched the golden pen from the shirt pocket of the guy sitting behind the wheel of the Lincoln. As the baboon examined it inquisitively with both hands, the red-faced man shouted out, "Put that pen back!"

This panicked the animal, which reacted by snapping the pen in two and for some inexplicable reason, he smartly returned the broken instrument to the man's shirt pocket. As he did so, the rubber tube containing the ink tore apart and splashed black ink over the white shirt and across the man's face and cheek.

In a fury, the man screamed at Freddy, "Look what your 'bloody' chimp has done!"

Freddy replied, rather calmly, I thought, "Well, he returned the pen like you told him to…he put the 'bloody' pen back didn't he?" Then raising his voice he added, "Walter does not like being called a chimp!"

With that, Freddy revved the powerful twin, let the clutch out, and the machine and its two riders took off against the light and were out of sight within seconds. I was quick to follow, as the driver of the Lincoln looked as if a stroke was imminent.

Whenever I recall this incident, I wonder what that guy Darwin would have thought if he knew that a baboon in South Africa could ride a powerful 650cc twin Triumph. No chimp had ever done that, but Darwin would have been impressed. Darwin originally thought that we had evolved from the orangutan! Now, I gotta tell y'all that I have seen many an orangutan in my life, and the thought of being their offspring makes me weak in the knees. Have you ever seen a pretty orangutan? Well, then Darwin changed his mind and decided that we evolved from the chimpanzee. Is that supposed to make me feel any better? I have seen many chimps in my life, and I challenge y'all to take a good hard look at what they do for fun in the zoo. They pick their noses and various other parts of their anatomy a lot. They are also not careful where they go to the bathroom…or how they go to the bathroom. When they appear on TV or in the movies, they are always wearing diapers under whatever clothing is provided. So, maybe the kamikaze pilots did learn something after all.

Well, no matter what Darwin said, this South African redneck is in no way, shape, or form related to the chimpanzee. If I was…how come I don't walk on my knuckles or pick my nose and 'udder' places of interest in company, and how come I am so tall? If I were part chimp, my butt would be closer to the ground. So, if someone insists that they believe in Darwin's theory of evolution, and that their 'Oupa' and 'Ouma' lived in trees…do not monkey with them. I must warn y'all that when we see how some jerks live, it may be possible that they are what they say they are. It is my duty to inform y'all that the world is made up of a many of 'them all' and that some of them find their way to the voting booths. The rest of us are just plain ol' rednecks. Thankfully!

This is the time! The time when I renew my claim that the South African has a stronger claim for the title of redneck than their American counterparts. The baboon riding a motorcycle incident goes one step further. Where in American redneck history can you find any animal like the South African redneck baboon? Not only have I presented individuals in South Africa who qualify for the title, but now a baboon adds to the weight of this claim. I feel sure that there may be Americans claiming a raccoon or opossum or rooster has been potty trained…but let's face it…no American wild animal can beat a baboon on a motorcycle. But, there's more. Much more! I am about to relate a South African redneck story that will top anything that their American competitors can come up with. It involves a big man and a bigger animal.

STOP THE PRESS! My publisher has advised me not to include this incident now. He warns that once this story has been told, the readers will conclude that this is the focal point of the book and stop reading…just like Kenny Rogers not singing *Lady* in the early stages of his live show in Bophutatswana for fear of the audience packing up and leaving after hearing his biggest hit at the time. Imagine all those Kenny Roger's fans streaming out the auditorium early and bumping into all those blind guys wearing dark glasses. And, if Kenny Rogers felt that way, that's the way it will be for me, too.

I must confess that the thought of 'some' of my books being returned for a refund so soon scares the shades off me.

The Not-So-Nifty Fifties
Time for Some Serious Reflection, With Respect

While my generation in South Africa and America lived it up in the fifties, some really serious 'stuff' was taking place...and I am not referring to rock and roll and the Hippie movement.

In South Africa, resistance to the newly passed Apartheid laws reached new heights. Boycotts by disgruntled black folk and organized protest marches were the order of the day.

In America around the same time, one hundred and fifty black citizens were indicted by a Grand Jury in Montgomery, Alabama, for taking part in a bus boycott. Some bad things were about to take place on both sides of the pond, but some other 'stuff' was also very interesting and very alarming.

First, some interesting 'stuff'. In May of 1952 the director of the USA Guided Missile Development suggested that the USA build space vehicles that could transport pilots through the solar system.

How preposterous! I thought. Next thing you know; some bright spark would say that we could get a man to walk on the moon. Boy, was Ms. Finklestein in for a surprise!

A few other tidbits of interest to ponder, which occurred during these years are: Field Marshall Jan Smuts died. He was the South African Prime Minister 1919-1924 and again in 1939 when he took South Africa into the war against Germany on September 6, 1939. His military background had included being a Boer general during the Boer War. During WW I, he thought up the plan for the League of Nations. At the subsequent Paris Peace Talks, he presented his concept in a pamphlet, which President Woodrow Wilson borrowed lock, stock, and barrel. The League was established in 1920, but finally failed and was replaced by the United Nations 26 years later. Ironically, for South Africa, this new forum would be the main instrument in the demise of Apartheid. In a November 1942 publication of *Life Magazine*, Smuts was considered one of the five most important individuals in the United Nations War effort.

There was plenty going on in the world around us during those years. In England, King George VI died and Princess Elizabeth, who thought that I was cute, was crowned Queen of England. Britain announced their ability to produce the atom bomb. In America, legislation was approved, which would limit future presidents to a maximum of two terms. Sometime later, General Dwight D. Eisenhower was elected President of the United States of America. He would be the president who would break ground on the March 10, 1954, for the first atomic power plant in history. Instead of using the traditional shovel, he broke ground using a radioactive and electronic device. A few weeks later on March 31, the US Atomic Energy Commission announced the development of a hydrogen bomb, capable of destroying any city on earth! On May 24, the US Supreme Court upheld the constitutionality of the Internal Security Act of 1950, declaring sufficient grounds for 'the deportation of aliens.' (WHAT?)

The Korean conflict had come and gone, but the constant flow of body bags returning to the USA had diminished the resolve of the American Administration. But, some other 'stuff' bubbled up to the surface…

Africa, in general was heading for turmoil during those years. In 1954, the British arrested over 700 Kenyon 'activists' who were extremist members of the Kikuyu tribe. This group had formed the Mau-Mau who had been opposed to European ownership and presences in 12,000 square miles of Kenya's highlands. They had killed both Asians and Europeans, but the greatest number killed were Kikuyu, who failed to support the Mau-Mau who were demanding an immediate surrender of the highlands. The British response came in a statement, "…to hit these people like they've never been hit before." British Air Force operations conducted the saturation bombing of Mau-Mau jungle strongholds. The Brits concluded that if the Mau-Mau had their way, the era of British domination would come to an end. Sure did!

In June of 1955, the AEC (Atomic Energy Commission) announced that the USA had the ability to build 'cheap' H-bombs of virtually limitless size. Now that really grabbed my attention…what did they consider 'cheap' and, more frighteningly, how did 'they' define 'limitless size?' Who were 'they?' It was no surprise, that the following month, in London, nine scientists led by Einstein strongly urged a ban on war, explaining that the newly developed nuclear bombs "threatened man's continued existence!" Not to be outdone, that December, the USSR exploded its most powerful H-bomb, which was equal to one million tons of TNT! At that time, they hinted that they were continuing with tests of "new types of atomic and thermonuclear weapons." In the interest of guaranteeing US security, I wondered how President Eisenhower felt about that as he recovered from a heart attack. Also, I did not think that his condition would be improved by the $44 million stock exchange loss a few days later! This was the heaviest one-day loss in the history of the stock exchange since its inception. Well, time would test that record. Has it?

Oh, and in October, South Africa walked out of a UN debate focusing on 'the racial conflict in South Africa resulting from the policies of Apartheid.' Ironically, the walkout took place on 'United Nation's Day,' supposedly a "happy occasion when nations were focused on cooperation."

Aaah, those were the days, my friend.

It was my intention to move on from the fifties to write stuff about the sixties, but I took a break to celebrate the arrival of the New Year 2010…and where better for a South African redneck to celebrate, but in the Blue Ridge Mountains. To be precise, in a cabin hanging off the side of a mountain wedged between the borders of Georgia, North Carolina, and Tennessee.

What follows is a detailed account of the collision of 'American Southern' redneck cultures and 'South African' redneck cultures. I felt that it was time to strengthen my case and cause, that the American Southerners could no longer claim the term 'redneck' as their sole or original heritage.

Cooling off" in Zinkwazi

"Water Conservation"

Have You Driven a Ford Lately?

While at the cabin, I went out for a walk and met Albert, the nearest neighbor, a really interesting, clean cut, forty-something 'can do anything' type of guy. *Not your typical redneck*, I thought. His 'little ol' cabin,' as he described his three-story four thousand square foot log home, was also precariously perched on the edge of a precipice. He and I became instant friends as did his dog 'Woody,' whose full name was Woodrow Washington. He was no ordinary dog. He could understand Mandarin. I'll 'splain later. Through this chance encounter, my wife and I were invited to a cookout at another neighbor's home 'to meet the locals,' who wanted to meet a South African. Albert described them as a group of 'good old boys.' He added that they were a little 'different,' but very hospitable. A 'little different' brought to mind my Willy Nelson experience, so this time I decided to do everything possible to fit in with these 'mountain folk.'

I dressed appropriately in faded jeans, not the torn type this time, and a red tartan shirt with long sleeves covering my tattoo to be revealed at a later stage as a conversational subject. *A nice touch*, I thought. I pulled on a pair of waterproof duck boots because we were expecting rain. Although I was told that all food and drinks would be provided, I carried a six-pack of 'Bud' to show my culture. My wife, who is always politically correct, wore a Belk's two-piece feminine outfit that matched the color of her eyes and the color of my six-pack. We drove to the cookout in my Subaru Baja with a wheelbarrow and two concrete blocks in the rear pickup compartment. I did not want to stand out in the crowd. All mountain folk drive pickups like those I had noted at the Willy Nelson parking lot, right?

The directions to the venue were not complicated. I drove down the mountain, descending about five hundred feet, then turned up another road and drove up the other side of the mountain. Did I mention that we drove up the mountain? The gravel road became steeper, and steeper, and steeper and we climbed so high that I became light-headed and my nose bled. Finally, as we crested the summit, the address came into view. I quickly checked the address on the mailbox and turned into a well-manicured driveway that led up to a massive and very impressive log home. It was not so much the size of the house that surprised me, but the number and makes of the cars parked at the front door. There were several Mercedes models in various lengths, all with tinted glass, a few imported SUVs, and an odd-looking Audi...no pickup trucks. I exited the vehicle gingerly and after extricating my wife from the passenger side with one hand (the other hand was trapped in that awkward shape six-pack package), I cautiously steered her onto the front porch. As I prepared to ring the doorbell, I became aware of background music floating through the house. I hesitated and listened, hoping that I could recognize the tunes. I had made a mental note of the banjo music played in a movie I had seen where some guys on a canoe trip down the Mississippi were rudely interrupted by some jerks that had a hard time distinguishing between males and females. I listened. 'No banjo music.' Instead, I heard some highbrow orchestral piece that you can't whistle.

My wife asked, "Why don't you ring the bell?"

I told her to 'Shoosh!'

She said, "Don't shoosh me!" It's a line she used before.

Then something caught my attention on the floor beside the front door. There were bunches (redneck word for lots'a) of shoes neatly arranged in pairs sitting beside one another. If it were not for the music, I would have concluded that we were outside a Mosque. I noted that most of the men's shoes were those modern seriously elevated leather slip-ons with those nerdy dingle berries hanging where shoelaces normally hang.

My wife said, "Looks like the other guests brought a change of shoes."

I knew that! But, I wondered why the guys were not wearing boots. On the other hand, all the women's shoes were flats. That sort of surprised me, but I figured it out. We were about to meet short men and tall women. Then the little woman spoke that 'little word' that strikes fear into the hearts of husbands throughout the universe. "Well?" she asked.

"Well, what?" I shot back. Husband lip biting time!

"Don't use that tone with me!" she snapped back. Then she pointed to my footwear and added, "You know what? Take off those dumb boots!"

"I can't, honey. I am not wearing socks!"

She froze, not unlike that woman in the Bible who turned into a pillar of salt. Then she gave me that tough-guy 'Bogey' look that meant I was going to have hot tongue and cold shoulder for supper for the next week. "Okay, okay, honey bunch, I'll take them off."

It took some effort to undo the knots in the heavy string that I used to replace the original laces during the previous winter when I went duck hunting with the vice president. I use white string for the right boot and brown string for the left boot...this way I make sure not to put the wrong boot on the wrong foot. I did that once. It takes the joy out of moon walking.

I removed my boots and placed them neatly beside the other abandoned shoes and my wife did likewise. Man, the moment that my bare feet hit the deck they started to turn blue. At least they would match my wife's eyes, I thought.

I was about to ring the bell when my wife interrupted, "Why don't you ring the bell, Biddie?"

It was not so much 'what' she said, but 'how' she said it that knotted my intestines. She knew how much I hated my middle name.

"Shoosh," I replied. Lip biting time again, I knew what was coming!

"Don't shoosh me," she said, right on the money.

I rang the darn bell and it played a melody that drowned out the nerdy background music and we heard a chorus of male and female voices singing out, "Someone's at the door." *You can't beat that with a two by four*, I thought.

A really big guy dressed like '007' opened the door, introduced himself as Jim (short for James?) and, after the usual formalities, he invited us into his home. My feet were praying for carpeted flooring, but no luck…all hardwood floors, except for one smallish Persian rug near the bar. *A good compromise*, I thought. It suited me, and my feet. The living room was huge and it needed to be because there were about ten couples scattered around drinking, kidding around, and laughing…until we made our entry. There was a deafening silence as Jim introduced us to the others. It only took one look for me to realize that I was the only one dressed appropriately…again! These dudes were sharp dressers, like my wife, except that she did not have anything on her stocking feet. Bless her heart y'all. I would hear more about that while driving home…if I lived that long. Nobody commented on my bare feet, but I felt compelled to set the record straight. So later, while standing on the Persian rug and leaning nonchalantly on the bar, I casually mentioned to our hosts, "I hope you don't mind my bare feet. This is traditional when attending functions in Zululand." That did it! My wife's jaw muscles tightened, causing her blue eyes to narrow and changing them to a color that brings out 'red eye' in photographs.

But, at least she did not turn to a pillar of salt.

Once the bare feet thing was settled, I started to chill out. That's different than your feet freezing. It's more like thawing out. Jim came over to serve me a drink, giving me a friendly slap on the back. Did I mention that he was a big guy with big hands? He handed me an odd-shaped glass, which he carefully filled with chilled white wine. Did this guy think I was gay? Before I could ask for a beer he said, "I always plan the menus according to the wines I have selected for the occasion. It is our custom." He looked down at my feet and added, "Something like your Zulu custom." My wife flinched.

He added, "I have chosen this wine because it is a three grape blend of Welschriesling, Riesling, and Gewurztraminer." That's a Gewürztraminer with a double dot thingy over the 'u.' I noticed a private smirk as he continued, "It is a 2008 Apatsagi Pannomhalmi Tricollis." That is an Apatsagi with a single dot thingy above the first 'a' and on the second 'a.'

The first gulp of the white wine tasted like stale vinegar and sent shock waves through my spleen, causing me to change from my usual gulping custom to sipping my poison, which lead to a great discovery…if you rinse your mouth in sour white wine, it removes yesterday's plaque from your teeth. The secret is not to let anybody know what you are doing. But, I figured that if my cover was blown, I could always enlighten them of the fact that this was another South African custom. A new thought crossed my mind; I wondered whether gargling with white wine would 'fix' Strep? 'Fix' is a redneck word covering everything from blocked drains, broken crankshafts, broken relationships, and Strep Throat. I was on a roll. But, in my considered opinion, no matter how many dot thingy's were over those letters, the wine tasted unfriendly.

As time moved on and my teeth became cleaner, I allowed my eyes to case the joint. I soon realized that the modern mahogany bar was not the only interesting piece of furniture in that huge living room. An imposing grand piano was strategically placed in the far corner. It was nothing like the piano that Wyatt Earp played. No, sir, this was a beautiful shining black instrument with some black keys and some white keys arranged so that the piano player would not mix up the left hand keys with the right hand keys…something like the way I identify my boots. I noticed that somebody had forgotten to close the big inspection lid over the top of the piano exposing the musical strings. Some were thinner than others and I assumed that they had been abused and would have to be replaced before they snapped. I decided to stand well back if some fool played the piano. Whoever had done the latest inspection had propped the lid open with a matching black stick in such a way that it reminded me of a sail on the little sailing boat that I made for my grandson that sank in our fishpond. I noticed a sheet of music that had also been abused in place above the keyboard. It had been written by some guy whose name sounded like 'Chop pan,' but was spelt differently, the way they spelled long ago before people learnt American. He had obviously died long before Elvis. There was a shiny blue electric guitar on a stand beside the piano, and I had picked up from general conversation that this was a 'Les Paul' original. I knew that. I wondered where they kept their banjo?

The walls were covered with weird paintings that I assumed were school art of their children that had been framed to make them feel good about themselves and boost their confidence. I noted that their children had signed their names on their work. These people were definitely mountain rednecks. Who else would have named their children Picasso and Leonardo?

About the booze…the bar was loaded with a variety of wines, but nothing to moisten the drought stricken lips of a seasoned party-guy…no Jack Daniels or beer. I wondered what had happened to my six-pack and when I whispered this question in my wife's ear, the one without the earring, she crunched heavily on one of my bare feet, the foot that wears the boot sporting the white string. I was glad that she was not wearing her stiletto heels.

About the snacks…there was nothing that looked familiar…no sandwiches, fish sticks, or jerky. There were warmed bread rolls, asparagus rolls, crackers, cheese, a variety of nuts, and a green paste called 'gwa-muck-amoly' made from 'hava-gotta' pears ground up and mixed with snake juice…but, no corn bread. While in a beer-deprived trance, I never noticed Jim working on opening a bottle of bubbly directly behind me. When the cork popped, it sounded like a rifle shot, so I immediately grabbed the woman with the big boobs, threw her onto the Persian rug, and used my athletic body to protect her. It took a while for normality to return, but the bottom line is that I had displayed my bravery and my concern for others by being willing to take a bullet for somebody else, not unlike those bodyguards who will willingly use their bodies as a shield and take a bullet if necessary while protecting the president. I am not sure that everyone in the room understood or appreciated my selfless and brave actions, but one look at my wife's face after I had returned the 'other woman' to her feet, convinced me to medicate myself so that I would not feel pain when we returned home.

To break the ice, so to speak, Jim announced that champagne was being served to enhance the main 'horse-duh-overs,' which his wife wheeled in on a dainty cherry inlaid Italian serving wagon. My attention was immediately drawn to what was being presented. A cut-glass bowl nestling on ice, which was arranged in another larger cut-glass holding bowl. On closer observation, I noted that the top bowl was filled with what can only be described as 'used dark axle grease' that had gone bad, because little slimy bubbles had formed on the surface. To my surprise, all the guests were carefully smearing small quantities of the grease with a little mother-of-pearl spoon on dainty crackers before snacking on them. As they all seemed to enjoy the taste, I decided to fit in, so I ignored the little 'cheap-o' spoon and dug a load out with a couple of fingers and smeared it on a bread roll because there was no bread for sandwich making. Then I took a Southern bite. The instant that the load passed through my pie trap and hit my tongue, all my taste bud alarm bells went crazy. Under normal circumstances, I would simply have spat out what tasted like fish giblets, but this was no ordinary circumstance. I did the next best thing. I grabbed an open bottle of that imported white wine and 'chug-a-lugged' it down, washing the contents of my mouth down my private septic line. I knew that my stomach would not be happy, but I figured that if that wine could remove yesterday's plaque, then surely it could also de-coke (short for de-carbonizing) my taste buds. Jim came over and, in an effort to comfort me said, "Let me guess. This is the way that you eat caviar in South Africa?"

I would have acknowledged this, but as my stomach was sending urgent messages to my brain, so I simply nodded in agreement.

I overheard someone commenting that Jim had imported this particular caviar from Iran. That was, no doubt, intended to impress the Iranian body shop guy…I could not figure out why, but I knew there was a reason. Jim had mentioned privately that he no longer buys Russian caviar. I figured the reason was because of Russia's support of Iran's nuclear program. When you mix with these rednecks…you've gotta be smart. I also caught the fact that the best caviar came from the Caspian Sea near Miami. All the fishing locations had Hispanic names, e.g., Beluga, Osetra, and Sevruga. The Iranian guy said that all caviar came from species that are not Acipenseriformes, including

Acipenseridae or Sturgeon Stricto Sensu and Polyodontidae that are not genuine caviar, but considered a 'substitute of caviar.' I knew that! Like I said, you gotta be smart around these ignorant mountainfolk.

Just when I thought that I had heard everything I needed to know about caviar, some 'bright spark,' the auctioneer, had to go one better and explained that the word 'caviar' was derived from the Persian words '*!tj#r-^#*' pronounced 'xdvjdr from khaya egg and qyaka,' diminutive of '*ava from *owya/*oyyoegg' + dar 'bearing.' And I had always thought it was derived from the Persian words 'lssl-#8sg (Xag-avar)' with a little thingy on the first and second 'a'…not on the third 'a' meaning 'the roe generator.' Soooo, how does roe get generated? I hoped not in the same manner as the way Zool was extracted!

Returning to the caviar dinner…my wife was spending her evening talking to the lady with the big boobs. She made a habit of this to keep me away from women of interest. Supper and the meal turned out to be even more interesting than the white wine and snacks. According to their redneck custom, all the guests were separated from their spouses, so that we could get to know individuals more easily. At first, I suspected that we were at a swinger's party. Maybe they were going to get us to swap wives, but as the best looking hunk ended up with my wife beside him, I knew that I was on the wrong track. The interesting thing, though, was that I was seated beside the lady with the big boobs. How about that, Mama? However, she informed me that she was gay and her live-in was an alligator trainer. I wondered whether she was just trying to put me off because of my bare feet. Now, I could finally figure out why my wife had that silly grin on her face. On the other hand, the guy seated on my other side was very friendly…very friendly. He mentioned that he was also gay, so I asked him if he had come with the lady who…you know…had the big boobs? He shook his head and said, "No way…she's gay." I am still trying to figure that out. Was he afraid of the alligator lady? As it turned out, these two were the only ones who came solo. The others were all normally aspirated couples.

Getting to know strangers during a meal can be very interesting. The only drawback is that you have to be sure your mouth is not full when somebody asks a question. It reminded me how my daddy used to fuss with us about our eating habits. He would often say, "Don't speak with your mouth half-full…fill it."

Now that's a real mouthful! You think? Returning to the redneck supper…we were all served with California red wine which, although not as palatable as beer, did not taste like mouthwash or liquid soap…more like warm liquid blood.

I noted that the table was laid with antique silver cutlery and even the nerdy napkins were rolled into silver napkin rings. Even from a distance, I could read my wife's signals…"Do not take any souvenirs!"

I discovered a lot about these rednecks while I attacked the salads. I mean about the men. The women did not seem to warm to me. Surely, it was the fact that I wore no shoes.

Jim was the retired D.A. of a major city. The only guy I know that has sent convicted felons to the chair. I decided then and there that my souvenir collecting days were over.

Michael, the guy married to an Irish immigrant without boobs, had retired from Enron. He was laden down with gold. He wore a pair of gold chains around his neck, one heavy one on his left wrist, and a gold Rolex watch on his right wrist. This made me conclude that he was left-handed. Maybe left-handed guys prefer skinny wives.

Manny, the 'all smiles' ex-Iranian guy with the cute wide-eyed wife owned and operated a successful auto body repair shop. He claimed to have learnt his trade before immigrating to America. Apparently, the Iranians don't rely on camels as much these days. He mentioned that his brother Ghanga Din was a 'nuclear scientist/rocket scientist' in his homeland. Yeah, right! I suspected that he was a phony all along. What would a nuclear scientist do for a living in Iran? Really!

Kenny, the guy sitting opposite me, was the only guy who spoke with his mouth half full. And he had lots to say. It turned out that he was an auctioneer. After ducking whenever he spoke, I made a mental note never to attend one of his auctions.

Sydney, the youngest of the men and the sharpest dresser by far, was a regional VP for a major heavy equipment hire company. He was the only guy who did not drink. He had also never ever personally operated any heavy equipment in his life, although he spent a night at the Holiday Inn.

Johnny, on the other hand…and I mean 'on the other hand'…had his two middle fingers missing on his 'other hand.' I am not really sure if a pun was intended. It came as no surprise to learn that he owned and operated a sawmill specializing in the preparation of logs for log homes. He lost his fingers while trying to remove his wife's cat from the jaws of his Doberman. There were several other interesting individuals around the feeding trough, but I need to move on to cover that night's menu.

Jim had told us earlier that he was preparing a surprise menu. I could hardly wait. Once the salad plates had been thrown away, Jim appeared with a huge silver platter of freshly cooked meat and announced that the rack of lamb was ready. I could not believe it. These mountain rednecks ate domestic animals! It was going to be a long evening with more than a bottle or two of dry imported white wine used for gargling.

We were the first to leave that evening. Actually, I had engineered this situation because I wanted to be sure that nobody had taken my boots by mistake. It was a very silent drive home until I started to say something romantic to my wife.

She told me to "Shoosh!"

I never did find out what happened to my six-pack!

Life After Caviar

The following morning, I woke up surprised at the fact that I was still alive after what can only be described as an eventful evening in 'redneck land.' Normally, sitting up first thing in the morning without waking the little lady required a special skill. However, it came as no surprise that I was alone in the feather bed. I concluded that my wife was preparing the usual Southern breakfast for her man. Wrong! The morning menu turned out to be cold shoulder and colder breakfast...cold milk over lifeless cereal. Did you ever notice how different milk tastes when coming in contact with overnight plaque that had been rearranged by expensive white wine?

That got me thinking...not easy until my fog-shrouded brain had been rescued and released from the 'morning after' haze by a strong cup of black coffee. Did you know that most marriages are reconciled by an early morning cup of strong black coffee? That is the golden rule of redneck marriages—young unmarried girls were taught that coffee came before sex. Let me rephrase that—that's the very first thing that redneck girls are taught by their mamas; if you want to avoid an early morning delight from the guy waking up smelling like a drunken chimney sweeper, hand him a hot cup of black coffee before he can make a move. The hotter the better! The longer he takes to drink it the more time the wife has to run a tub for him...or run away!

Back to my 'morning after' thoughts about milk...

"Why milk?" I asked my battered brain.

My brain replied, "Think about it." So, I thought about it and came up with these conclusions: At some stage in life before anybody had ever considered drinking milk from an animal (Ughhhhhh!), a couple buddies were sitting under the shade of a tree chilling out and drinking moonshine. Moonshine came before milk. In fact, moonshine came before sex. That's why all babies were born unsteady on their feet with poor eyesight. Back to the shade tree guys and moonshine, and 'Rosy' the cow that strolled by with a leaky udder. Luckily for mankind, the two bosom buddies were 'going like a Boeing' and to overcome boredom, they dared one another as to who would be the first to drink (Ughhhhhh!) milk from the cow. Remember, this was not even a pretty cow—just a plain Jersey, but she did have those big brown eyes. That's where a songwriter got his inspiration for the lyrics, "I dream of 'Jersey" with the big brown eyes."

Oh…and a nice 'unusual' pair of…pair of…y'all know!

What took place next and 'how' the milk was extracted is a subject well left alone. My imagination played havoc with this subject. How about yours? The bottom line is that if at some stage in our evolution (progress?) it became popular to 'pull' or 'squeeze' milk from a cow and then to drink it…Ughhhhhh!…MILK TASTES LIKE COW…RIGHT? If y'all think this is gross, just think on this. Who was the first person to say, "See that chicken there feeding on those cow droppings…I'm gonna eat the next thing that comes out its bomb-bay." Ughhhhhh!

At least in the case of egg production, nobody is required to squeeze the egg out, unlike those poor unfortunate Cephalopods who had the Zool squeezed out of them. Sorry about that…again.

On reflection…How come eggs don't crack when they land?

This leads me into a private subject that I would not normally share with others. I am an 'expert,' defined as: "Someone who has a special skill or knowledge in a subject." When it comes to removing a hard-boiled egg from its shell without removing the shell, having a special skill and knowledge…that's me! I'll 'splain using the formula: "Who, Where, What, When, and Why?"

Who?…Yours truly.

Where?…In the 'First & Last Bar.'

What?…What was I doing? Working as a barman…not drinking…I did not want to be brained by Harry.

When?…When I was still innocent (stupid). That's why I shelled eggs during the fifties.

Why?…Hard-boiled eggs were provided free of charge. Why…to encourage patrons to buy more beer to wash them down. The only downside was that patrons burped a lot and passed gas louder.

So, about my egg shelling expertise—Harry boiled five-dozen eggs every night and it was my job to remove the shells. That takes a lot of time and also entailed a lot of cleaning up of all the bits and pieces of eggshells that splintered off. My answer to the problem was to make a small hole in both ends of the shell and then blow the egg out of its shell. No kidding! You cup the egg in one hand, wrap your lips over the top hole and blow really hard. The shell expands and the egg pops out into your hand all nice, shiny, and smooth as a baby's butt. The empty eggshell, although cracked all over when it expanded, remained intact and was conveniently tossed into the trash. J.D.

Job Done! I hasten to add, oops, that the eggs were washed before presented to the bar patrons. When I demonstrated this technique to the guys in my Community College Body Shop 'Lab' class, the professor gave me extra credits. He confided, "I was amazed that the 'busted' (redneck term for screwed) eggshells had not exploded."

He declined to eat any of the eggs. He did not fancy eating anything that had been blown out by human lips. Had he never seen eggs being blown out of the chicken lips?

I wondered if he drank milk? MILK TASTES LIKE COW…RIGHT?

QWB 1: WHAT ARE 'CHICKEN NUGGETS'? Are they only laid by Golden hens?

QWB 2: WHY DON'T EGGS TASTE LIKE CHICKEN…Like milk tastes like cow…right?

So, finally, to return to the caviar. Just as we have discovered the origin of cow's milk and the 'incredible' egg, we must once again ask some of those important questions that I have been telling y'all about. Let 'us all' consider 'Who' was the first individual to extract (Ugh!) and eat (Ughhhhhhh!) raw fish eggs? And, more importantly, 'How' were the fish eggs first extracted? History did not record who was the first, but a diligent search of the Scriptures when I spent a night at the Holiday Inn revealed 'How' the fish eggs were extracted. But first, my original thoughts…

I had wondered if the fish eggs had been squeezed out the fish in the same manner as Zool was extracted from those poor Cephalopods, but my fine tuned thought process would not buy that. Think about it; how on earth could one squeeze a slippery squirming fish without it shooting out of one's hand? Like the way my perfumed pink soap bar shoots out my hand when I take my Saturday shower. By applying all that thought logic that I have 'splained to y'all, I came up with the answers to a multitude of questions that have eluded mankind for generations. The very first consideration to overcome would have been, if you eat fish eggs would they not become tadpoles or little fish in your stomach? Those little critters would have created more gas than boiled eggs or bald peanuts. Don't you think?

The solution was very simple; you need to eat only 'non-fertile' fish eggs. The next step was not so simple. Where were you going to get gay fish? The answer…off the gay coast. How on earth could y'all not 'sea' that coming? That's pretty 'punny.' My sincere apologies to the gay community, but as a redneck who has endured more than my fair share of ribbing, I suspect that all is fair in love and war.

Now, for the final piece of the puzzle—How to stimulate fish to release their eggs? Very simple; y'all stun them by clubbing their heads…something akin to braining them. I am not exactly sure what they are clubbed with, but I don't recommend using a baseball bat—that's too severe and will render the hitting surface of your bat too slippery for home runs.

To continue, after they are stunned, somebody must extract their ovaries by Caesarean section to remove their baby baskets. Their incisions would then be stitched closed, enabling them to continue producing non-fertile eggs when released.

So picture the scene at the fish nursery. Gangs of guys armed with bats stun every fish that comes to the surface for air; another team catches the semi-conscious fish in nets and delivers them to a team of gynecologists, who deliver the eggs by Caesarean section before they can be born. I must mention that my wife's Rock Hudson look-alike gynecologist completed his internship in one of these locations. I wish he had found an Eskimo wife and settled there.

On with this 'fishy tail.' The collected eggs are frozen, canned, and sent all over the world where big guys like Jim slurp them down with cold bubbly to impress guests from all walks of life. I still can't figure out why none of the other guests at Jim's party burped and/or passed gas after ingesting chilled wine, chilled champagne, and frozen fish fetus, all while standing up. I bet that they fired up at bedtime. That's why older married couples sleep in separate beds. My wife and I don't have that problem. We have not shared the same bedroom since I started watching NASCAR races on our black and white TV in our master bedroom in the unfinished basement.

Caviar and the Environment
Serious Stuff

Listen up! Did you know that there is a connection between caviar and the environment and, in particular, to global warming?

Returning to the collection of caviar from those cute fish, think about the cycle of events starting with guys stunning them with clubs and ending with those post-operative egg-empty fish being released back into their habitat. These pathetic semi-conscious fish are easy prey for polar bears that gobble them up by the ton. Now, this in turn makes catching fish so easy that the polar bears become lazy and overweight from overindulging. Instead of spending most of their time fishing, they do the next most enjoyable thing. Y'all know…all males care about is food and sex…not in that particular order. So, the bear population has been increasing by leaps and bounds, no matter what Al Gore tells us. But, despite the increase in population, the 'green guys' will not allow any polar bear hunting. The result of all this is a huge increase in bigger, fatter, and lazier polar bear populations.

Now the ugly part, there are tons of polar bear poop all over Antarctica and the carbon 'paw print' of each individual polar bear is greater than that of a Volkswagen Beetle. So, the more fish we club on the head and then release with brain damage, the more polar bears will have to eat, the more they will poop, and the worse the carbon footprint will become. Maybe it's time to refrain from eating caviar and start cooking polar bear steaks.

Over to y'all. After 'all' the digression, we must now return to the South African scene following the 'Fifties.'

The Sexy Sixties

After running the successful taxi business in the fifties, Harry sprung another of his surprises. He sold Bunny's Taxi's business 'lock, stock, and barrel,' and purchased 'The First and Last Bar' lock, stock, and many, many, many barrels. Ella threatened divorce, but Harry cut her off at the pass when he bought her a pump organ and made a sizable donation to her church. In exchange, she agreed not to burn the bar to the ground. The bar was appropriately named the "First and Last" because, when it was built over fifty years before Harry bought it, it was located on the 'first' intersection when entering the city from Johannesburg in the north and it was the 'last' watering hole when entering the city from Durban in the south. In those days, the route between Johannesburg (the largest city in South Africa) and Durban (the largest port in South Africa and the whole of Africa) passed through the very heart of PMB and the welcoming front bat-wing doors of the 'F & L' as it was aptly nicknamed by the regulars.

As for me, my taxi driving days were over, but I was about to embark on a colorful career as a part-time barman. Surprisingly, it would prove to be more physically demanding than I had anticipated. For example, my regular job at the aluminum factory ended at 4:42 P.M. and I had to drive the ten miles from work like the devil to be in time to serve behind the bar when the first wave of thirst parched patrons shoved through those bat-wing doors. The bar was ideally situated between several factories and when those five o'clock whistles blew, the game was on! From 5 P.M. through the 11 P.M. closing time, cases and cases of cold beer were pulled from the fridges and poured into thankful mouths, down drought-stricken throats, and siphoned through hundreds of kidneys and livers of those seated around the bar. Imagine *Cheers* without air conditioning and four times the size.

Strict government liquor laws governed the hours of operation and because the F & L was licensed as a workingman's bar for males only, it was restricted to serving only beer and wine at that time. We called 'last round' at 10:45 P.M. and closed the doors at 11 P.M. Then, as Harry cashed up, I rushed home to shower off to combat the smell of beer, sweat, and stale cigarette smoke.

American TV viewers are familiar with *Cheers* and its characters, so it will no doubt be of interest to those dedicated viewers to compare *Cheers* with real life barflies in South Africa. What I am about to relate are memoirs taken from my personal experiences as a barman in a South African redneck bar.

While there are some similarities between the *Cheers* patrons and those of my experience, the South African setting in the "workingman's bar" was a little more on the rough side. Sure, as in *Cheers,* a 'Norm-like' character burst through the doors and ambled toward the bar to the spontaneous chorus of, "Hi, CHUCK," from those in the early stages of transformation from working guy to 'king of the road.' But, unlike an hour TV show, the real bar room activities took place over several hours…and a heck of a lot can happen during that time. One thing an experienced barman learns is once the initial rush is on, all is well, but after things slow down the biggest problem becomes boredom. So, how do we keep up the spirits of those winding down without interrupting their serious drinking arrangements? The answer was to occupy them with challenges, usually pitting them in a friendly contest to arrive at a winner. (Champion sounds better.) These contests ranged from serious snooker games, darts, and push halfpenny to less serious and light-hearted activities.

While it is a fact that among the regular patrons there were many who possessed unusual skills, the one guy who was most in demand was Vinny, the tonsorial artist, affectionately referred to as the barber of the 'F & L.' He routinely set up his private salon in the stockroom at the rear of the bar, and accepted drinks in lieu of payment for his grooming efforts. It worked like this: The guys who lined up for haircuts brought Vinny a beer then took a seat on a huge wine vat. Vinny, always the professional, would proceed to cover them in a crisp white sheet before taking up the comb and scissors. Between gulps of beer and friendly banter, Vinny worked diligently at the task at hand. It soon became obvious, however, that after six beers, professionalism of his workmanship deteriorated. Nobody lined up after number six! A new guy did not know the rules and nearly received a Yul Brynner cut instead of the Tony Curtis style he requested. Vinny's excuse was that he had seen Tony Curtis several times in *The King and I*.

More than anything else, the camaraderie established between friends in the bar never ceased to amaze me. Despite obvious differences in language, culture, and backgrounds, they bonded into what can only be considered a 'brotherhood' relationship and their loyalty to each other was set in concrete. When one hurt, they all hurt, and many a dollar was tossed into a hat for one of their own in need. The amazing thing about this bond was their willingness to put words into action. A club was formed by the regulars aptly called the 'Kennel Club,' because these guys were always in the doghouse on Friday nights…according to their wives. Fellow members banded together taking care of home and car repairs and other stuff. The only guy whose expertise was not called on was Steve, the mortician, but he did the cooking at the Kennel Club Christmas cookout.

Bartender 101

There were strict rules of conduct for a barman in those pubs. Rule number one, no drinking on duty, an easy one for me as I never took a drink until my twenty-first birthday. A pretty dumb tradition in those enlightened days and also because my father said that he would 'brain' me if he caught me drinking. Now there's a new slant to the word tradition.

The biggest advantage about being the only sober guy in the place was the fact that you learned to anticipate the customer's needs. In this way, you were able to lend them a friendly hand with some of those tasks that became awkward to carry out as the evening moved along. For instance, when you noticed a guy fumbling for matches to light up, you instinctively moved in and gave him a light. Then you quickly moved away to avoid that first powerful blast of a mixture of exhaled smoke, beer, and really bad breath, but you knew that he would tip you later. That way, you more than covered the price of lavender soap, which all off-duty bartenders use to freshen up.

On rare occasions, a barman came over to the customer's side of the bar. Although this practice was not encouraged, there were times when a good old boy needed a helping hand to make it to the bathroom…'to' the bathroom…not 'into' the bathroom! They could work their zippers without my help. On rare occasions, a patron needed assistance to make it to a waiting taxi. I never helped with that because as an ex-cabdriver, I learned to personally help many a guy into the back seat…and that was a sure way to a earn a good tip for the cabdriver. I was not about to deny a cabbie of this tidbit. I also did not want to get 'brained' by a cabbie who ate nails for breakfast.

As a part-time barman, I was reminded that I should never encourage an already tipsy patron to over imbibe, but become his friend and find ways to ensure his safe departure home. This did not present problems when the guys lived within walking distance of home. They were simply helped out the door and pointed in the right direction. Those patrons who arrived on bicycles presented more of a challenge than others. There is no 'Bicycle 101' where nightbike drunks are concerned. It takes even more skill to help a drunk onto a bicycle that is stationary but unsteady one moment and rearing to go the next, when you help getting the two going with an expert shove on the rear. It takes even more skill for the drunk's brain to work out which leg is which for the 'get go' and further skill for him to aim his iron steed in the right direction to get him on his merry way.

In all my years at this experience, there was only one guy who simply could not get his act together on a bike after only a few beers. I refer to old Reg Maple who had collided with every object that was not moving when I launched him on his way. He hit the first lamppost once, rode into the cherry hedge twice, and rode back into the front door three times…and three times and you are out! So using my Influence with Bunny's Taxi's new owner, I arranged for both Reg and his bicycle to be transported safely home on Friday nights. It was a regular sight to see the taxi heading away with the front wheel and handle bars of Reg's bike hanging out of the trunk of a bright gold Hudson taxi. For using my ingenuity, I was awarded the coveted 'Wyatt Earp Temperance' (WET) Award of a silver-plated bottle opener for 'service above and beyond the call of duty.' As a proud recipient of the 'WET' Award, I thought it appropriate to relate the history of the 'original' WET Award and, in order to do this, we must return to the piano playing Wyatt Earp incident previously covered.

The barmen of those early Western saloons were just as dedicated as the modern barman to ensure the safety of departing patrons after a bout of regular drinking. However, when 'Cactus Joe,' the three hundred-pound 'plus' stagecoach shotgun rider needed help onto his horse for the umpteenth time, the barman 'Wagon Wheels' Williams (nicknamed 'Wee-Wee'), solicited the help of Wyatt Earp to get the big guy into his saddle on 'Randy,' his trusted steed.

Wyatt Earp, who had just cleaned some axle grease from his hands, was already more than a little irritated and, in his haste to help Cactus Joe into the saddle, he accidentally flipped the rider onto the saddle facing backwards The term 'accidentally' is loosely used in this context because some said privately…that nobody in their right mind would argue with a gunslinger whose cigar had just been converted to chewing tobacco by the irresponsible shooting by a young recently 're-adjusted' cowboy who was at that moment trying his best to ride home sidesaddle. A timely slap on Randy's huge rump launched both horse and his confused rider into the cold night in a shower of dust. That is what is termed as 'killing two birds with one stone.' In this instance, one cowboy was riding backwards and the other cowboy riding sidesaddle. While there is nothing to be learnt from riding a horse backwards (rodeo riders do it often), one could well ask once more, "If men are smarter than women…how come men are not the ones riding sidesaddle?" (That way we will ensure a greater presence of bass singers in choirs.)

There is an interesting sequel to Joe's reverse saddle ride home. The following Friday afternoon he arrived on foot at the saloon with an unusual, but sad tale regarding his horse. It seemed that when he mounted his horse outside the saloon the previous Friday night, he noticed that somebody had cut off his horse's head. He immediately stuck his foot into Randy's jugular to keep him going as long as possible in an effort to reach home. He was surprised that the horse reached their destination, and to spare Randy, his faithful steed, from further suffering, he shot the poor creature!

As a fan of the popular TV show, *Cheers*, I was surprised that none of the characters had nicknames. That was the only serious flaw in the show. Let's face it, can anyone imagine a group of guys meeting regularly and not having nicknames for one another? It can't happen. Even at school, no matter what grade, nicknames were common. In most cases, they reflected something of the individual's character or unusual name and even their habits. Here are a few bar nicknames…

'Banana Fingers'…John Coetzer, the six foot seven, three hundred-pound ex-cop, whose fingers were so big that he could not pick his nose. I always wondered what the Red Indians would have named him…Chief Small Nose? Maybe…maybe not. 'Blackie'…the tall, skinny, pale-faced, extremely blonde character with matching blonde eyebrows. 'Blondie'…the short, stocky, dark-complexioned plumber with a shock of jet-black hair. 'Shorty'…the only guy taller than 'Banana Fingers,' but able to pick his nose. 'Curley'…the bald guy without eyebrows. It was rumored that he never had a hair on his body. 'Flash'…the slowest snooker player that ever lived. You only played snooker with him if you were lonely. 'Ginger'…the redheaded guy with freckles. 'Freckles'…the redheaded guy without any freckles. 'John Boy'…the John Boy look-alike. 'Fuddy'…Fred Fudrucker. I always wondered why they never considered calling him 'Freddy?' I must add that all these nicknames referred only to males. No self-respecting guy would think of nicknames for females, right? Remember how the press referred to Elvis as "Elvis the Pelvis." It's lucky that his sister Enis was not musically inclined.

Let's take a look at the definition of a bartender. I have deliberately replaced 'barman' with 'bartender' because in this enlightened society, bartenders could be either male or female. In my time, a barman was a barman…definitely not a bar person, but a man tending a bar. The true professional barman in a workingman's bar was many things to many guys. A friend with whom you could share 'anything,' even those things that you could not share in confession. Why was that? It is because no self-respecting drunk would be seen dead in a confessional. Think about it; a drunk can tell a barman where he went to have a good time with some interesting ladies knowing that his secret was safe, but would he tell a priest this? That would have been cruel because, unlike the barman who knew where to go in the first place, the priest had to live with this secret information without going there. I am not going there either. Get it? I could expound on many barroom clandestine activities, if it were not for the fact that I am a 'S.O.B.' having personally sworn the 'Sacred Oath of a Barman' (S.O.B.) never to divulge anything heard in confidence while on active duty. That oath, however, does not exclude activities that made the press, which I will reveal down the line.

Another thing about *Cheers* that surprised me, was that neither of the barmen did any tricks. All South African barmen are trick artists in one form or another. Like my counterparts, I performed many tricks…many of the more dramatic ones for a few bucks or, in some cases as a bet, and in rare instances just to show off. Some took years of practice, while others were discovered in the course of growing up…like making sousaphone sounds by quickly squeezing my right hand palm under my left armpit. By reversing the procedure, I could play sounds in a higher scale with my left hand palm under my right armpit. To play my favorite tune, I would have to strip to the waist and call on my superhuman agility to enable me to speed up the procedure of alternating arms, palms, and armpits, and deliver such a perfect rendition of *God Save the Queen* that all the drunks would stand to attention.

Another physically demanding trick entailed me walking on my hands along the length of the broad mahogany bar counter. These two tricks almost paid for my 'night school' tuition. After college, I continued my education in the dark, because I was not very bright. I developed a repertoire of card tricks, coin disappearing tricks, snooker tricks, and many others that I have employed to baffle and amuse my grandchildren for hours without them ever being bored with my company. Who would have thought that many (not all) of those tricks that I learnt during my misspent youth could satisfy the minds of these electronic wizard children. Harry had always said,

"No matter what, BS baffles brains." Harry was a good teacher and I was a good student. Harry never did any bar tricks, but on the other hand he arranged some very interesting inter-bar competitions…not unlike those old Sheppy and Bedford Inn days. Those experiences were, in fact, his apprenticeship for his new First and Last activities, which are too many to completely cover. I will, however, mention two, which involved animals and gambling…not betting on horses, but on tortoises and frogs! Yep, Harry held tortoise races and frog jumping competitions in the F & L.

Tortoises were lined up on the barroom floor and their trainers were all on their knees, scratching the tortoises on their shells to encourage them to move across to the finish line. At first the races took forever for the critters to reach the other side, but in time, the trainers found newer and more exciting ways to get them moving. Benny Axlerod laid on the floor directly behind "Happy" his tortoise and blew…you guessed it…with his mouth within a whisper of the rear end of Happy he blew his lungs out. Happy became champion by a gale and Harry the bookie made a killing.

However, not to be outdone, Harry's frog "Leaping Lena" took the Frog Leaping Championship by jumping nearly two feet farther than Clancy Coughburn's "Cutie Pie." The local press ran a picture of the final jump off with Harry's shining face in the background. In later years, Pinky Plyler insinuated that Leaping Lena jumped so far because as the starter's whistle blew…so did Harry…on the poor frog…after downing a pint of bitters. Have you ever been near a guy's breath after downing a fresh pint of bitters?

Not all barroom activities were light-hearted. There were a few ups and downs, but for all intents and purposes, there is no need for them to be expounded upon. It will, however, be criminal not to mention some of the antics that were instigated and acted on by Harry during those crazy years after WW II. So, let's go down the line…

Rock around the Block

During the rock and roll era, most of the big cities experienced the emergence of the ducktail gangs. These guys, mainly awkward pimple-faced guys in stovepipe pants, white socks, and James Dean windbreakers, slicked their hair back in a ducktail-style glued down by axle grease.

Our city PMB had little contact with the big city influences and, as TV was unheard of, none of the youth in PMB were influenced by this new craze. A few guys dressed in similar fashion, but there was no evidence of gangs; that is, until a Durban (the big port city sixty miles south) duck tail gang decided to spend Saturday nights at 'Dino's Café,' the only jukebox equipped Café in PMB that stayed open until midnight if patrons lingered to drink milk shakes and sodas, etc. This was the only venue for 'after movie' goers to chill out.

Dino, the owner, was a close buddy of Harry's, to whom he had expressed his concern that the influx of out-of-town ducktails was hurting business. He said that these ducktails never brought females with them and they harassed female customers. He felt sure that they were drinking in their cars because they were forever going in and out to them. Harry discussed the problem in the F & L war council room behind the toilets, and it was agreed that if Dino needed them they would be on their way immediately.

Sure enough, the very next Saturday night the call came through from Dino. He said that a bigger group of about thirty ducktails had virtually taken over the café and were interfering with his normal customers. It only took ten minutes for two carloads of F & L boys to reach Dino's! As if happened, I was not working that night and was on my way with a date to chill out at Dino's. As I approached the area in my MG TD, I noticed several ducktails hanging around, drinking beer outside the café and then out of the blue, a '46 Ford and a '51 Hudson screeched up to the curb and, to my amazement, a dozen members of the F & L Kennel Club rolled out of the vehicles and made for the café. The 'duckies' outside ran into the café. Bad mistake! Our boys went in after them. In a matter of seconds, a group of the unwelcome guests came pouring out the café with the F & L boys in hot pursuit. It was a massacre!

Duckies were felled like trees. Some made a run for it and, as I climbed out the car to assist, a duckie was running right toward me, but the poor guy was overtaken by my brother Bob (the fastest sprinter in his school days) and I watched as he cuffed his fleeing prey behind the head and I swear that the guy did a somersault before landing in a semi-conscious heap on the sidewalk.

The action only lasted about five minutes before the cops arrived in a paddy wagon, but by then the war was over, except for Banana Fingers, who had a guy upside down banging him on the sidewalk. The guy was screaming and a woman leaned out from an upstairs apartment and shouted encouragement. Another cop van appeared and all activities stopped. What a sight! There were duckies lying battered and bruised all over the place. Most had torn clothing and one had been knocked clean out of his shoes. In short order…no charges were laid, all the duckies collected their wounded, climbed into their cars, and left town in a hurry. The next day, the local newspaper *The Natal Witness* carried an account of the action under the headline "Hundred Angry Men Take the Law into Their Own Hands." It is on record.

The news carried far and wide and, the more it spread, the bigger it got. Finally, no self-respecting ducktail ever set their foot back in PMB…after all, who would dare to take on 'one hundred' ex-military roughnecks. Well, that night the 'one hundred angry men,' all twelve of them, all without injuries except a few raw knuckles, drank a toast and sang the F & L 'rallying call.'

> "Here's to Harry. He's so blue. He's a drunkard, through and through.
> He's a bastard…so, they say.
> He tried to go to Heaven…but he went the other way!
> Drink it down, down, down, down!"
> And they drank it down, down, down!

On another 'too quiet' evening at the F & L, Harry and some of the regulars decided on some action to break the monotony. They engineered a most incredible and daring stunt. A military complex left over from the WW II era was located about a half mile from the city center. An officer's mess was open in the evenings and old soldiers gathered from time to time, to shoot the breeze and enjoy the drinks at special low prices. The complex was several acres in size and, basically, was a storage complex for old military equipment. Occasionally small commemorative parades and the like were held there…also, some basic training was held periodically. The old and poorly maintained buildings were scattered around the perimeter with a large parade ground in the center. An aging high wire fence enclosed the whole complex. The area was poorly lighted and sentries were only posted during times of activities. Wire gates that were padlocked usually secured the complex.

Rising to a challenge, good old Harry decided to remove a WW II cannon and tow it to the city square. Very late one night, he and several accomplices breached the old perimeter fence at the rear of the parade grounds. They then manhandled a fair-sized cannon out of the complex. It is hard to believe that this could be achieved, but there is more. They hooked the cannon to the rear bumper of an old truck and slowly hauled it in the general direction of the city square, carefully avoiding the main streets by using quiet side streets.

Their objective was to haul the steel monster to the city square to win a wager arranged with some other crazy idiots. Traveling cautiously through side alleys, the convoy reached a point within two blocks of their destination. They were then forced to travel on one of the main streets entering the city, which passed by the main cemetery. At this point, the road became slightly steeper and, in an effort to compensate, my father pushed harder on the gas…a little too hard, unfortunately, as the sudden acceleration, although minor, ripped off the rear bumper of the truck and the cannon broke free. To their horror, the old warrior slowed, stopped, and immediately started rolling backwards down the incline.

In panic, the guys jumped off the truck and attacked the monster from all angles trying to stop it, but the old girl was running free once more like a horse heading for freedom. As it picked up speed, the cannon wobbled and jerked, sending the men flying in all directions. Although they did not impede its movement, they somehow caused it to spin around completely and it headed toward the cemetery barrel first. There was no stopping it now, but at least it was going to clear the road. As it reached the sidewalk, the two huge rubber wheels smacked the curb and bounced the monster a few feet into the air, sending it over the low brick cemetery fence. The barrel cleared the fence, but unfortunately, the wheels did not. They crashed against the fence, causing the barrel to jerk earthward and, as the fence disintegrated, the old warhorse burrowed its barrel into the soft earth with its wheels spinning in the air. The weight of the wheels and the undercarriage drove the nose of the barrel deeply into Chuck Bailey's grave, whose headstone read, "Rest in Peace." Chuck's peace was about to be disrupted and as the saying goes, "It's not over until the fat lady sings." Well the fat lady took the stage. The weight of the undercarriage once more came into play, jerking the steel monster back to the ground. As it crashed back onto its wheels, the barrel scooped a huge chunk of soft dirt from the grave, catapulting it into the air sending sod across the graveyard. So much for "Rest in Peace!" The men were horrified and scared out of their wits. Stealing a cannon was one thing, but the desecration of a grave was quite another story! They loaded the damaged bumper and took off, leaving the cannon sitting at an angle with its barrel pointed to the heavens.

Something of interest…the late Chuck Bailey's death was the result of three light-caliber bullet wounds inflicted by his redheaded wife, who had caught him in bed with his secretary (the lady shall remain nameless), who also took a slug in her behind and left town after medical treatment. It was said that after Mrs. Bailey's trial and sentencing, she had remarked, "I should have used a cannon on the old bastard!" Poetic justice? Makes one wonder.

The brotherhood in bars was not 'the only game in town.' All sorts of shenanigans were cooked up by guys trying to outdo other idiots in other 'big boy's' organizations. Rugby players, water polo players, cricket players, etc.,

etc. were all vying for the 'dumbest guys in town' trophy. Matters were made worse by the fact that many guys were members of more than one of those institutions. The focus is on the word 'institutions' in which many belonged...although they did not realize it...but their wives did. One such sporting body was the 'Motorcycle and Car Club' whose members included some of the craziest guys in town...I was the only normal guy in the club.

Some of the most competitive racing in the world took place on our racetracks, which included world motorcycling, motor racing, and Formula One big names. I'm tempted to mention a few, but fearful I might omit someone important and get brained.

Organized parties and cookouts after major racing events were the best! After the checkered flag, competitors and pit crews mixed with the officials and let their hair down. I could recount many, many interesting stories around this subject, but for now, just this one.

One evening during a braai, which is a South African term for a cookout with 'real meat,' a drunk somehow crashed the party and did his best to drink the place dry. He staggered around and eventually passed out in the pits near the rigs that towed the racecars around the country. Two of my buddies, who should remain nameless, unzipped the canvas cover over a Porsche racer, which was owned and driven by a highly respected doctor from Pretoria. I won't mention your name, Dan; it would not be professional. The drunk was carefully lifted and slid into the cockpit of the Porsche and then they slowly re-zipped the canvas cover. They watched carefully when the rig with the covered Porsche on the trailer behind pulled out. There was no indication that it contained an inebriated hitchhiker.

The story goes, during a gas stop a few hours later, someone noticed the canvas cover being punched desperately from within and heard the most awful sounds and cursing coming from the Porsche. The car owner, whose name I will not divulge, rushed to his trailer and unzipped the cover and, as he did so, the drunk came out swinging, but lost his balance and fell out of the car. As inquisitive spectators gathered around on the forecourt, the two got into a shouting match. The drunk was unmanageable and crazed and, noting his strange surroundings, he shouted, "Where the hell am I? You bastards have kidnapped me. Someone call the police!" The Porsche owner had no idea what had happened and absolutely no idea what to do. Some 'Good Samaritan' became involved and took the now recovering drunk into the convenience store to buy him black coffee and calm him down. Our doctor friend walked over to zip up his beloved silver racer and, as he looked in, he groaned, "He threw up on my seat!" Although the tale does not end there...the culprits were never discovered. If you are reading this, Varnie and Stevie, don't worry, your secret is safe with me.

I hesitate to include military pranks for fear of undermining 'State Security,' but what the heck. How about this...

In South Africa, it was customary that a military cannon be fired to signal the opening of annual Agricultural Shows. These 'shows' were something similar to American State Fairs, except for our lack of cotton candy and the presence of a big military cannon like the one Harry and his F & L boys borrowed that fateful night. A small contingent of military personnel was on hand to fire the heavy cannon at the opening ceremony. This monster was towed into an open and safe location and, at an appropriate time, a blank shell was fired when the show was declared open by some government representative. The resulting percussion shook the air as thick black smoke and flames flashed out of the barrel.

On one particular occasion, I was on hand taking care of the bumblebee cake that I had made, calling on my confectionary skills learnt from my days working at Anne's Confectionary. It was entered in the cake baking section. After firing the cannon, the small contingent of young military personnel towed it to the side of the arena close to my room in the adjacent 'no tell motel' and parked it near a new white travel trailer that was on display. Young military men were on hand to tell the little people all about this instrument of mass destruction. As usual, kids lined up all day long to have their pictures taken with the gunnery sergeant and the cannon. This was before South African kids had heard of Santa. It was a fun day.

Around midnight something incredible happened in the arena. I had just showered and was about to hit the sack in my motel room, when I heard a deafening explosion that rattled the building. There was a flash of light across my window and I rushed outside in my briefs. My attention was immediately drawn to the arena, where the perimeter lights provided sufficient lighting to reveal a cloud of smoke drifting across the area. I, like most, suspected a bomb blast and despite the hour, people were appearing from everywhere and heading toward the arena. I was in the lead. Once inside, it was obvious what had happened. Some idiot had fired the cannon! Unfortunately, the cannon had been parked too close to the travel trailer and the resulting percussion had blown the side windows to kingdom come. In fact, the blast was so fierce that fragments of glass and tattered curtain material were imbedded in the interior, and the outside wall of the vehicle was bowed in and covered with black soot. Fortunately, the trailer was only for display purposes and nobody was inside at that time, otherwise who knows what would have been the result. Two young military types were running around in their socks and briefs trying desperately to restore order. This was a sight to behold! There is much more to report on this crazy event. A subsequent military enquiry established the fact that a few ex-military types had snuck in with a blank cannon shell and fired it as a prank. There were very serious repercussions, which I believe are best left to rest…and as for those young soldiers…Bless their hearts…y'all.

Bless Their Hearts

It is time to reflect on how far we have come in comparing American rednecks with South African rednecks. To this point, everything has been concentrated on 'male' rednecks. The question is: Were there any redneck women way back when…and, if so, is there any documented proof of their existence? During my research, I stumbled across an incident that may throw light on this issue. I will, however, not reveal on which continent this incident took place. That will be left to your imagination. To make it easier, I will tell you that this incident either took place in South Africa during the Boer War, or in America during the Civil War. I must warn you not to jump to any conclusions. Now where have I heard that before? Do not take anything for granted.

This is the setting: A small group of soldiers that had been cut off behind enemy lines were slowly and carefully making their way back to 'their side' when they came across an isolated farmhouse. It was late at night and candlelight indicated that the house 'was occupied'…I must remind you that this was either during the Boer War in South Africa or in America during the Civil War…Okay?

The group of four men hid in a grove of trees and carefully cased the joint. After being convinced that there was no enemy troops in or around the farmhouse, the sergeant in charge made a fateful decision. He and two of the men would sneak up on the house and the remaining soldier 'Lips' Lipstein, their sharpshooter, would remain on guard until dawn at the ready 'in case!' When the three men reached the house, the two regulars hid in the shadows as Sergeant Greene tiptoed to the front door and, revolver in hand, knocked on the heavy wooden door. Within seconds, the door was eased open revealing a middle age rather rotund woman dressed in a well-worn cotton dress. The sight of the revolver scared her and she cried out, "Don't shoot me, sir!"

The sergeant took a careful look around and, noting that the woman was alone, he returned his revolver to its holster, removed his hat (Is that a clue?), and spoke gently to the woman. Addressing her with respect, he said, "Please do not be afraid, ma'am. I will not harm you. I wonder if you can spare some food for me and a couple of my men and, perhaps, allow us to sleep in your barn overnight."

Her reply surprised him. She straightened her dress, brushed her hair from her face and replied softly, "I will be happy to provide food and it won't be necessary for your men to sleep in the barn. As you can see, I have plenty of room for y'all." Then, she added rather coyly, "I will welcome some company. I have been alone for so many years." Then she asked, "How many other men can I expect to sleep in the house?"

The sergeant replied, "Two without Lips."

She sighed, "Bless their hearts."

In revealing the history of the 'original' female redneck, we can't deny that we have taken 'One HUGE step for WOMANHOOD, and one GIANT step for MANKIND!' There is little doubt that the dear lady who, in her innocence, had opened her home to strangers qualifies for the title of 'Woman Redneck"...maybe even 'The Queen of Rednecks.'

Having introduced a female redneck the thought came to mind, *What about a juvenile redneck? How about this?* A Tennessee farmer drove to a neighbor's farmhouse in his Fargo and knocked at the door. A boy about ten years old opened the door.

"Is your pa home?" asked the farmer.

"No, mister, he isn't; he went to town."

"Well, is your ma here?"

"No, she went to town with Pa."

"How about your brother Charlie? Is he here?"

"No, mister, he went with Pa and Ma."

The farmer stood there for a few minutes, shifting from one foot to the other and mumbling to himself.

The boy asked, "Is there anything I can do for you? I know where the tools are, if you want to borrow some...or I can give Pa a message."

"Well," said the farmer uncomfortably, "I really wanted to talk to your Pa. It's about your brother Charlie getting my daughter Betty pregnant."

The boy thought for a moment. "You will have to talk to Pa about that. I know he charges $300 for the bull and $50 for the pig, but I don't know how much he charges for Charlie."

Now that's a good contender for juvenile redneck...I wonder if he could have been kin of the woman in the previous story? Could it be that blood is thicker than water?

Prepare yourself for a shocking thought... Is there any evidence of 'toddler' rednecks?...Try this.

A young Tennessee boy heads off to school for the first time as his toddler brother waves at the cabin door. The first day of school turned out to be a nightmare for the elder boy who, because of his unusual given name, came under severe ridicule from all the other children. To make matters worse, even the teacher could not believe the boy's name...a bad day all round!

Later that day, as the boy made his way disconsolately home, his younger brother rushed out to meet him. The little brother was very excited and called out loudly, "Wagon Wheels, Wagon Wheels, how was your first day at school?"

The elder sibling replied, "Boy, have I got news for you, Chicken Shan!"

Having dispensed with 'juvenile' and 'toddler' redneck and a woman redneck referred to as the 'Queen' of rednecks, who can qualify for the title of 'King' of rednecks?'

In order to come to the correct conclusion, we must first consider who qualifies as the 'King of South African Rednecks,' after which we can look at all the contestants in America for the title of 'King of American Rednecks' and compare the two in order that we can arrive at the overall winner of the title "Redneck King."

You will no doubt recall my reference to a South African story involving a big man and a bigger animal? At the time, my publisher had suggested that I delay the story until the final pages. In his opinion, this delay would keep you guys reading feverishly until the final page. However, I disagreed because I know that some readers would simply check out the final pages and return the book for a refund. But, I knew something that my publisher did not know because he never reads my stuff. (Y'all know…that I will bring in the American redneck challenge down the line.) Meanwhile, now the big South African one! For the setting we must return to the fifties, Harry and his beloved First & Last Bar…

A circus came to town from time to time and they always set up on the show grounds one block from the First and Last Bar. As expected, the circus generated additional business for Harry, which included some of the circus performers, one of whom was the world-renowned German animal trainer Karl Schmidt.

One night after their opening performance and several beers, my father persuaded Karl to bring a young elephant to the bar as a publicity stunt. Karl agreed and my father joined him as they coaxed the huge animal with peanuts. On reaching the bar, the men had a few more drinks after which, at my father's suggestion, they walked the beast several blocks to the Plough Hotel in the center of the city.

On the way, several intrigued pedestrians followed and by the time they reached their destination, there were dozens of followers. Arriving there just before closing time, they caused a sensation as the animal was guided through the swing doors into the main bar off the street. On entering, they approached the bar with crowds stumbling in behind them and bedlam broke out as customers reacted. All were taken by surprise; a few were scared, but more than one inebriated patron called for another round. It was rumored that Joe Brown swore off drink for life after seeing his first pink elephant. He was colorblind.

In a panic, the barman rushed out to call Mr. Janes, the manager, who immediately responded. On entering the crowded room, he was shocked to see the elephant, however, he was not surprised that my father was involved. He had seen this big clown in action many times before. He reacted favorably, but he called for order!

Mr. Janes was a well-groomed middle age man who sported a Hollywood-inspired D'Artagnan beard and mustache. He was always immaculately dressed and spoke cultured English. He walked over to Harry and Karl, requesting that they remove the beast. By this time, the animal had picked up an empty beer bottle and was waving it around with her trunk. The manager was perturbed, but not angry; however, fearing the animal's behavior he insisted that the young elephant be removed immediately. The many amused patrons tried to convince him otherwise, but he insisted, "The elephant and the two clowns have to go!"

Karl turned the animal around in the room lining her up for the door. As he tugged to guide her out, the beast passed massive wind and dropped a wet load. The steaming parcel landed directly in front of Mr. Janes and splashed across his shiny shoes and into the cuffs of his trousers. There was an immediate mass evacuation! Harry gave that bar a wide berth for several months, but he had once again provided the local newspaper with an interesting story.

This true story should achieve two things: First, it must be agreed that it overshadows the amazing elephant story that was related at the beginning of the book; and, second, it leaves the field open for a counterattack from the American side to come up with a stronger challenge.

As the writer of this book and the only person who knows what that challenge is, I must confess that I am beginning to doubt whether South Africa can wrench the redneck title from American. The American response is short and sweet, but not to be divulged just now. If it were…even I would not care too much about the rest of this book. But, don't go anywhere, because there is lot's a interesting stuff about immigrant redneck activities that needs to be shared before the final American redneck counterattack…how's this?

At dawn the telephone rings, "Hello, Senor Bob? This is Pedro the caretaker at your country house."

"Ah, yes…Pedro. What can I do for you? Is there a problem?"

"Um, I am just calling to advise you, Senor Bob, that your parrot, he is dead"

"My parrot? Dead? The one that won the international competition?"

"*Si, Senor*, that's the one."

"Damn! That's a pity! I spent a small fortune on that bird. What did he die from?"

"From eating the rotten meat, Senor Bob."

"From rotten meat! Who the hell fed him rotten meat?"

"Nobody, senor. He ate the meat of the dead horse."

"Dead horse! What dead horse?"

"The thoroughbred, Senor Bob."

"My prize thoroughbred is dead?"

"Yes, Senor Bob, he died from all the work pulling the water cart."

"Are you insane? What water cart?"

"The one we used to put out the fire, senor."

"For the love of...! What fire are you talking about?"

"The one at your house, senor! A candle fell and the drapes caught on fire."

"What the hell? Are you saying that my mansion is destroyed because of a candle?"

"Yes, Senor Bob."

"But there's electricity at the house! What was the candle for?"

"For the funeral, Senor Bob."

"WHAT BLOODY FUNERAL?"

"Your wife's, Senor Bob. She showed up very late one night and I thought she was a thief, so I hit her with your new Ping G15 204g titanium head golf club with the TFC 149D graphite shaft."

SILENCE...LONG SILENCE...VERY LONG SILENCE!

"Pedro, if you broke that driver, you're in deep 'shan'!"

The question is: Who is the redneck? ...It's not the parrot!

I 'threw' in this tale for a couple of reasons...to challenge the intellect to answer the above question (The answer is not the parrot!), or to challenge the theory that golfers are somehow considered smarter than the rest of us...in which case there could not be such a creature as a 'redneck golfer,' Heaven forbid. You tell me, how's this?

The husband takes his wife to play her first game of golf. Naturally, the wife promptly sliced her first shot smack through the window of the largest house adjacent to the course. The husband was mortified and said, "I warned you to be careful! Now we will have to go up to the house, find the owner and apologize, and see how much your lousy drive is going to cost us."

So they walked up to the front and knocked on the door. A warm voice called out, "Come on in." When they opened the door, they saw the damage that was done: glass all over the place and a broken antique bottle was lying near the pieces of window glass. A man reclining on a couch asked, "Are you the people who broke my window?"

The husband replied nervously, "Uh, yes, sir, we are very sorry about all this."

"Oh, no apology is necessary. Actually I need to thank you. You see, I'm a genie and I have been trapped in that bottle for hundreds of years. Now that you have released me, I'm allowed to grant three wishes. I'll give you each one wish, but if you don't mind, I'll keep the last one for myself."

"Wow, that's great," replied the husband who pondered for a moment and blurted out like an Irishman, "I'd like a million dollars a year for the rest of my life."

"Done," said the genie. It's the least I can do for you. Check your bank for the deposits. And you, young lady, what can I do for you," the genie asked.

"I would like a gorgeous home in every country in the world complete with servants," she replied.

"Consider it done," the genie said and added that the homes would always be safe from natural disasters.

"And now," the couple asked in unison, "What's your wish, genie?"

"Well, since I've been trapped in the bottle and haven't been alone with a woman for so many years, my wish is to spend some time alone with your wife."

The husband looked at the wife and said, "Golly, honey, the genie has given us a fortune and all those lovely houses you want. What do you think?"

She mulled it over for a few moments and said, "You are right. Considering all we are getting I wouldn't mind, but what about how you feel about it?"

"You know I love you, darling, and I would do the same for you," replied the husband.

So the genie and the woman went upstairs where they spent the rest of the afternoon enjoying each other's company. After several pleasurable hours the genie looked directly into her big brown eyes and asked the woman, "How old are you and your husband?"

"Why, we are both thirty-two," she responded breathlessly.

"No kidding," he said, "thirty-two years old and you both still believe in genies?"

So, who y'all calling a redneck golfer?

Ever wonder what golfers talk about as they play their rounds?

Male golfers talk a lot about Tiger and his scores. Some even have the audacity to compare their scores to his. But, no golfer can top Cody Hilton's scores. He is considered the ultimate 'sailor golfer,' a score in every port.

Female golfers also talk a lot about Tiger's scores and where 'they' shop and how 'they' dress. Concentrate, Stanley...not everybody plays golf.

I have a question that I am almost too scared to ask, Why do golfers call out 'fore' to warn other golfers of a golf ball on its way? I have pondered on this for years and come to the conclusion that as the Scottish dudes have still not seen the joke about bag pipes, then how in the world can we blame them for not knowing the difference between 'Fore' and 'Oops!'

More laxatives for Christmas from my family in Scotland!

If it were me, I would simply have called out "!KCUD"...short for, "RUN FOR YOUR LIVES!"

Back to Reality

Having related some of the unusual shenanigans that involved South African rednecks, I feel that some of the more serious 60s history should be included to bring the reality of those difficult times to the fore…and to compare events in South Africa with those in America and, in some instances, the rest of the world.

Sixties Ups and Downs

In South Africa:
There were two assassination attempts on the South African Prime Minister, Dr. Verwoerd, in the sixties. The first in 1960 was unsuccessful when a local white farmer David Pratt fired two light caliber shots at close range, hitting Dr. Verwoerd in the cheek and in the ear. In a remarkable recovery, he returned to work two months later. The second and successful attempt on his life took place in 1966 in full view of the assembled Parliamentary Chamber. A messenger walked up to Dr. Verwoerd and, instead of handing the Premier a message, he pulled out a knife and stabbed his victim repeatedly in the neck and chest.

In America:
John F. Kennedy, the Reverend Dr. Martin Luther King Jr., and Robert Kennedy were assassinated.

In Russia:
The Russian's successfully launched a space capsule containing a dog named Laika. Then a little later in 1961, they launched a space vehicle containing Air Force Major Yuri Gagarin and returned him safely back to Earth.

In the Rest of Africa in General:
During the 60s, trouble was brewing in many parts of Africa. Congolese rebels viciously turned on the white population. Hostages were taken, many of whom were murdered, including Dr. Paul E. Carlson, a well-known and highly respected American missionary. U.S. Air Force planes dropped six hundred Belgian paratroopers into Stanleyville in a hostage rescue attempt, but, unfortunately, eight hostages had already been brutally butchered.

For the moment, we will leave the activities of 'so-called' South African rednecks and move out of that period between WW II through the sixties. In so doing, we will depart from Harry and those crazy-hazy, hazy-crazy days to embrace the period from the seventies through today.

America or Bust!
Redneck 102

In the sixties, for personal reasons like millions of others all over the globe, I made a decision to explore the possibility of immigrating to America. The next step was to visit America to 'check the place out.' I start with my first of many visits in the bi-centennial year of 1976.

From the moment I stepped onto US soil, I had the strangest feeling that I arrived in a make-believe land. Allow me to 'splain, lest you burn this book. Remember that America had worked hard over many years to turn this country into a showcase for the word to discover the 'land of the free.' Tourists arrived in the millions to be greeted with, "Have a Nice Day," by helpful courteous smiling citizens who were spontaneously embracing one and all to show the world that since their independence 200 years earlier, this democracy was the poster child to the world. And, what a poster child! You could eat off the floor! The whole country was as clean as a whistle. Over a four-week period, my wife and I covered many states to get a feel for conditions and to mix as much as possible with the 'man/woman in the street' to help us devise a future strategy on immigration considerations.

During that American visit, I tried as best as possible to assimilate with the American culture and I made good progress, despite the one unexpected hindrance. My accent! For two reasons, we were thought to be Australians, Scottish, or Irish. When we declared we were South Africans, we were inundated with questions. It was obvious that most were surprised that we were white. The fact that we were tri-lingual and could muddle our way through a few other languages was also the source of interest. The first lesson I learned early in life is 'not to judge a book by its cover.' We have been there. Just because Americans had their understanding of my background…I too had some pre-conceived notions of the American lifestyle. I was about to learn 'American Culture 101'!

Once I returned to South Africa, I started gathering personal and important documentation that I anticipated would be required for immigration purposes. I needed to get my act together. From my initial American observations, I realized that there were many employment opportunities in the transit industry. As a realist, I figured that I should at least be prepared to take any opportunity to make a living 'if' and 'when' I immigrated, and driving a taxi or truck seemed like a good starting point. I was in possession of every driving license category from motorcycle to extra heavy-duty vehicles. Then the thought occurred to me...what were the opportunities for someone with a pilot's license?

I'm including the following story because it gives a glimpse of the desperation facing any immigrant to be prepared for any opportunity to make a meaningful start in a new country. At the same time, by relating this story you will find further understanding of my culture, even some humor, at my expense.

Although I was a qualified C-150 pilot, my particular license excluded me from carrying passengers, so I decided to convert and upgrade my license to carry passengers. I made arrangements for an instructor to put me through the course in a new more powerful C-172 and waited for an appointment, which would take some time to book. Over the next few days, my working activities were hectic and all thought of the pilot conversion slipped away until a few days later at around 10:00 A.M. I received a call from Mel, my flight instructor. On answering the call, it went something like this: I said, "Hi, Mel. What's cooking?"

"You're cooking, pal. I've booked your conversion for 4:00 P.M. today."

I was elated and replied excitedly, "Okay, Mel, I will meet you for flight check at 4:00 P.M. sharp," then he said something interesting...

"Be sure to bring two more passengers."

I was startled, but trying not to act dumb (been there, done that), I answered, "Sure thing, Mel, can I bring anybody I choose?"

"Sure, anybody will do," he answered. Then he suggested with a laugh, "...Even if you have to pick up a couple of those poor guys who stand on the street corners hoping that someone will give them a day job." His last comment, before ending the call, was, "As long as they don't throw up!"

The minute I replaced the phone, I went into a cold sweat. Who could I get at short notice to be my passengers? In a flash (well, after *some* thought), I remembered that Tully the Zulu gardener down the road who finished his shift at 2:00 P.M. daily had asked me to consider him for any part-time work in the afternoon hours. I had, on occasions, recommended him to others and he had always come through for them.

I had once done Tully a personal favor and given him my old bicycle, so that he could ride to work and save on bus fare. At the time, he had reported late for work several weeks in a row on Mondays. His excuse was that the bus was always late on Mondays.

Tully was easy to like. He spoke some English and had a great sense of humor...and he liked an extra buck or two. *He's my man...* I thought. I rushed over and found Tully watering plants on his job and I discussed my situation regarding my need of two volunteers. The first thing I needed to know was, "Are you scared of flying, Tully?"

His quick reply, "No, I am scared of nothing!" That response did not surprise me. Tully was the most over-confident guy that I had ever encountered…so I asked the sixty-four thousand dollar question, "Have you ever been in an aircraft before?" Silly question! He answered with a flourish, "Sure, I have. I once flew to Zingkwazi…" and before I could comment on the fact that there was no airport or any landing strips in or anywhere remotely near Zingkwazi, he quickly changed the subject and offered, "I will get my cousin Sam to be your other passenger. He is also not scared to fly." Time, would tell.

After several formalities, it was agreed that Tully and Sam would meet me at my car at 3:00 P.M. I must mention the 'formalities.' Tully asked for $15 so that he could pay Sam $5 and retain the remaining $10 for arranging the duo. He was quick to add, "Those who are desperate for work will normally charge $3 per day, but this is not normal work, so I will pay him $5 and for the same reason I will need to charge you $10," and he added slyly, "because you helped me with the bike." That said, it was a 'done deal,' but he did not look me in the eye.

At precisely 3:00 P.M. as arranged, Tully presented Sam. His condition shocked me; he was painfully thin and obviously undernourished. He was dressed in tattered clothing—a faded shirt with torn collar tucked into threadbare brown longs. He wore shoes without laces and no socks, and he only spoke Zulu. I thanked him for offering to help and asked if Tully had explained what was expected of him. He never answered me directly, but after a quick glance at Tully, he nodded his head in acknowledgement. As far as I was concerned, it was now between him and Tully. On the drive over to the airport I wondered what the 'veteran flyer' Tully had told him, but we rode in silence…each to his own thoughts.

When we arrived at the airport, I signed in and did the pre-flight checks as my passengers watched intently. Sam blinked a lot. When my instructor, Mel, arrived he looked us over and said, "Have these guys been up before?"

I replied, "Sure they have. Tully over here is an old hand…."

He squinted, "They better not throw up on us."

I opened the passenger side door and told Tully and Sam to get in. Sam froze and, for a moment, I thought that the day was over, but Tully quickly reminded him about the money by making that thumb and finger gesture that is universally known as 'payday'…and then hustled the unsure man into a seat behind the instructor's seat. Tully then hopped into the seat beside him. Getting the two passengers to belt up was not that straightforward. Sam somehow managed to get the safety belt hooked around his neck and Tully 'somehow' managed to click Sam's belt into that position. I had never seen that before. How was that possible? After some tugging and rearranging, I managed to finally get both the passengers secured in their safety belts. I was glad that Mel was preoccupied in a conversation with a nearby mechanic at that time and had not taken in the boarding scene.

I settled in the pilot's position and Mel came over and eased his agile body in beside me. Before Mel gave the okay, he checked that the two passengers were correctly secured and, after a final look over, he asked once more, "You sure these two clowns have flown before?" Before I could answer he added sourly, "They better not throw up on me!"

Once strapped into the cockpit, I went through the flying rituals and finally, after the 'clear prop' was called, I pushed in the throttle slowly and, after moving ahead, I set it around 1,000 rpm. I tried the brakes and then moved along a little faster than a brisk walk. Before takeoff, I went through the required checks including the radio settings and we were ready to go. At this point, I don't want to labor on the details of flying procedure…basically this is how it went; before taking off, I increased the power of the engine with the brakes fully depressed to test the rpms. As the cabin vibrated and the engine roared, I glanced into my mirror for the first time to take a good look at my passengers. Their faces showed a little more than normal concern as the noise level of the engine increased and the aircraft continued to vibrate from the surge of the powerful engine. After my radio call, I sent the sharp blue and white C-172 hurtling down the runway and, as we left the ground, I glanced at the rear view mirror and I did not like what I saw. I had no doubt that this was a new experience for the two mummies who sat bolt upright behind me. I prayed to the 'Flying Fairy,' "Do not let them throw up!"

My conversion flight exercise required me, among other things, to execute several perfect 'touch-and-gos' in succession. That meant that after flying a circuit around the flying area, I was to make perfect landing approaches, but instead of actually landing the plane, as soon as the wheels touched down, I would accelerate off the runway and become airborne for another circuit. Although I had been through this procedure countless times in other aircraft, I had to concentrate to insure that I would perform satisfactorily as I was flying under the critical eye of my very experienced instructor, whose presence made me nervous. But, if I was nervous, you should have seen my passengers. Each time the landing wheels touched the ground, they seemed relieved, but as I punched the throttle to speed up to takeoff, they froze.

The more I flew, the more they reacted. On one occasion, when I landed a little awkwardly against a slight side-wind, Sam actually covered his face with his hands. Sam worried me because he was turning gray…a sure sign that he was going to throw up…and he was sitting directly behind my instructor. However, he held on. Finally, when Mel was satisfied with my performance, he called it and I landed, slowed down on the runway, and taxied to the parking area where, after the usual checks, I cut the engine. We all unbuckled and stepped out of the plane and, to my astonishment, as Sam stepped out the plane, he threw up! Big time!

I quietly thanked the 'Flying Fairy' for the fact that Sam had held off until after the show…but Sam was not through, yet. As he composed himself, he

turned on Tully and shaking his fist, he got in his face and he cursed in Zulu, ^*$#^&*(>>>(*%#%@!*(^%&**(*&*^^%%$$%
^^&&&&&&^%$##@##@@@##$$%%%^^

The cleaned up translation, "You are no longer my cousin. You put me in a plane with a fool who does not know to fly. It took him five tries to land that plane!" Then Sam added the most interesting tidbit, "You should have paid me more than the $3."

The question is: Is there such a thing as a 'redneck' Zulu? If so…could it be Tully or Sam? Or Heaven forbid…both!

Pilgrim's Progress

From this point on, the focus will shift to my personal redneck efforts to immigrate to America. In doing so, the mantle of 'South African Redneck' *may* have to pass from Harry to me something like, "The acorn does not fall far from the tree." We have to reach the point where we acknowledge the fact that certain traits continue from generation to generation…and, in my case, my blood line from those original South African redneck roots. Modern DNA supports this. That is where we find similarities in the American Southern and South African Colonial traits. Both groups are acorns from the same trees.

This book started with my personal challenge to the American Southerners' claim to the exclusive right to the term 'redneck'… This necessitated traveling back in South African history to explore the first 'documented' proof, wherein early pioneers to the 'dark continent' were actually referred to as 'Redneck.' This is a strong challenge to America where the term 'redneck' seems to be more of a nickname for certain Southern folk, rather than an actual documented historic term.

No matter who the original rednecks were in early history, we now need to decide who are the real redneck survivors in this modern age? Are they Americans or South Africans? The only way to determine 'whose who in the zoo' is to pit a candidate from South Africa against the 'best in the business' in America. This is an exercise of massive proportions…particularly in view of the fact that this competition must of necessity take place on hallowed American soil, which in normal circumstances gives America the home advantage. But, I hasten to add *again* that this is no 'normal circumstance.' May the best redneck win. Good luck, y'all. Soooo, here's the challenge.

South African Redneck Challenge in America

In my efforts to prepare for a new beginning in America, my wife and I crossed the ocean on many occasions to spend time in as many different locations as possible. This entailed air flights to and from the two countries via the least expensive international airlines. Cheap is not always a good way to fly between continents. Another factor was that South African airways (due to United Nations regulations) were not permitted to fly over countries to the north. These flights were, therefore, routed around the Western coastline of Africa (the bulge) to destinations in the rest of the world. For these and other nebulous reasons, we chose to 'go with the flow.'

There was, however, one advantage about having to fly via different countries' airlines. During flight changes in foreign countries, we were able to spend time as visitors in many of the world's most captivating locations. There is nothing as stimulating as rubbing shoulders with different cultures on their home turf. In most cases, language barriers proved less of a problem than anticipated; we managed to mull our way around Dutch, German, and Italian situations…and found that people in Spain and other countries helped us through their general English knowledge…except for France! Why is that? As previously mentioned, we never spoke English when within hearing distance of the locals…in particular, when wanting decent service in restaurants, etc. Being fluent in other languages, other than French in our case, was our saving grace many times. Once you have had the experience of ordering a chicken sandwich in France, only to be served a boiling hot plate of onion soup that sticks to your lips and burns off your ability to plant a romantic kiss on your beloved, will you understand why you should avoid being recognized as English speaking when in France.

So, what can happen to a pair of hapless South African rednecks in foreign lands? Well, that depends. In a hotel in Rome, we shared a bathroom 'down the passage' with the United Nations. Did I mention that we traveled 'cheap?' Oh, and somebody stole my bottle of South African wine that was an intended gift for an American friend. Now that's cheap! Here are a few of the other interesting travel moments...

On one occasion, when attending a bullfight in Madrid, I was filming everything possible with my new movie camera. At one point between 'kills,' I had to go to the bathroom. As I walked down the passage, I continued to film the colorful people moving around. While walking along the oval sunlit walkways, I was so engrossed that I was still filming as I entered the men's public bathroom where I caught several men on camera with their hands full. Realizing my mistake, I immediately dropped the camera from my eye, but the last glimpse of the frame revealed an angry mob starring at me in disbelief. I was out of there like greased lightning and I can only assume that the time delay involved in men's final bathroom rituals, gave me the time to make my escape.

I rushed back to my seat, crouched beside my wife, and cuddled her like the other couples did between kills. Are woman sexually stimulated by bullfighting...like those who watch wrestling? Not my woman! She pushed me aside and muttered, "What's the matter with you? Stop fooling around...it's too hot to mess around." A short time later as the crowd screamed, "Ole!" I told her that I had to go to the bathroom again. She looked at me and said, "You had better have a prostate check."

Once when waiting for a flight from O'Hare, we were informed that the aircraft had mechanical problems and we could expect a two-hour delay. My wife and I wandered around the concourse and returned an hour later. The clerks were irritated at us because they had been calling our names for an alternate flight, which had just departed. Have you ever heard and understood a public announcement in an international airport? With that, six others from our original group arrived and also received the bad news. An hour later, our small group boarded a slightly smaller aircraft and we lined up for takeoff.

I was surprised at how few passengers were on board, which included a honeymoon couple on their first flight to paradise. They were cuddling together as we took off and in their bliss, they were not even aware of flight. As the plane took to the air, I became alarmed. We did not seem to be gaining much altitude, and then there was a sudden shudder through the cabin, the plane veered to the left, and as one wing dipped slightly, the passengers were jiggled around. The honeymoon ended...the couple started to pray. The plane leveled with another lurch and despite the fact we were nose up, the aircraft was struggling to gain altitude. In time, we slowly climbed into the sky.

The engines were roaring and the plane was vibrating, and then out of the blue, all the oxygen masks popped out above us and I knew that we were in big trouble. The sight of those dangling masks scared the heck out of the young bride and she became hysterical. Suddenly, a male attendant came stumbling down the passage and, with his hat at a comical angle, he announced, "There's no cause for alarm!" He could have fooled me. He added with a quiver...something like this, "We will, however, be making an emergency landing and all passengers must adopt the heads down safety procedure when we land." I assumed he was referring to the position, which made it physically possible to kiss your butt 'goodbye.' He made the sign of the cross and the bride fainted!

At this point, I noticed faint traces of smoke filtering through a square vent directly behind the cockpit and I swallowed hard. It took a long time for the plane to complete a turn, however when completed, we went in for a direct landing. I worried because I could not believe that at that crowded airport, a runway was cleared.

As we landed, the emergency vehicles accompanied us on the ground with lights flashing and sirens screaming. By the time we stopped, there were dozens of rescue vehicles moving into position on both sides of the aircraft. The instant the plane came to a stop, we were evacuated through emergency procedure and the minute our feet touched the ground, we were whisked across the runway. When we entered the terminal building, one of our numbers complained about being rushed off the plane. A flight attendant replied dryly, "Rather be rushed than dead…" Amen to that!

Once during a return flight from Paris, our French airliner was diverted to one of those African states connected to France at the hip. It was an unscheduled and unexpected detour and we were not told the reason for it. At the time, South Africans were not welcomed in many African states and this turned out to be one of them. On landing, the aircraft was boarded by military personnel who were armed with Uzis (automatic weapons). One sweaty uniformed officer informed the passengers that we were to be escorted to the terminal where we would be made comfortable during our stopover. He made a point of telling us that we were to leave all hand luggage on the plane. When my wife and I reached the exit, a soldier grabbed me by the arm and remonstrated over the fact that I had my camera hanging around my neck. He called his superior, who roughly removed the camera and then asked for our passports. The minute they realized that we were South Africans they became excited and rude. We were separated from the other passengers, who were being directed to the terminal and two armed men escorted us to a separate room in the facility. Although these people were French speaking, the man left with us spoke reasonable English. However, he would not answer any of my frantic questions. In time, two men in civilian clothes entered the room and, without saying much, gave us a body search. It was a humiliating experience for the two of us and once it had been concluded, we were ushered out the room and under armed guard we joined the other passengers on the hot and humid walk to the aircraft. To my surprise, I was handed back my camera, but the film had been removed. It was obvious that during our absence from the aircraft, everybody's hand luggage had been roughly searched. We eventually took off and resumed our flight to South Africa and, to this day, we have no idea why any of this happened. From that moment, we have avoided anything French.

There were some lighter moments. While traveling in Italy, which became my favorite stopover, we joined a happy throng of soccer supporters at an important playoff for some or other championship. It was a cold evening and we were advised to carry a bottle of good red wine for sustenance; I would have carried two, but there were certain boundaries that I dared not violate while accompanied by 'the little woman.' Not really a problem because none of the women in my life ever partook of the juice of the vine…leaving that chore to me.

The soccer final was a 'sight.' There were bands supporting each team and, whenever something exciting happened, both bands took turns to outplay their opponents…and when a goal was scored, the place went crazy with fireworks flashing everywhere and bands playing their lungs out. All this activity created a great thirst and supporters of both teams chug-a-lugged on their comforter bottles…me included! It soon became obvious why I should have brought two bottles. Whenever a goal was scored all the spectators took a good swig from their supply…and as the final score ended at three goals to two, my wine ran out just after half time. At the conclusion of the game, we were entertained all the way back to our hotel by street revelers in high spirits. What a night! Hic!

England was easy on the eye, and they speak proper English! Well, not in all locations, as Dr. Doolittle discovered.

Did I mention that we lost our eldest son Wayne somewhere in Harrod's…a somewhat 'harrowing' experience until we discovered him in the women's underwear department? What do they say about a falling acorn?

Holland was pretty…and expensive.

Welcome to America
Redneck 103

However, all things taken into consideration, I must confess that there were also some 'interesting' events awaiting me in America.

Because South Africans traveled on restricted amounts of foreign currency, we needed to find a way to minimize our regular frequent land travel expenses in America. The solution was to ship an automobile from South Africa to America, and leave it there with somebody when we returned home. The only problem was that American importation rules excluded any and all vehicles that did not conform to the strict fuel emission and safety regulations. This excluded every vehicle except those built in America. To cut to the chase, I bought an imported left-hand drive American Rambler from an American citizen, who was returning home after several years on assignment in South Africa. It was not cost effective for him to pay for the cost of shipping a vehicle back to the states where its value was less than the shipping charges, and when I replied to his advert…he knew instinctively…'here comes a ripe one.' It was a sweet deal for both rednecks. He got a good price and I found a way to reduce traveling costs in the states. The added advantage was that this big comfortable station wagon could also cut down on overnight digs…and y'all know what I mean.

Without going into all the details of how I eventually managed to ship the wagon, which could have me glued to this cotton picking keyboard for hours, I will fast forward to the 'interesting' factual story regarding my experience when collecting it from the Savannah port authorities. You may well ask, "Why did you chose Savannah?" Simple; at that time, Savannah was the only port of entry for South African shipments of all descriptions.

At that time, we were considering the Southeastern coastal region as a possible new home in America, so we arranged to stay 'cheaply' in a travel trailer park in Fort Lauderdale to await the arrival of the wagon. Sounds spooky, but we had developed a sound relationship with the owners, who eventually became close friends…and who kindly offered to store the soon to arrive wagon for us. 'Soon to arrive' spoken in haste because while we waited in a travel trailer during a hot and uncomfortable summer, somebody re-routed the ship carrying the wagon via Australia. No kidding! That's a long story best left alone. Fast forward…once more.

I am taking the liberty to relate in detail the events surrounding the clearing of the wagon in Savannah, because it will show many sides of America…some expected bureaucracy, some quirks, but most importantly the refreshing certainty that you will always find somebody who cares in America. Just as important, when reading this account, give a thought to the underlying emotions of a complete stranger in a foreign environment at the mercy of red tape issues and add the fact that my 'Southern' redneck accent never came near being understood in the heart of the American South.

I called the South African shipping agents almost daily to keep track of our cargo, so that I would be prepared to fly to Savannah the moment the ship docked. Three weeks after settling in, the ship docked and I flew to Savannah to personally clear the wagon. I flew out on a very early flight dressed warmly, because the weather had unexpectedly turned cold. It was my intention to clear the vehicle that day and start my long drive back immediately. I traveled light and carried one strong hand suitcase onto the plane. Besides a change of clothes and a small bathroom kit, I added some tools, a pair of jump leads, and an empty two-gallon plastic container for gasoline that I intended to buy on the way to the port. I carried the heavy case into the plane, shoved it into the overhead storage, settled back for the flight, and arrived for breakfast.

I called a cab and went to the first gas station and filled my plastic container, and then shoved it back in the case and spent several minutes explaining to the cab driver that I was not about to blow up the world. I explained in detail that I needed the gas to crank my car that had been shipped after all the gas had been drained. I was unsupervised when draining the gas at the South African shipping terminal and knew that a few gallons remained. In fact it is almost impossible to completely drain a tank…and as far as the danger of a fire is concerned, it is the gas fumes that remain that are more dangerous in the event of a spark ignition. As you know, in a fire the existence of any amount of gas could be an issue…not sure why I threw this in.

The cab driver agreed to continue the fare on the condition that the suitcase rode up front with him and me in the back seat. We agreed and I told him to take me to a particular area in the docks where I had been informed my car had been unloaded. I took careful note of our route and especially the security gate number where we were to enter. We were stopped at the gate and I produced my papers. The security guy was small and skinny, and constantly whistled under his breath as he checked through my documents. During this time, I paid the driver, who kindly gave me specific details on how to get myself onto the highway to Ft. Lauderdale. He made a point of advising me to exit from the same gate…the other exits were to be avoided, as they would head me in the wrong direction. I thanked him, paid him, and he drove off.

The guard told me to go to the harbor office, which he pointed out some distance away. I picked up my case and walked off briskly, leaving the man as he softly whistled to himself…I could not make out the tune. I covered the distance to the office within ten minutes, looking all over for my wagon as I walked…but no luck.

When I entered the office, several clerks were on hand assisting a few people ahead of me. As I waited, I realized that all the other customers were clearing agents and seemed to be well received by the clerks. There was much friendly banter and I began to feel at ease. These guys were very friendly. My turn came and the huge guy with the shiny shaved head and red round face came over and said, "You must be new around here…which clearing agency do you work for?" I smiled and replied, "I do not work for an agency; I am here to clear my own car." Everybody turned and looked at me. My clerk went a shade redder, "That's a little unusual…we don't like to deal with civilians who don't know the rules…that's when things get all screwed up." I pulled out my documents and said politely, "I don't want to cause any inconvenience; I did not realize that agents were necessary." Oops! All eyes were on me and I quickly corrected, "What I mean is that I did not realize that I needed an agent…I am inexperienced in these matters." Did I really say that? I continued, "I am sorry…I did not mean any disrespect." He took the papers from me and started to check them, but a group of workers came in and interrupted him; they were talking loudly and flopped into chairs at the end of the room. My guy then dropped the documents on the counter and said, "It's lunch break. Come back in forty-five minutes."

I felt a complete fool, picked up my papers and suitcase, and walked outside…I needed some air! I pulled out some cookies from my jacket and sat on a pile of boxes for my lunch. While sitting, I looked around for my car…still no luck. As I chewed, I noticed a police car cruising the area and its presence gave me a feeling of security.

In a while, a man came out of the office and walked toward me. I recognized him as one of the customers and I guessed that he was a clearing agent…he made me nervous. He was young and walked very upright.

"Hi. I am Tony; I thought I would keep you company," he said with an unexpected smile. I introduced myself and he offered me a candy. I was beginning to like the man. He smiled widely and told me, "Don't worry about old Jock, he is a stickler for correct procedure; if your documents are in order, he will take care of you. I am an agent; let me take a quick look at your stuff." He noted my initial reluctance and he added, "No strings attached…I only want to help you." I felt embarrassed and handed him my documents. He turned to the first page and looked up, "Are you from South Africa? I thought you had an unusual accent."

I replied in the affirmative, adding, "I only arrived last week."

"You sure don't look African. Are your folks missionaries?"

"No, they are not, but I have been asked that question before."

He recognized my discomfort and returned to the documents, "Your stuff is perfect, you will have no trouble with Jock," the man told me.

We returned to the office and Tony called out, "Hey, Jock, I have done your job for you. This African's paper's are perfect."

Jock turned around to take me in and asked, "What African? Who are you talking about?"

Tony put a hand on my shoulder and said with a laugh, "This 'pale face.'"

Jock looked at me and replied, "He don't look African to me. Are you a missionary?"

Within minutes, we were all friends and Jock explained that my car was in an open shed one-half mile farther along. He gave me documents, including some duplicates and an envelope containing the car keys and he asked, "Will you be sending a wrecker to collect it?" You should have seen his face when I replied, "No. I intend driving it out." His expression was priceless, but very worrying. I thanked Tony and Jock, picked up my case, and headed for the shed. All eyes were on me as I closed the door.

The temperature had dropped considerably and I shoved the documents into the inside pocket of my heavy corduroy jacket and zipped it closed. The jacket felt warm and its length conveniently covered my 'cute buns.' That is how my wife referred to them one night after a late New Year's party. I pulled out a woolen 'boggan,' stretched it over my ears, lifted my collar, and headed into the cold wind. It was a long walk to the shed and on the way I noted workmen checking and moving cargo around with forklift trucks. I exchanged friendly waves to many and swung my suitcase to help me along.

Within a short distance from the shed, I heard a car approaching from behind and I glanced back and noticed the cop car cruising slowly toward me. Not wanting to obstruct the car, I moved out the road and stepped behind a huge pile of timber and as I did so, the driver switched on the siren and accelerated. Thinking that he was going to speed off to assist somewhere, I jumped further behind the timber. Then to my utter amazement, the car suddenly turned toward me and screeched to a stop, blocking me between the timber and the front bumper. I nearly wet myself and dropped the suitcase heavily on the ground with a thud. I noted workmen vanishing in every direction.

As the car rocked to a stop, the siren faded like a sick goat, and a cop jumped out and shouted at me, "Don't move!" I was not about to go anywhere! I was surprised to see that the cop was actually a female. Not a big female, a tiny thing. She had a big voice and an even bigger firearm strapped to her side. She shouted, "Don't move! What ship did you jump, Sergei?"

I realized that she was confusing me with someone else and I replied sharply, "I have not jumped ship. I am clearing my car, let me show you my papers."

With that, I reached into my breast pocket for the documents and she went ballistic, screamed, "Freeze!" and she jerked her Smith and Wesson from its holster. I was definitely going to pee my pants! She was a little thing, but the more I looked at her piece, the taller she got. She stood at her open car door and shouted hysterically, "Place your hands behind your head and turn around." I hesitated. She screamed, "Now!" I did very quickly! I heard her speak on her police radio, "Joe, I need backup on pier 20…I got us an illegal…he speaks funny. I am sure he is Russian." Then to add insult to injury, she added, "He is mean-looking…he has a beard and is wearing a funny wooly thing over his head, and he has a suspicious suitcase, which he tried to hide when I stopped him. No, no, I'm not kidding, ten four." I heard her approaching from behind and she said firmly, "Place your hands on the timber in front of you at face level and lean forward." I obeyed and she said softly, "Now move your legs back a foot, spread them, and assume the position." Did she want sex? She added sharply, "And, I mean right now, Sergei." As I assumed the position, another car arrived with sirens screaming.

A male police officer arrived and after a brief exchange between the two, the man said,

"Okay, pal, put your hands behind your back."

Without moving I called out, "You are making a mistake…take a look at my papers, I am clearing a car." I was surprised that there was no angry response from the newcomer and I sweated despite the weather. The male voice remarked, "You sound Australian. What are you doing here?"

I pleaded, "Please help me, your friend thinks I have jumped ship. I can't believe she thinks that I am Russian. Do I sound Russian?"

He replied, "Turn around very slowly and remove your headgear." I turned slowly and removed my wooly thing. The two stared at me and I spoke slowly and deliberately, so that they could understand me.

"When the lady stopped me, I tried to get my papers out of my inside pocket and she thought I was going for a gun. That's why she called you for backup; please check my papers."

Moving cautiously, I put my hands behind my head and the male cop came forward and carefully removed my papers. He read them and asked, "Show me your passport." I produced it and handed it over with some additional paperwork. He examined them closely and said, "So you are from South Africa. You don't look like an African. I thought you were an Aussie."

I replied, "I have never been in Australia. I was born and raised in South Africa."

The woman looked me over said, "You sure don't look like an African."

I took a deep breath and muttered "And my folks are not missionaries."

The big cop handed back my papers and passport, and glancing at his companion, he said, "It looks like somebody made a mistake. I will be getting on my way." With those few words, he slipped into his patrol car and pulled off. As I stood there a little distracted, the woman stared a while and walked to her car.

I was relieved, but furious, and as she reached the car, I said, "It would be nice if someone who made a mistake would say sorry." Then I bit my lip.

She stopped abruptly, turned, and said, "You are pushing your luck, Buster." Then with a forced smile she added, "What the heck. Sorry, pal…but it's all in a day's work. Welcome to the real world!"

Now, I pushed my luck. "How about a lift to my car?"

That came as a surprise, but she recovered and replied in a friendlier manner, "Sorry. Not permitted, except for suspects, and you are not a suspect, right?" I backed off and she left the scene. I reached the shed and caught my first glimpse of the wagon, which was standing in front of a line of cars and farm tractors. It was filthy and I noticed that the wheel caps were missing. My heart sank…what else would be missing? Using my spare keys, I unlocked the driver's door and made a quick check. I was relieved to note that everything in the wagon was exactly as shipped. I then did a thorough check of the vehicle. The tires looked good, but the radio antenna was broken off and the passenger mirror was cracked, otherwise, all seemed in order. I unlocked the glove compartment, removed some rags and window cleaner, and wiped all the heavy grime off all the glass. I then realized that the wipers were missing and I took a quick look at the sky and hoped that it would not rain. I popped the hood and checked…nobody had been in there. I removed a few tools from my suitcase and tested the battery; the strong flash across my screwdriver scared me, but encouraged me. Using a wrench, I connected the battery terminals, checked the oil, transmission, water, and brake fluid levels. I was ready, but very impatient and nervous. I did not wait to pour my gas into the tank because I was too eager to see if it would crank on the gas that remained in the tank. I slipped behind the wheel and pushed the key gently into the column. I pumped the gas pedal several times and said a prayer. I turned the ignition key and the motor fired instantly. I got such a shock that I nearly stalled it. The steady throb was music to my ears.

The fuel gauge was between empty and a quarter, so I poured in my two gallons while the car was idling. I was not about to cut the motor, but I knew that I would need gas soon. The inside of the vehicle was surprisingly clean. I adjusted the mirror, pulled out carefully, and headed for the gate. The speed was limited to ten miles per hour and I complied, watching carefully for any signs of 'Cinderella' and her Smith and Wesson. Although I drove slowly, I became conscious of a strange intermittent vibration coming from somewhere under the car, but I kept going. When I passed the port office, someone waved. I soon reached the security gate and when I pulled up, a tall overweight woman in uniform called me over with the words, "Cut the motor and let's see what you've got."

I climbed out with my papers and she shouted, "Cut the motor. Those exhaust fumes are killers." I reluctantly complied and handed her my documents. She scanned them and then said curtly, "Let me see your gate pass."

I blinked. "What gate pass?"

She lit up, "You don't have a gate pass?"

I replied honestly, "No, Ma'am."

She seemed shocked, "How did you get in here?"

I replied confidently, "A cab brought me." That did not sit well with her.

"Don't mess with me. We don't allow cabs through here. If you really came through this gate you would have been issued with a temporary pass." I tried my best to explain and I became excited as I spoke. Not allowing me to finish she said, "Hold it, boy. You talk too fast and you talk funny." Look whose talking!

I tried again slooowly, "When I came through, a little white guy with a mustache checked my papers and let me through."

That raised her eyebrows and the pitch of her voice, "Don't tell me that Rufus did not give you a pass. He never would let you in without one."

I took a breath, smiled weakly, and asked, "Well, how am I going to get my car out of here?"

She snapped back, "I don't know, but I sure as heck ain't letting you through here without a pass."

I asked, "Because whistling Rufus screwed up?"

She pulled up on her belt and looking me in the eye she said firmly, "Watch your mouth, young man. This has nothing to do with Rufus. Anyway, my friend, somebody in the harbor office forgot to stamp both copies of your papers. So, I suggest that you go back there and get them to do their job right."

I retrieved my papers, jumped into the car, and turned the key…nothing! I tried again…nothing. I started to sweat and the woman came over, stuck her head in the window, looked everything over, and said, "If it don't go, you will have to push it back, look at the traffic backing up here."

I turned the key again to no avail. The woman then stuck her head through my window and said, "Hey, you need to select neutral or park to give her life. Don't they teach you nothing in Australia?" I sheepishly selected park, cranked the car, and drove slowly to the office.

When I walked in Jock groaned, "Oh, no. Now what?"

I explained what happened and he cursed, "That woman is crazy. I stamped your release."

I frowned, "She wants the duplicate stamped."

He turned the pages, stamped one, and handed the pile back to me saying, "Look, take my advice go through the south gate past the shed where your car was stored. That way you won't be delayed. Just look at the congestion at her gate. The way she operates, it will take you all day to get out of here."

I left through the south gate and had no idea how to find the interstate to Florida, but I had a more pressing problem. The car started to vibrate and I stopped and crawled under the car, but could not locate the problem. I noticed a small gas station nearby and limped onto forecourt. I located a mechanic, told him my problem, and asked him to examine the car. He was a greasy little man with a wad in his cheek. He looked me over and said, "It will cost you ten dollars." I agreed. He walked around the car and came back to me. "That will be ten dollars," he repeated.

"What for?" I asked.

"Found your problem."

"What problem?" I asked.

He spat out something into a trashcan and repeated, "Ten dollars."

I asked, "Can you fix it?"

"Sure, for another ten dollars."

I handed over a few bills, he thanked me and said, "Somebody was trying to steal your front wheel. All the wheel nuts have been loosened. It's just as well that you stopped; it could have tore off." He added, "Just wait here. I will take care of it." He went through the workshop door and returned dragging an airline behind with an air wrench attached. In five quick movements, he tightened the wheel and stepped back to look me over.

"You ain't from around here, are you? Where you from?"

Not wanting to go through the missionary thing I replied, "From Australia."

He smiled and replied, "Thought so. Had you pegged from the get-go. We all like you Aussies 'cause you were some of the few who helped us in Korea."

I caught my breath and replied courteously, "Glad that we could help in Korea," and I added wryly, "what goes around comes around."

I pulled up at the pumps, and filled up. As I got in to leave, the man came over and asked, "How do you know that the other wheels are tight?" He noted my look and he laughed, "Don't worry, I have checked them" and he stood showing his yellow teeth.

I reacted with, "Don't tell me another ten dollars?"

He laughed until he rattled, "No charge. What do you take me for? We Southern folk don't take advantage of tourists."

I pulled out at sundown and drove in circles for hours before finally hitting the interstate. I drove through the night and stopped occasionally to catch a few winks, and after some delays, you guessed it…it rained! I finally pulled into the trailer park late the following night. I was welcomed home like a sailor!

If at First You Don't Succeed, Do You Quit?

While spending time in Fort Lauderdale, I discovered a new phenomenon…a flea market operating on Sundays on a drive-in theater site. I was amazed at the activity and the throngs of eager customers. Items of every description were snapped up in the friendliest commercial atmosphere that I had ever seen. Everything from sewing thimbles to used auto parts. One of those guys mentioned that there was a huge market for used English Jaguar parts because of the exorbitant prices charged for imported parts. Then I noticed a most unusual section. Some guys were offering used beer cans for sale. I could not believe this. Why would there be customers for used beer cans? It did not take long for me to learn that beer can collecting was the latest collector's craze. Most cans were sold for a dollar, but many imported cans went for as much as five dollars. I noted that there were no South African cans among the thousands offered, so it occurred to me…Why not bring some South African cans when I next came over to the States. Better still…why not ship thousands of cans? The question was…how and, more importantly, at what cost? With the clearing of the wagon from the port still fresh in my mind, I got to thinking. Maybe I could ship over a few used English Jaguars for resale as 'used' parts and fill them up with old beer cans for a free ride. You must remember that this was still in the dark ages.

On our return to South Africa, I had no problem finding a few cheap used Jag XJ6s. This was when we were struggling with UN sanctions and oil embargoes, which resulted in very expensive gasoline prices at the pumps. People were downsizing their auto choices, favoring small inexpensive cars…cheap French, Italian, and those Japanese rice burners. Any gas-guzzlers, including expensive cars like Jags, were being auctioned off at fire sale prices. There was one further advantage about these Jags…there had not been any significant changes to the models for years. All body parts up to ten years old could be utilized by body repair shops in America as replacement parts for the current models. I was at the right place at the right time.

Collecting used beer cans in South Africa was no problem. Within a few weeks, we had collected thousands of cans from various sports venues. It is only when you clean up after one of these events that you realize how much money is spent on beer. The organizers of these sports events were delighted that they did not have to pay for this service and getting something free is 'good!' We washed the cans, sorted them, filled six enormous grain bags, and stored them. I was ready to roll!

Fast Forward

Six months later, we were indeed ready to roll, this time with the aid of clearing agents at both ends. I arranged to ship two 'used' Jags to America. The agent, Allen, was flabbergasted at the fact that I wanted to pack the cars with sacks of beer cans. He mentioned that using a vehicle as a container was frowned on. I told him to frown as much as he liked, but to include the cans in the manifest. He also seemed uncomfortable about me personally delivering the vehicles to the docks.

Despite everything, a few weeks later, a driver and I drove the two Jags to the docks with my wife following. She was very amused as the cars were so packed with sacks of cans that she could not see who was driving. I personally prepared the cars for shipment and once again managed to leave a reasonable amount of gas in each tank. I also included new additional batteries for the cars. There was, however, one major difference this time around. The cars had to be shipped to Jacksonville, Florida, and not Savannah. This did bother me some, as I had hoped to clear the cars in Savannah, where I not only knew the routine, but also felt more secure about the relationships I had forged with the officials there.

A few weeks after the cars and cans were shipped, we returned once more to take up residence at the trailer park in Fort Lauderdale. As before, we received special low rates and to show our appreciation, my wife and I volunteered to do some tasks for them. My wife 'struck it rich.' She helped tend the flower gardens and water the plants. For her, this was pure pleasure. I 'struck out!' My main job was to help hook up the 'honey sucker' to the septic tanks…and this was one big trailer park!

In time, the Jags arrived in Jacksonville, Florida, and I hired an acquaintance that lived in the park to assist me and keep me from getting lost. After hitching a hired trailer to the wagon, we set off one morning long before daylight. On arrival at the port, we joined a clearing agent who handled all of the formalities, after which I paid him and took it from there personally. I was delighted that the cars had arrived without damage. I negotiated with the supervisor to have the cars released. His name was Louis, a heavy

Italian-American, who insisted on checking the vehicles personally before releasing them. As we walked to the cars, he sweated heavily and wiped his brow constantly. Once he noted the sacks of cans, he complained about me using the cars as a container, but as they were legally noted on the manifest, he okayed them, provided that he check them out. To my annoyance, he started removing the sacks and, to my amazement, started pouring out the empty cans all over the place, and began roughly examining them. All this time, he sweated and wiped. The more he sweated, the more aggressive he became and many of my precious cans were damaged. After about an hour of this frustrating exercise, he made me repack the cans in the sacks and then reload them into the vehicles. He was not the only one sweating.

Finally, out of the blue, he said, "We have a small problem…these vehicles do not comply with the fuel emission and safety regulations of the USA. I am going to impound both of them."

I was stunned, but replied politely, "They have been imported for used parts and I intend dismantling them."

He did not go for that. "You will never convince me that you are going to strip down these two beauties. If I release them, you will clean them up and sell them, and that will be illegal."

I protested, "I guarantee you that I intend dismantling them for parts."

He shook his head and said gruffly, "The road to Hell is paved with good intentions; once these cars leave here, you could change your intentions. These babies are worth a pile!"

I insisted, "But, the manifest clearly identifies them as scrap vehicles."

Wiping his sweaty brow, he retorted, "I don't care what the manifest says. I say you won't dismantle them and, pal, these cars are going nowhere!"

In desperation, I asked civilly, "What can I do?"

He told me, "They can stay here for twenty days, after which time you pay demurrage per day. Then after a certain reasonable period, if you have not shipped them back to South Africa or elsewhere, they will be crushed right here at the docks!"

In shock, I inquired, "Any other options?"

He replied, "Yep, you can lodge fifteen hundred dollar bonds per car in escrow with us and take the vehicles and modify them to comply with our regulations within thirty days. Once you prove that you have done that, you can apply for me to release your escrow bond and then everybody will be happy. But, I must warn you that you will not be permitted to drive any of these vehicles from here or anywhere. If you do so, the vehicles will be confiscated."

I thought for a while and said, "It will cost me a fortune to convert these cars."

He half smiled, "You are right, it will cost you more than they are worth."

I considered for a moment and enquired, "I don't know anyone who I can get to do the work."

He jumped in, "My brother Angelo can do it. I could get you two together. How about this? He converts one for you and one for him. That way you get one converted and he takes the other as payment." Go figure.

I answered slowly, "I'll pay the bond into escrow."

He replied curtly, "No problem. It's your funeral."

I needed time and suggested, "How about me paying a fifteen hundred dollar bond and take one car in the meantime and then I can decide what to do."

He looked up and repeated, "Okay, it's your funeral."

The subsequent documentation was prepared and my friend and I loaded one car onto the trailer and removed the bags of cans from the other car. To my surprise, Louis stopped me and asked, "What do you think you are doing?" I answered, "I'm taking all the bags on this first trip." He sneered, "Not without my authority."

I replied, "Okay, will you please authorize this for me?" Back to the office we walked where further documents were provided allowing me to remove all the sacks of cans. We eventually left, towing the Jag and its precious beer can cargo on the trailer.

I could write a chapter on how this situation was resolved, but for now…through a contact, I eventually sold both vehicles at a handsome profit to a buyer who transshipped both cars from Jacksonville to the Bahamas. This turned out to be more convenient and a blessing in disguise, as I not only saved time and effort to dismantle and market parts, but saved valuable time for other matters. The buyer was obviously very well connected. Once the cars were shipped, my bond was immediately released by the sweaty official, who commented, "Too bad. You win some; you lose some." Who lost…who won? I now had a new exciting contact in the Bahamas. Don't you just love it when a plan comes together?

Regarding the beer cans, how's this?" I sold about 50 percent of the cans at $2.25 each. You can imagine how much cash this generated when you consider the number of cans in a carload! Our friendly trailer park owners kindly allowed me to store the remaining bags of cans for sale in the future.

During this trip, I visited an immigration lawyer in Philadelphia. He was sharp and bold. He surprised me during a bathroom break when he tapped me on the shoulder while I was busy at the urinal.

He asked, "Do you have a thousand dollars cash on you?"

I cut it short, pulled out all the cash I had and counted out a thousand. As the money crossed his little palm, I mentioned, "Careful, I never washed my hands." We both washed our hands. He was expensive, but he was good.

So who are the real rednecks? You tell me.

On subsequent visits to America, we sometimes stayed with ex-South African friends who had immigrated earlier. I recall the first American home where we stayed in New Jersey. We were given a very elegant upstairs room and guess what was the first thing we did? Open the windows for fresh air. All South Africans apparently do this because they are not accustomed to homes whose temperatures are regulated. So, I went over to the window and tried to release the 'roll up' blind that covered the window. I gave it a gentle pull and nothing happened. So, I gave it a harder tug and the darn thing went crazy! The recoil spring was so strong that the dumb blind took off and wound itself up so aggressively that even after the thing was fully pulled into its chamber, it kept on spinning with such force that the whole apparatus tore off the frame and took off across the room. What a dilemma! It took me an hour to replace the blind with the aid of a nail file from our traveling kit.

The next private home that we stayed in did not have blinds, but no matter how hard I tried, I could not pry the windows open. Apparently some jerk had set them up that way. Makes you think, don't it?

America – Getting to Know You, Getting to Know All about You

America sure was different to anything I had seen anywhere; I had never seen a ride mower. But, even more interesting, I had never seen a woman on a ride mower. I was so engrossed with this spectacle that I asked my friend's neighbor if I could take a photograph of her on the mower to show the folks back home. She obliged, but I later heard that she thought that the South Africans were 'kind of strange.' Well, I don't know about that. If I had a ride mower I would want to drive it myself. That could be fun. That's something else I discovered about Americans, they have a way of having fun doing everyday things. Like their garbage cans…they had wheels…and you could race them to the curb and back. With a little ingenuity, you could even hitch a ride with one foot and propel yourself with the other as was my custom with the supermarket buggies; that is, as long as my wife was not around. And, what about dishwashers…are you kidding me? And those garbage disposals that gobbled up food waste through the kitchen sink. I wondered what would happen if you accidentally stuck a few fingers down there when it was grinding and 'mashing up' unwanted goodies.

What about American TV? Sooo many channels and all in English (er…American). I missed the Zulu news.

Although the Americans have a gadget for just about everything, my personal favorite was the leaf blower. Man, could I have used one in South Africa. What could beat a leaf blower when you had to clean off your kids after a day at the beach? Why, you could blow all the beach sand and salt off in a hurry. The first thing I bought when we finally settled in our own home in America was a leaf blower.

One day while my family was out shopping, I decided to help out with some of the housework to relieve my wife of some of the chores. My wife was always on me about how she wished that I could sometimes do the dusting. So, what's with this dusting deal? I watched her carefully remove everything, dust the items, then carefully replace them. It took her forever. I was about to change all that. I opened all the windows, hooked up the hundred-foot extension cord to my new leaf blower, and stepped into the house ready to roll. I must admit that I had not read the operating instructions on my new toy, so I somehow overlooked the fact that my model had two speeds…'Fast' and 'Furious!'

I dragged half the cord into the living room, pointed the blower at the carpeted floor, and hit the big red button. That crazy machine jumped into action and almost ripped itself out of my hands. In that instant, I was so shocked at the power that I forgot what I was pointing at. As the machine spun me around, I hit everything full blast. Drapes flared up toward the ceiling, all the flower arrangements were destroyed as they were 'bazookered' into the air, magazines took off from the coffee table and landed all over the place. Family pictures were knocked over onto the floor.

I must confess that the leaf blower incident casts me in a 'dim light'…remember 'night school?' But, in my defense…you must not lose sight of the fact that when a South African redneck is confronted with some new and/or unknown contraption, he will rise to the occasion and take it on…it's called a learning experience…and I learned in a hurry. In the same way when tourists arrive in South Africa and ask, "Where is the jungle?"…only to awaken to the realization that no jungle exists in South Africa…some unkind remarks may be offered. Or, when a tourist arrives in South Africa with a suitcase full of Bibles for distribution to the barefoot population residing in the bush, only to find that more Bibles are printed and are available in South Africa than any other book, and that South Africa is the largest producer of footwear on the continent. Makes one think, don't it? Should I mention that I personally hardly wear shoes at home now that I have been Americanized? Or my wife, despite the fact that she had more shoes than the previous first lady of some large island country in the Pacific. Walking barefoot makes the feet strong and healthy, as long as you wash them, which brings me to another interesting South African ritual.

We all are proud of our cars (usually an older model) and personally wash and polish them regularly, usually early on Saturday mornings to shine those babies before driving to town to strut our stuff! For us 'jungle bunnies,' car washing is a ritual…a ritual that I continue even to this day as an American citizen, except in winter! (Regarding my American citizenship experience, I have saved that 'saga' for inclusion at the end of this book as a conclusion…and, in my opinion, an eye opener.) Sooo, on with the home car wash.

My car washing ritual commences with arranging all the necessary washing paraphernalia (toys) in their respective places—water hose with a variable spray fitting, buckets, sponges, rough cloths, gentle cloths, imported leather waterproof cloth, window cleaners, interior car spray laced with nice smelly flower scents, car polish, black tire polish, and my newly discovered 'toy' for removing those stubborn drops of water that hide away until you drive off…and then they splash on the windshield. I am referring to the 'leaf blower.' What do you think that those automatic car wash machines use to blow your car dry as you exit? A GIANT LEAF BLOWER! So, was I really that dumb about using that baby for dust removal! Oh, well.

The first thing that I do before washing the car is set the radio on my favorite country station and turn it on loud real loud! With the music howling, I prepare myself. I strip off all my clothes except my '50s' gym shorts. I turn the water on full, take a firm hold of the pistol grip chrome spray, and go to town on every surface of the car. From time to time, I turn the spray onto myself with a 'whoop and a holler.' When any member of the family (including dogs and cats) comes near, I shoot them from the hip and add a quick step to my 'whoop and holler.' After the initial rinse, I apply buckets of soapy water with a sponge and then, once again, rinse off the car and anybody in shooting distance. Then I dry the car off with the imported leather waterproof cloth, followed by various other soft and gentle clothes, clean all the windows and FINALLY, I crank up the leaf blower, set it on crazy, and take care of any drops of water that may be hidden. Then I carefully pack away all my toys…and as always, that is a signal for my wife to appear with an electric hand vacuum and the advice, "Hey, Biddie, you forgot to clean the inside of that mobile junk shop!" Things have improved. She bought me my own hand vacuum for my birthday. Ah! Peace in the land…at last.

Having completed the car washing exercise, I always cool off by stripping behind the Edsel and showering myself with the hose, after which I quickly wrap a towel around my athletic body before anybody can see the rest of my anatomy. That's a sight for sore eyes! I noticed an increase in traffic past my house around 8 A.M. on Saturday mornings…the general time that I complete washing the car and me. My neighbors are all very friendly. As they drive by, many honk their horns and some even wave their hands. I noticed that some did not use all their fingers.

Time Out for Rednecks Everywhere

Some sunny weather found me once again sitting on that hard wooden bench in Albemarle listening. Not really eavesdropping, but hearing those two Southern friends Tom and Tom, who meet every Saturday to discussing matters of vital importance.

This is how it went on the subject of 'globalization'…

Tom said, "Hey, Tom, you hear all this talk about globalization?"

Tom shook his head, sniffed, and replied, "I heard about it, but I have a question." "What's the question, Tom?

"What is the truest definition of globalization?" asked his friend.

"Princess Diana's unfortunate death. That's my answer, Tom."

"How come, Tom?"

"Look at the facts, Tom," Tom replied and continued as I hung on every word. "An 'English' Princess with an 'Egyptian' boyfriend crashes in a 'French' tunnel, riding in a 'German' car with a 'Dutch' engine, driven by a 'Belgian' who was drunk on 'Scottish' whisky, followed closely by 'Italian' paparazzi, on 'Japanese' motorcycles, treated by an 'American' doctor, using 'Brazilian' medicine. That is what I call 'Globalization!' Can you beat that?"

Tom scratched his ginger beard for a moment, then rising to the challenge, he came back with, "That's very interesting, Tom. I'll have to run that by my other brother, Tommy. He enjoys hearing from me because his job at that nuclear facility in New Mexico is very boring. He enjoys it when I send him e-mails."

"That's my point, Tom. That way, you will be sending it via e-mail, using 'American' Bill Gates technology on his 'Chinese' computer using 'Taiwanese' chips and a 'Korean' monitor assembled by 'Bangladeshi' workers in a 'Singapore' plant, transported by 'Indian' truck drivers, hijacked by 'Indonesians,' unloaded by 'Sicilian' longshoremen, and trucked to you by 'illegal Mexicans.'

"That's my point, Tom."

There followed a time of reflection before Tom changed the subject and asked Tom, "So, how do we describe 'Political Correctness,' Tom?"

It was time for Tom to finally wrap up the conversation. He said softly, "Political Correctness is a doctrine, fostered by a delusional, illogical minority, and rabidly promoted by an unscrupulous mainstream media, which holds forth the proposition that it is entirely possible to pick up a turd by the clean end." He sighed, adding wistfully, "Regarding that drunk 'Belgian' driver. I am not sure that what he drank stated, 'Scottish' whisky on the bottle labels. After all, we need to be sure of our facts."

Were Tom and Tom on the same page?

Just as the two started to discuss 'bowling,' Tom's cell phone jingled *What's New Pussycat* and he answered, "This is Tom." He listened intently and muttered, "So, sell the Bank of America stocks and buy a bunch of 'Wells Fargo." After a short silence he said, "Oh, crap!"

The conversation ended abruptly and Tom and Tom stood up and walked off. As they parted Tom said, "See you later, alligator."

Tom replied, "In a while, crocodile."

I knew then that neither knew the difference.

End of 'Time Out'…for now.

How about the following WOWs regarding newspapers and shoes?

WOW 1: IT'S ALWAYS DARKEST BEFORE DAWN. So, if you are going to steal your neighbor's newspaper that is the time to do it.
WOW 2: BEFORE YOU CRITICIZE SOMEONE, YOU SHOULD WALK A MILE IN THEIR SHOES. That way, when you criticize them, you are a mile away in their shoes reading their newspaper.

Try this QWB. WHY IS THIS? While sitting at your desk in front of your computer, lift your right foot off the floor and make clockwise circles. While doing this, draw the number '6' in the air with your right hand. Your foot will change direction! Congratulations! You have passed a critical redneck test with honors.

Oh…to those of you who flunked the redneck test…"Bless your hearts, y'all."

As someone who has passed all the redneck tests thus far, I feel that I should include my favorite South African redneck story as a salute to my countrymen and women.

You will recall that in the South Africa Colonial mix the Boers, the mainly Dutch farmers, and the British settlers were always on the opposite ends of the totem poles. Not unlike the American Northerners and Southerners, except for one huge difference…language. The Boers spoke Afrikaans and the Brits spoke the King's English. There were times when they could not understand each other. This situation caused serious problems, but in some instances, it was a blessing, e.g., after the Boer War, a Boer farmer walking through his field noticed a man drinking from his pond with his hands. The Boer shouted, "*Moenie daaran drink nie. Die kooie en varke het daarin gemorse!*"

Translation: "Don't drink the water. The cows and pigs have crapped in it!"

The man shouted back, "I am an Englishman. I don't understand, nor do I care to understand your gibberish. Speak English, you stupid Boer!"

The Boer shouted back in English, "Use two hands. That way you'll get more."

Did I mention that the British settlers were referred to as rednecks?

You no doubt noticed that both the 'Tom and Tom' discussions and the above Boer story mentioned one thing in common. I don't quite know how to 'delve' into this subject for fear of sounding somewhat coarse, but here goes. The subject is 'animal waste' (sounds better than the poop that I so carelessly mentioned when the first commercial ink was produced). Some would say, "Remember the Alamo." I say, "Don't forget the Cephalopod!" And just why do I bring this 'poopy' subject up? It was something that Al Gore said, regarding his conclusion that more than any other 'human' factor, the gas-guzzling SUV (Sport Utility Vehicle) is responsible for creating more carbon footprint than anything else. I have news for him; I have just read an interesting report on this subject in my NASCAR magazine. Where else?

According to Professor Igonna Slitzyoo, "The carbon footprint of a pet dog creates a carbon 'paw print' (love that) more than double that of the gas-guzzling SUV!" Here's the proof...

An average size pooch annually eats popular pet food consisting of about 360 pounds of meat. Add 95 kilos of cereal they woof down each year. I threw in kilos for brain exercise. The land requirement to generate food for a medium size doggie creates an annual footprint of 0.835 hectares...some 2.075 acres...once more saving your precious brain cells. This is 'twice' the 0.41 hectares required by a 4x4 vehicle driving 10,000 kilometers (6,000 miles), including the energy to build the vehicle. That's bad enough, but wait; there's more animal statistics to tempt your brain cells.

Let's look at cats. They have an eco-paw print around 0.15 hectares, which is a little less than driving a Beetle for a whole year. How about your two pet hamsters? They equate to a 45-inch plasma TV. And, my goldfish 'Bubbles' burns enough energy to operate two mobile telephones. The fact of the matter is that my cousin Ralph's two dogs and seven cats are the equivalent of a small fleet of cars.

Pet's environmental impact is not limited to their carbon footprint; they devastate wildlife, spread disease, and pollute waterways, y'all! Take Britain's 7.5 million cat population, for instance, and compare this...187 million wild animals are hunted down, killed, and eaten by feline predators each year averaging 24 mammals, frogs, and birds per cat. Where is the outcry from the bird watchers? Do some of them also keep cats?

Back to domestic animal waste...where do most dogs drops their loads? Some on neighbor's property, but most on their walks around their neighborhood. Ask any runner how often they have to clean their running shoes after slipping and sliding through the tulips. Dog feces (acceptable word for poop) actually cause high bacterial levels in rivers and streams. That's why I no longer skinny-dip in the creek. These high levels make the water unsafe to drink. The bottled water producers love this. Finally depletion of oxygen kills aquatic life.

Now about cats…their poo (dropped the last 'P' to save ink) can be even more toxic than puppy poo. It is a fact that many cat owners flush their litter down the toilet. (Ughhh!) This way, they infect a variety of animals with toxoplasma gondii, which causes a killer brain disease. There has been an alarming increase of this problem in sea otters.

Ever wonder how the German honky-tonk piano player came to be known as 'Crazy Otto?' Y'all may be too young to have heard him hit both those white and black ivories without missing a beat…he played better stuff than that whistle proof 'Chop pan' music Jim played in Blue Ridge, Georgia.

It is no wonder that, in some countries, they eat dogs and cats. Mr. Gore should commend them for saving the planet. I wonder if he has any dogs and/or cats in that green mansion that he calls one of his homes. If so, I suggest for the sake of all things 'nice' their dogs be confined within their property and their cats indoors. What about training cats to use the bathroom? That would save the otter. Another thought…kill off the polar bear and feed those brain-damaged fish to the cats. That should kill two 'birds' with one stone. Y'all know what I mean.

Another suggestion…if we must have pets…why not get a hen? That way the kids will discover where their eggs come from, and after the egg basket is depleted, the hen becomes dinner. Then how about rabbits? They also taste good.

Before departing from this 'waste-full' subject, I must bring in the joke I promised about the hypnotist at the senior center…that took a turn for the waste. Er…oh, well.

It was entertainment night at Sunny Days, the old folks' home, and over 300 seniors came to see the show. Stanley the hypnotist exclaimed, "I'm here to put y'all into a trance; I intend to hypnotize each and every member of the audience so that y'all will obey all my commands."

The excitement was almost electric as Stanley withdrew a beautiful antique pocketwatch from his coat and announced, "I want every one of you to keep your eyes on this antique watch. It's a very special watch. It has been in my family for over five generations." He began to swing the precious watch gently back and forth, back and forth, while quietly chanting, "Watch the watch, watch the watch, watch the watch."

The crowd became mesmerized as the watch swayed back and forth, back and forth…the light gleaming off its polished surface. Hundreds of pairs of old eyes followed the swaying watch, until suddenly, it slipped from the hypnotist's fingers and crashed to the floor, breaking into several of pieces.

"CRAP!" said the hypnotist.

If only he had said Shan…poor guy…he was asked to 'clean up' his act.

As is always the case, one story leads to another, and so we return to senior citizens and the dilemma that they find themselves in because of poor choices these old timers made in their youth.

There is more money spent on breast implants and Viagra today than on Alzheimer's research. The result is that by 2040, there will be a large elderly female population with perky boobs and older men with newfound glory, but absolutely no recollection of what to do about it.

Connected at the Hip

Right from the 'get go,' I mentioned how the early American settlers and those who immigrated to South Africa were largely from the same stock. Certain world events like the two World Wars, Korea, etc., had citizens from both continents working together for the benefit of mankind in general. A bond was formed and there were some who traveled between these two countries, even in the days of sailing ships. These movements created some interesting mutual trivia.

In 1981, Ronald Reagan became the fortieth president of the USA and his occupation was listed as 'Motion Picture Actor.' He was the first Hollywood actor to become the president of the USA, but not the first Hollywood actor to become president of a country. That was the distinction, if one can call it one, held by a South African, the Honorable Charles Robberts Swart who served as president of South Africa from 1961 through 1967. This tall, dignified statesman who stood six foot seven in his socks, had appeared in several cowboy movies in the 30s and 40s. It is an interesting fact that both actors appeared in 'cowboy' movies.

There is some other interesting trivia regarding the 'Old West' in the USA and a connection to South Africa. In 1867, Henry M. Stanley, an adventurous news reporter, had tracked down Wild Bill Hickock and after an interview, he wrote and published newspaper articles on his new hero. The very same Stanley was sent to Africa to search for the famous English missionary, David Livingston, who was reportedly missing in Africa according to an article in the *New York Herald* on April 9, 1869. Stanley's expenses were covered by the *Herald*.

After many exciting and dangerous experiences over 236 days and covering thousands of miles in Africa, Stanley eventually came across Livingston in the bush and recorded the now famous quotation, "Dr. Livingston, I presume." How could he presume otherwise? After all, Livingston was the only white man lost in Africa at the time.

Then, a further surprising link to America...prior to this historic event, a few years earlier Livingston's son Robert had traveled to America to fight in the Civil War. He was wounded at Laurel Hill in Virginia, captured, and died in a prison camp at Salisbury, North Carolina, on December 5, 1864. He was eighteen years of age.

Some interesting South African Facts and Trivia:

Sport
South Africans have beaten the best of the world in many sports. Here are those that come to mind: rugby, golf, cricket, boxing, swimming, athletics, Olympics, surfing, skateboarding, and 'Jukskei'…look it up.

Unusual Sporting Venues: The 19th hole of The Legend Golf and Safari Resort situated on the Hanglip Mountain is very unusual. The tee is constructed over 500 feet vertically above the green below, which is in the shape of the African continent. It is the longest par three in the world. Oh, and the only way to access it is by helicopter. You bet!

The Giants at Dungeon's at Hout Bay Beach produces 70-foot waves for surfers to revel in.

Biggest Races in the World: The Cape Argus Cycle Tour has boasted over 34,000 riding the grueling 109 km route around Cape Town and is the world's largest individually timed cycle race.

The Dusi Canoe Marathon with over 1,400 paddlers carries the competitors 125 km through KwaZulu-Natal and the impressive Valley of a Thousand Hills where the Msudusi and Umgeni Rivers meet. Rapids and whirlpools present serious and dangerous challenges to the hardiest and fittest.

The Comrades Marathon of 90 km is run between Pietermaritzburg and Durban over an unusually hilly course. The writer has had the honor of seconding Gordon Baker, my oldest friend and the first competitor to win eight consecutive Gold Medals. Those were in the years when 'seconding' meant accompanying the runner as a passenger on a motor cycle and jumping off occasionally to hand him a drink or splash water over the sweating hero. A second had to be fit because there were times when the runner needed to have him run beside him for encouragement during those inevitable energy lapses. During Gordon's last run, I ran beside him up Polly Shorts, the last of the soul sapping hills before entering Pietermaritzburg. I was personally relieved to learn that Gordon had run his last Comrades Marathon. I was getting too old for riding sidesaddle on the back of a motorcycle. Oh, and running up Polly Shorts.

I need to add that on retiring from ultra distance running, Gordon took up cycling and was soon chosen to represent South Africa in veteran events. That crazy guy! Here's to you, Gordon, my now Aussie mate and to Lynette, your dedicated and loving wife. Oh, I must mention that his wife, Lynette, can do more press-ups than her old man! That's some achievement for such a petite gal.

The Midmar Mile Swim, held annually across Midmar Dam, situated twenty-five miles north of Pietermaritzbug on the Umgeni River, just above the Howick Falls, which drops 365 feet. *The Guiness Book of Records* claims it to be the largest open-water swimming event in the world with as many as 17,000 swimmers churning across the water. The writer has swum it several times up to age fifty, however, I personally know someone who completed the swim at age 80! My three sons, Wayne, Sean, and Rafe took part at a young age. (Rafe, my youngest son, when he was only seven years of age.) Wayne, my eldest son, was beaten into second place in the senior event one year before immigrating to America. I have attended many a Midmar Mile prize giving, having personally donated the trophies for 'The Iron Man' and for 'The Iron Woman.'

"Barker" Gordon Baker

How about this?

The Biggest Manmade Hole

The manmade 'Big Hole' dug in Kimberley for over forty years, produced in excess of three tons of diamonds. The hole is so large that Table Mountain could fit in it.

Speaking of diamonds, the biggest diamond was discovered near Pretoria and named after Sir Thomas Cullinan, the owner of the mine. The stone was cut in three parts. The largest (after polishing) is 530.2 carats and is named the 'Great Star of Africa.' It is mounted in the British Royal Scepter and another piece weighing 317.4 carats is mounted on Queen Elizabeth's hat…the British Royal Crown. In my opinion, these polished gems should be returned to South Africa where they belong. Enough already!

Gold

South Africa has 40 percent of world's gold resources and is the second highest producer of gold in the world. Only China produces more.

On a sad note, more people in South Africa are living with Aids than in any other country in the world.

On a brighter note, The Baragwaneth Hospital near Johannesburg is the largest hospital in the world.

Back to America

First impressions somehow always remain fresh in the mind. I have previously mentioned my first and lasting impressions of America when I first stepped on USA soil. However, as over many pages I have revealed my inner person, you will no doubt understand something else that often comes to mind and makes me smile. The first joke I heard in America came early after my first arrival in New York. I was waiting for the baggage carousel to start up and deliver my two suitcases. There was some delay and, while sitting among other passengers, I overheard a joke that I will never forget. Okay…I was eavesdropping.

Two golfing buddies returning from a Vegas fling were shooting the breeze when the older of the two told this joke:

There was this handsome middle-aged Casanova golfer who spent every possible moment playing golf and a few other sports away from home. His wife constantly nagged him about this, but being too caught up in his own life, he simply ignored her. As time went on, the nagging increased and the couple was fast approaching divorce court. Then the husband suffered a heart attack and died.

In an instant, he found himself at the 'pearly gates' confronted by St. Peter, who greeted him warmly and explained, "Before you can gain entry into Heaven you are required to spell a word that is very important in Heaven."

The new arrival swallowed hard. He never was good at spelling and he enquired, "What is the word?"

"Love" replied St. Peter.

"L, O, V, E," the man spelled.

"Correct, my friend," replied St. Peter. "Welcome in."

Once in, the man found that Heaven was full of the best golf courses in existence. He was no doubt in 'Golf Heaven.'

Several days later, St. Peter approached the man and asked him to take over his position at the pearly gates for the afternoon. "Remember that all you have to do is get the newly arrived people to spell the word LOVE."

Within a few minutes of St. Peter's departure, the man was shocked to find his wife arriving at the gate. She was happy to see him. He had mixed feelings. He quickly explained that she had to first correctly spell a word before gaining entrance. She, like her husband, was not a good speller and nervously she asked, "What is the word?"

"CZECHOSLOVAKIA," he replied.

Welcome to America…Now Go Home

At this 'point in time' and thankfully for the last time I, like all writers, am penning the 'conclusion' of my book. The question is how? My purpose for writing was to entertain with 'tongue in cheek' humor, directed mainly at myself and my South African redneck background. I am not sure that including some of the more serious 'stuff' was wise, but in recalling many of the incidents that I shared, I was simply not able to shut out local and international memories that had such a profound influence in my life. Somehow, I believe that immigrants experience this more than others. Who can tell? My decision to relate in some detail the journey to American Citizenship is not intended to tug at the reader's heartstrings. Far from it! I have already acknowledged the fact that our experiences were not as traumatic as those early immigrants whom we followed. I have included it…not to cast aspersions on the system…but, hopefully, to relate with some anxiety, some frustration, and more importantly, with some humor, a real life experience that changed our lives forever…and for the better! Maybe you have never given this much consideration. Why would you? Without my experience, I probably would never have given it a thought either. There, but for the grace of God, go I.

Here goes…

It starts with 'one small step,' etc., etc., moves on to several 'small steps,' and finally 'One Giant Step'…all the way from the country of my birth to America.

Fast forward…our sons had immigrated to America earlier and after several years, they received their green cards. Their permanency was the signal for their parents to join them and continue working on our own immigration efforts on USA soil, which we correctly assumed would eliminate 'cross-pond' negotiations. Something like a hometown advantage…maybe…maybe not.

We took up residence near Charlotte, North Carolina, to be close to our sons and to share expenses. From a location point of view, it suited our plans as the Charlotte immigration department in Charlotte was within a forty-mile drive…but what a drive…road construction almost every inch of the way to the big city! Experience soon dictated that we hit the road before 6 A.M., if we had any hope of making on 8 A.M. appointment. So it was that we started our own 'Pilgrims' Progress' that would take us down the road (many times) through the process necessary to first obtain 'Resident Alien' status (a pink and blue card), then to be granted 'Employment Authorization' (a maroon and brown card renewed annually), to later receive Green Cards (them 'white' cards'), and then several years later receiving American Citizenship. However, I am moving too fast. I'll back up the wagon and now cover the whole story.

'Yours truly' reached that critical 'point in time' where this South African redneck joined the legal immigration sausage machine to face the biggest hurdle that life had to offer…applying for American Citizenship.

Some personal family history update is relevant at this stage…my three sons had immigrated several years before my late wife and I were finally able to disconnect from our complex and busy working schedules. Selling up everything was heart wrenching…but at least we had something to sell, unlike millions of less fortunate immigrants who over the years had arrived with little more than the clothes on their back…and maybe a trunk or two at the very best. I must repeat that no matter what emotions we lived through, we were more fortunate than the majority of others who landed in America. I knew that it would be difficult, but I had made my bed and I was going to sleep in it. What I am about to relate are simply the honest facts of our immigration experience. It was truly a roller-coaster ride, even for a hardened South African redneck!

By the time that we arrived in America, our three sons were in possession of their green cards and had applied for American Citizenship. Encouraged by this progress, my wife and I initiated our own pursuit of obtaining American Citizenship. This was the beginning of many visits to immigration offices. As the showman says, "This is only the beginning!"

On our first visit, we left home at 6:00 A.M. to ensure that we would arrive early. It was a ninety-minute drive and although we were early, we were late! The line outside the immigration office stretched for about thirty yards. Once the door opened, we took numbers and sat and waited our turn. Several clerks were on duty and handled people in strict numerical order. Anybody not arriving at the counter within thirty seconds of their number appearing…was out of luck…and many were.

On that occasion, we made the counter just before lunch and the clerk quickly answered our questions and then handed us a set of documents, but I felt that I needed to clear up further questions. She was not very forthcoming and said, "Just fill out those forms. You will find all the answers you need from them." With that, she punched the next number and a young man shot out of a chair and flashed to my side. Talk about Speedy Gonzalez!

I did not move and asked politely, "I would like to ask you some further questions."

That seemed to upset the clerk who replied, "You had your turn to ask questions. Your time is up and you are holding up the others. Just fill in the forms."…Right!

We drove home in a hurry to start working on the immigration papers. That night, we laboriously filled out the forms and finally hit the sack around 2:00 A.M. Those forms were something else!

A few days later, we once again lined up outside the immigration office. It was 6:00 A.M. and I was number ten in line. After they opened, my number was called within forty-five minutes and despite having all the forms filled out, I needed to ask some questions. On this occasion, a different clerk did answer some questions, but she rushed me and, consequently, I missed a few. Noticing my documentation, she said, "Oh, you did not need to bring them personally, you could have mailed them. Let me have them and I will submit them for you." With that, she placed our forms in the 'out tray,' punched the number, and Speedy's brother appeared at my side as if from nowhere. When I left that time, I took a good look around and made some plans for the next visit.

Several weeks later, I received a letter from the INS and I was elated thinking it contained good news, but just the opposite! The notice informed me that I had not included form G-325A (Biographic Information). This surprised and upset me; we had filled out all the forms that the clerk had handed us.

The next morning, we lined up number twenty despite our even earlier arrival in the dark. This time, I carried a list of questions and after I took a number, I hung around and returned to the number machine on two further occasions and pulled additional numbers. I was determined to get answers to my questions.

When my first number came up, I rushed to the clerk and showed him the letter about the missing document. He inquired why I had not filled it out and I replied, "Because the person who gave me the documentation did not include it."

He replied, "I doubt that. Maybe you mislaid it." I bit my tongue. He selected a document from a pile beside him, handed it to me, reached to punch up the next number, and I stopped him abruptly and said, "Don't change the number, yet. I need to ask further questions." I was too late. Speedy's cousin had seen the clerk's familiar hand movement toward the number changer and appeared directly behind me; he stood so close that I could smell his aftershave.

To my surprise, the clerk scolded him saying, "Excuse me, but you have not been called; please stand back and wait for your number to appear."

With that, his number came up at the next cubicle and in his haste to take the one step necessary to that clerk, he stumbled and dropped a pile of papers on the floor. Fearing losing his place, he scooped the papers off the floor and tossed them on the counter in front of the clerk, and the force of his thrust, sent the documents fluttering against the clerk and onto the floor on that side. Nobody smiled.

In the confusion, my clerk brought up the next number and another zombie appeared from nowhere. I was frustrated, but I had an 'ace in the hole.' I had two additional numbers. I was so smart, but was I? My next number came up a little later and to my horror, it appeared at the same clerk that I drew before! Just my luck, of seven clerks on duty, I had to draw the same guy twice. As I had another number, I never moved, but sat silently in a corner and watched as the next number came up and someone rushed to take my place. Sometime later, my last number came up. You guessed it, I drew the same clerk, but I was committed.

When I appeared he recognized me and said scowling, "You were here earlier…how come you took two numbers?" He underestimated me. I had taken three numbers! Then I heard myself say, "My wife needed to ask some questions and I am standing in for her." He shook his head and I wondered if he had ever heard that one before? However, thankfully, he politely answered my questions.

Two days later, I once again lined up in the dark and finally reached the counter as number twenty-six. I handed the completed form G-325A to the clerk and asked him to check it. He placed it in a tray and said, "You could have mailed it," and with that, he brought up the next number. As I had no further questions, I discarded my other two numbers and left.

A month later, our son Sean who had been transferred to Austin, Texas, became an American Citizen and his inducting official confirmed that he was now legally permitted to petition for his parents to become US residents. This was wonderful news and we would take advantage of this unexpected opportunity, but first we had to get the appropriate forms from the immigration office!

We once again drove to the immigration office and we were shocked at the long line of humanity stretching into the parking lot. We took our places and waited, listening to the chatter around, but they were talking in tongues. Nobody was speaking English or American. As I stood there, I felt like someone from outer space who had just arrived at a picnic. In this microcosmic gathering, everybody else looked like aliens to us…aliens.

When the doors finally opened, officials called for silence and you could have heard a pin drop. They had instituted a new system of control. Groups were admitted and the overflow remained lined up outside. There simply was not sufficient space inside the immigration office to accommodate the numbers that jostled for position outside.

We just made the first group and were soon standing at the counter. A young and friendly slim woman greeted us, "How y'all, today?" I wondered where they had found her. She listened carefully, understood our needs, and gave us a pile of documents, some of which were for our son to complete. She answered our several questions politely and as we left she called out,

"Now y'all have a nice day. God bless you." This time I retained my unused numbers as keepsakes.

Once we had gone over the new documents, we decided to drive to Austin, Texas, to visit our son Sean who had accepted a transfer there by his company. The main reason for that long drive was to fill out the documents together, as he was preparing to sponsor us in our Citizenship bid.

The journey to Austin took two days in our much used rice burner. Over several nights, we completed the many immigration documents and I was alarmed at the amount of information that Sean had to provide. Sponsoring a new citizen required convincing proof that Sean was not only financially able to support us, but that he would be responsible for all and any debt that we incurred in America during the immigration procedure. Many hours of visits to his bank and insurance companies were necessary to obtain certified proof of all the information requested. Finally after a week we left with all the documents duly completed and certified safely locked in a brief case that was never out of my control at any time from that moment on.

On our return and after a day to recover from the long and tiring journey, we once more arrived at the immigration department two hours early, but as usual we joined a long line. Once seated inside, we went over our documentation once more for the umpteenth time. We had everything and we were in good humor. We chuckled when we viewed our fingerprint charts and my wife said jokingly, "I hope the Feds don't have anything on you." My feelings were hurt.

When our number came up, we walked to the counter with confidence. A clerk greeted us civilly and I said proudly, "Our son is on American Citizen and is petitioning for us. We have completed all the documents and would like you to please peruse them to insure that they are in order, and also that we have completed every form necessary."

She smiled broadly and replied, "Sure, I can do that for you. Let me look them over." I handed the file to her and she smiled broadly as she opened it. Her friendly and helpful attitude was refreshing and we stood silently as she inspected the file. As she scanned the first page her smile changed to a frown and she remarked, "Your son lives in Texas; that's where you need to apply…not here in North Carolina."

We were shocked and I stammered, "But we are resident of North Carolina and this is the North Carolina Immigration office."

She replied firmly, "I'm sorry, but as your son lives in Texas, that's where you must make application." With that she took the file, snapped it closed, and with both hands slid it to me and said, "I'm sorry."

I was shattered and asked lamely, "What must we do now?"

She answered, "As I told you, file it in Texas." Then she added, "Let me give you some advice, Texas will not accept your fingerprint charts made here in North Carolina or any medical examinations made outside of Texas. I will give you new forms to complete in Texas before you submit anything down there. This way I am saving you unnecessary problems. I hope things turn out for you." With that she produced the form and punched the next number.

The next day we set out on the long drive to Texas and, as before, I never let the brief case out of my sight. Getting documentation redone in Texas proved to be tedious and time consuming, and the heat wave conditions did little to improve our dispositions. When we visited a large police precinct for fingerprinting, the duty officer seemed surprised at our request and told us to wait until he made some inquiries. After a long wait, we were interviewed by a senior officer who questioned us at length to ascertain our reasons for wanting the fingerprinting done in Texas. I related the whole story to him and, finally, he called in a baby-faced young officer and told him to take care of us. And as he left the room he muttered, "I don't understand these immigration people; nothing they do makes any sense anymore."

The young man led us to an adjoining room and 'took care of us.' He was obviously a rookie and by the time we finished, our hands were covered in dark black ink. When we left and we walked past the duty officer he seemed amused and on reaching the car, my wife burst out laughing and giggled, "You should see your face." Somehow down the line, I must have rubbed my nose during the fingerprinting. Looking back at me in the car mirror was a clown. We laughed for the first time in days.

Having a medical examination was truly a new experience. After considerable difficulty, we located a medical facility that was on the official immigration list. Not many were listed and authorized to carry out the examinations. Finding our way and locating the facility was a nightmare, but the best was still to come…or, should I say the worst was still to come?

After a considerable wait, first my wife and then I were escorted to different examination rooms. My blood was drawn and, in my case, the medic struggled with English and I wondered how my wife would do considering her hard to locate veins. The fact that she was in remission after breast cancer was also a source of concern. Once my blood had been drawn, I was ushered into another room where I was told to strip for a medical examination…I did not like the sound of that. I stripped and slipped into the back-to-front flimsy paper gown and took a seat on a chair. There was nothing to read and the room was sparse.

In time, a man in a white laboratory coat walked in with the distinguishing stethoscope hanging from his neck. He was short and lean with receding hair and a sallow complexion. He spoke with an unusual accent and did everything in a hurry. He was a clumsy fellow. He went through the rituals of the usual examination procedures and made hurried notes on a clipboard. Finally, when I thought he had finished he said, "Stand and face me." I smiled weakly and stood before him. He crouched down and felt around where no man had been before. While handling me there, the clumsy oaf unexpectedly tripped and tried to regain his balance, but unfortunately for me, he still had my man parts in his possession. A shock wave tore through places that I never knew existed. I yelled at him in pain and instinctively lined him up for a knuckle sandwich, but fortunately for both of us, I needed time to catch my breath and, in that moment, Doctor Strangelove made an apology. He rushed to the door where he hesitated a moment to call out, "You okay, I finished." With that he disappeared before I could finish him.

Another person then entered and told me to dress and return to the waiting room where I found my wife sitting in a chair disconsolately gazing without focusing. As I approached, I asked worriedly, "Are you okay?"

Without looking, she replied sullenly, "I will live." I kept silent, but I was fuming inside. We were later handed sealed envelopes for immigration and were told that the results of the blood tests would be forwarded later. We returned to the boiling car and drove back to our Texas family in silence.

That night as we prepared for bed, I noticed with shock huge purple bruises on my wife's arm where the blood had been drawn. She explained that the person who drew blood was completely incompetent and had dug around in several places in her flesh before finally getting the job done. When the needle was withdrawn, blood had escaped under her skin and finally some had squirted on her. It looked like somebody had beaten her arm with a baseball bat.

The following morning we were up at 4:00 A.M. and on our way to the immigration offices in San Antonio. We arrived at sunup, located the huge facility, and drove into the spacious parking lot, which was crowded with vehicles, mostly pickup trucks (many with their tail gates open and people standing around eating breakfast). It resembled a picnic on black top. Although the sun was not fully up, there was a line of people stretching from the entrance over the sidewalk and into the parking lot. I shoved my wife out the car almost without stopping and told her to get into line. I followed with the briefcase and took my place beside her and in this short time, several people were already behind us. It was going to be a long day.

As we waited alternating from foot to foot, we both fell silent and retreated into our own thoughts. During those few hours in line, I never heard English spoken. Finally, several uniformed officials appeared at the entrance and an excited buzz spread through the crowd, but someone called for 'quiet!' and everybody immediately fell silent; it was as if we had been switched off.

The officials moved down the line giving instructions, but I could not understand anything that was said because the instructions were in Spanish. As one official came near, I called out, "Please, I don't understand Spanish." Those standing around looked in disbelief, but the official came over and said in a friendly tone, "Don't worry, we will repeat everything in English." As she promised, we were soon given clear instructions in English. They explained the procedure and it went like this, "When the doors open you will enter orderly and quietly and everybody will pass through an area where someone will direct you to the relevant counter once they have ascertained the nature of your visit." She then added that no food or beverages were permitted inside the premises. At that comment, several people shoveled food into their mouths and chewed and swallowed hard. One poor guy choked on his sandwich and took a coughing fit.

Despite the fears of spending the day in that cauldron of agitated humanity, we were pleasantly surprised at the efficiency of the proceedings. By mid-morning, we presented ourselves to one of many clerks at our specific counter. The mild mannered, well-manicured lady greeted us with a wide smile as I handed her our file. She opened it and read a few lines and with a puzzled look she asked, "You are permanent residents of North Carolina?"

"Yes," I replied. "Our son who is petitioning for us is a permanent resident of Texas."

She hesitated and said, "Well, you must file this in North Carolina."

My wife nearly fainted. I felt sick and in desperation, I explained, "But we did file in North Carolina three days ago, and they told us to file it in Texas where our son resides."

She shook her head, "Well, I find that hard to believe, but you should have called for a supervisor." She obviously anticipated my next question and offered, "I can call my supervisor to explain it to you, if you wish."

I immediately answered, "Please do." She referred us to a supervisor who took time to carefully explain the correct procedure, but the bottom line was…our petition had to be filed in North Carolina.

I asked if he would mind giving me his name and he willingly obliged and added, "The North Carolina people can call me about this anytime and I will be glad to set them right."

The next day we hit the road to return to North Carolina and my wife had to remind me several times about the speed limit. I was in a hurry to talk to the people in North Carolina!

Three days later, we were once again sitting in the North Carolina Immigration department; I was fuming and ready to roll. I was prepared to have it out with the clerk who had sent us all the way to Texas, but she fortunately was not among those at the counter that day. When our number came up, I walked aggressively to the counter and my wife struggled to keep up with me. Before I could say anything, the pretty little thing behind the counter said, "Let me take a look at your documentation and I will see what you need, honey." I caught my breath and automatically handed her my thick file. I watched closely as she paged through the file and I was ready for action. She spent several minutes checking the documents and finally she looked up at us and I was ready.

She said sweetly, "Everything is fine, honey…you will hear from us soon…have a nice day."

That was it? That was it! I wanted to speak, but my wife dragged me away and she said, "Don't say a word…and I mean it. I can't take any more! I feel sick. Please take me home, Biddie." Where was home?

Nine weeks later, we received a letter from Immigration advising us to attend an interview the following Tuesday. The interviews were painless and within an hour, we walked out with our green cards. Finally, we were now granted permanent residence. We had come a long way. We were finally on our way to becoming American citizens. If I was a drinking man…that would have been the night!

That night we shared our good news and when I mentioned how relieved I was, my son piped up, "Well, Pa, at least you did not have to waltz across the Mexican border or swim ashore at Miami."

But a lot of water would flow under the bridge before I would finally be sworn in as an American Citizen. Some Good, some Bad, and some Ugly!

Five years later, I finally took the oath and received my American Citizenship. That was 'Good!' However, the return of my dear wife's cancer deprived her of the one thing left in life for which she had sacrificed so much. That was 'Bad!'

Remember... "You cannot truly laugh, until you have truly cried."

I make absolutely no excuse for including this sad event...it's the truth. It has happened before and it will happen again. That's life. You and I have become friends during this reading experience; otherwise you would not be reading this now. That is why I have shared this with you, just as I have shared my South African Redneck experiences to entertain y'all.

Now here's some other news of interest. Y'all may not believe this...I completed a two-year auto body repair course at Community College 'in two years,' and I took over a small mobile home park...so 'who all' are 'y'all' calling a redneck?

If it were not for the fact that I consider this book sufficient for y'all's gray matter, I could have written as much covering the experiences at the auto body repair shop and life in a mobile home park. If this book gets published, I will be back.

I have covered the "Good" and the "Bad," so what about the Ugly? There is no ugly. There is only me and the final challenge by an American redneck for the title of 'Redneck King.' This is what is pitted against the South African argument...it's short and sweet!

There's this guy Cecil in Tennessee, who had an invisible fence installed around his yard to keep his two pet goats on the property.

After the fence had been buried around his yard, the guy who installed it placed collars around each of the goat's necks. Unfortunately, no matter how much they tried to coax either of the two goats to attempt crossing the electric fence line, those stubborn critters would just not cooperate. The installing technician grew impatient and told the couple to let him know if the goats crossed the fence. If so, he would return and increase the electric charge, but he mentioned that the electric power in the fence was 'pretty powerful.'

For three days those goats never went near that fence line and Cecil grew impatient, so he made a decision to personally test the fence. How? He would take the collars off the two goats and he persuaded his wife, Hetty, an impressionable woman, to buckle one collar around her neck and he followed suit himself. The two then brazenly walked across the hidden electric fence.

Now, we have a man and his woman both with permanently red necks. That's a hard act to follow even for a South African redneck. I ask you with tears in my eyes, "Who are the real rednecks today? Those pale-skinned South African immigrants with necks that have been burnt red by the midday sun...or that Tennessee couple sporting permanent red rings around their necks?"

You will find the definitive answer in a few pages, but please do not turn there now! What you read before that page will prepare you for the answer. Trust me! You have thus far, so why not now?

Today

So, where is this South African redneck today? If you drive about forty miles northeast from Charlotte, North Carolina, you will pass by my home at the entrance to a little town of less than three thousand residents. I recently re-married…'took' me a Southern widow. We live in a 'double wide' on a few acres with a fenced-in portion where my wife personally tends to her garden, which produces many varieties of fresh vegetables, including them 'greens' and something sounding like Oprah. The garden has an eight-foot fence to keep out the deer population. My wife cranks the tiller and prepares the soil. I tried to work that little monster, but it has a mind of its own! We have home cooked 'everything' from our daily bread to chicken and dumplings…and deer meat when my aim is working.

Between us, we share five married sons, a 'bunch' of grandchildren, one and a half 'great-grand'un' and have been introduced to their seven dogs and twelve cats. Yes, this 'displaced and replaced' redneck has come a long way. In fact, like Donny of 'elephant fame,' I attended the local Community College. Yep, sure have. At age 60, the oldest 'pupil' and first South African to graduate (with a 4.0 average).

Been in some hot water with my wife because of the demolition derby. Let me restate that…'hot water' is 'cool' compared to the wrath of the little woman over my involvement in the local demolition derby. Well, it was not all my doing. My neighbor 'Mad Mike' Kucera had a lot to do with it. In fact, he had a 'whole lot' to do with it.

One Friday night after some liquid refreshment, Mike talked me into attending a demolition derby. At the conclusion of the automobile massacre, as we were making our way to his car, Mike surprised me by suggesting that we enter the next demolition derby. In my innocence I replied, "Why not?" BIG MISTAKE!

'Mad Mike' lives up to his name…a professional man from Monday thru Friday…but a Jekyll and Hyde over weekends and days off. Get the picture? Why even his delightful knitting crazy wife 'Nancy with the velvet voice' is still trying to figure him out after forty years of marriage…and the rest of us are rednecks?

Soooo, we acquired a brute of an old Caddy two-door (the ex-pride and joy of a Sunday school friend), we converted this beautiful sleek V8 into a mechanical gladiator (the end of my friendship in the Sunday school class), and entered it in the derby at the official driver's meeting cookout. Now, I must confess that there were signs that Mike and I were somehow not too warmly received by the rest of the competitors…even the one 'lady' driver, seemed 'stand-offish.' And, to make matters worse, few could understand my accent. Look whose talking! Have you ever listened to a demolition derby driver 'splaining the rules with a wad of chewing tobacco straining at his cheek?

During the cookout, Mike overheard some interesting remarks. Some quotes:

1. "Them two fancy speaking city boys are out to steal the $1,000 prize money." In fact, a news report in the local newspaper the following day included specifically mentioned that for the first time a couple of 'out-of-towners' had entered for the prize money.
2. "They won't last one minute!" They were wrong. It took them one minute and thirty-eight seconds to completely destroy the Caddy! We filmed the whole thing. When the flag was dropped, every other competitor immediately zeroed in like a swarm of angry hornets on the Caddy and wrecked it so severely that it took a road-grading vehicle with a scoop to remove it from the arena.

I should mention that as Mike and I were considered too old to personally drive the Caddy, Mike's son Andrew 'Rambo', an avowed mountain climber and all-around outdoorsman, did the honors. When extricated from the remains of the Caddy, he was not in the least fazed, but that night during our Victory party it was noticeable that he was only using his left hand to lift a bottle or two. It took about a week for him to straighten his right elbow. Cheers, Andrew…a true son of Mad Mike!

I promised my wife that I would not entertain competing in anything unusual again, but despite this assurance, Mike (Who else?) and I are preparing to compete in the International Conch Shell Blowing competition. That should blow her mind!

My wife has also made me promise not to offer to help anybody without her clearance…er blessing. All because of what happened when I 'helped' Larry deliver his boat to his other brother Larry in the mountains. Because the vessel was much larger than the average boat used for pleasure on the nearby lakes, I used a powerful Ford 'dually' to tow the sturdy trailer and boat up the steep mountain road. The words 'up' and 'steep' are used loosely.

Well, I reached a point of no return and was forced to 'rush' the last fifty yards of the rough steep (Did I mention steep?) incline. The 'dually' made it, but the boat did not! Now when asking the locals for directions to Larry's cabin they say, "Take 'High Mountain Road' until you see a boat hanging in a tree, then hang a left, etc."

"Before and After"
Mad Mike Kucera's Cadillac

"Demolition Dolls

The kids in the mountains refer to it as the 'Ark.' They know their Bible up there...being so close to Heaven.

Friday nights, I cook out and sip on strawberry wine. Saturday mornings, I wash and polish my '55 Chevy pickup 'after' vacuuming the interior. Not many people cruise by anymore...only a few senior citizens now and then...but I noticed that the late Billy Tallendish's widow next door does most of her bird watching using his hunting/military binoculars around 8 A.M. on Saturday mornings. Not sure what she can see, but she always gives me a friendly wave. That's how redneck neighbors are...always 'looking out' for one another.

I have passed 'the three score and ten years' mark and am 'gainfully' employed as a greeter at that supermarket with the biggest parking lot in town. I'm the guy at the door who welcomes one and all y'all with a friendly smile and a, "Have a nice day," as y'all exit. My duties include collecting those buggies that y'all leave all over the place in the parking lot. I'm the guy who rides them with one foot while propelling them with the other foot. My fastest time from the top of the parking lot to the store entrance is twenty-six seconds. Jimmy from the paint section did his best to beat that record, but was disqualified and 'let go' for entering the shop without giving the automatic doors time to fully open.

We have now completed the redneck cycle from the dawn of the redneck beginnings, over centuries, through different continents, and finally arrived at the same place from where we started this honorable quest for answers about our redneck heritages.

So what is the answer? Who can make the claim of, "Who are the original rednecks?" But more importantly, "Who are the rednecks today?" The answer is very simple…South African rednecks and American rednecks are essentially of the same breed, except on different sides of the globe. We are from a common bloodline, which stood side-by-side, shoulder-to-shoulder in the two great wars, Korea, and in conflicts unfamiliar to many. We are those people who produced brave men like the young, land-loving, baby-faced Audie Murphy…the bravest and most decorated of all American soldiers who overcame everything that a human being encountered on a hill in some forsaken foreign land…who stepped up and took on a group of determined and well-armed enemy single-handedly and saved not only his fellowmen, but helped save a world. He and millions like him have never faltered when having to step into the breach for America and the Free World. This same 'America' where dreams became reality, the wilderness was tamed, and the mightiest nation that the world has ever known was spawned.

And as in America, the Colonial South African has served with honor, converted coal to oil, oil to gasoline, and developed a nuclear capability that was the envy of the world. And, yes, from a sun-parched desolate area of South Africa came Dr. Christiaan Barnard, the humble farm boy who attended school barefoot, and rose out of the desert sand to conduct the first successful heart transplant in the world. From these very same bloodlines came the greatest of all world leaders. One man who inspired the American people and the whole world…the man of the land who lifted his fellowman to freedom…George Washington. That is why we can say with humility and pride, "GOD BLESS AMERICA."

So, be careful who you call a redneck, unless you use the term with respect. That is all 'we all' want…respect.

To those who do not understand so-called rednecks, I have some sound advice. Take the opportunity while you can to understand and embrace them. You see, one day when you depart this earth you will arrive at a place that is inhabited by more rednecks than you have ever seen and as you will have to live with them, prepare now to ensure you have a happy time.

In the meantime…some redneck advice…

When you are challenged at the pearly gates…remember how to spell 'Czechoslovakia'…otherwise you may end up in that place where someone dressed in black plays banjo music in the background.

"Bless your hearts, y'all. Y'all have a nice forever."

Forgot to mention, I have a horse named 'side saddle.'

QWB: WHAT IS THE DIFFERENCE BETWEEN AN IMMIGRANT AND A REFUGEE? Timing!

MISSION ACCOMPLISHED!!!
(I REST MY CASE)

'SOUTH AFRICAN' REDNECK AND 'AMERICAN' REDNECK FROM THE SAME BLOOD LINE DOING WHAT COMES NATURALLY!!

The author and "mad Mike" Kucera THE 2011 JOINT WINNERS OF:

THE CONCH
SHELL BLOWING CONTEST
At the Hollerin', Conch Shell Blowing and Whistling contest held annually at:

SPIVEY'S CORNER VOLUNTEER FIRE DEPARTMENT IN SAMPSON COUNTY NORTH CAROLINA.

SEE Y'ALL AT SPIVEY'S CORNER VOLUNTEER FIRE DEPARTMENT
SAMPSON COUNTY NORTH CAROLINA …3rd Saturday JUNE

South African History Lesson

Africa…the very word conjures up visions of jungles and wild animals! Then there is the concern for the living conditions of the indigenous peoples of this vast continent, so often referred to as 'the Dark Continent.'

This enormous landmass is comprised of many different countries embracing vastly contrasting cultures and cultures within cultures, which include diverse religious beliefs and tribal customs. It is also a fact that, although many religions and faiths are practiced, millions of its inhabitants have never heard 'the Word,' or any word at all! However, Africa has many, many faces and I intend introducing you to an Africa that is unlike anything generally perceived by the majority of 'first-world' cultures.

I am about to introduce you to a 'tribe' of white Africans, consisting of people drawn from many different parts of the globe, who finally settled in what is now referred to as South Africa.

The history of the white peoples of Africa and, more specifically, of South Africa is fascinating and intriguing. It is, however, not possible for me to adequately cover this enormous subject in this book, but as these people are the central characters in immigration, it is imperative that I briefly cover their history for you

The first white settlers arrived by sea in Table Bay Harbor, now known as Cape Town Harbor, in 1652. The contingent of ninety men, mainly Dutch, were under the command of Jan van Riebeeck, an ex-ship's surgeon, who was commissioned by his employers, the Dutch East India Company, to establish a 'post' for the exclusive use of their mariners.

Jan van Riebeeck was not sent to colonize or exploit. He was instructed to merely tame the wilderness in the surrounding area, build a hospital within a fort, and provide meat and fresh vegetables for passing ships. He was also expected to keep the peace with the Hottentot cattle breeders with whom he would have to barter for his meat supplies.

In 1657, many of those released from service elected to remain in the country and were allowed to start farming to supplement the production of vegetables and sometimes, the uncertain barter of cattle. The married men were joined by wives and children and soon a regular flow of Dutch and German settlers were arriving joined from time to time by British, Portuguese, Greeks, Italians, and Jews.

Not surprisingly, from these roots, a new language was spawned…enter 'Afrikaans.' In 1688, a group of French Huguenots arrived after fleeing religious persecution in France. They were followed by small groups from the United Kingdom, injecting the colorful characteristics of the Scottish, Irish, and Welsh into this delicious mixture of humanity, and together they evolved into what soon became known as the 'Cape Colony.'

It soon became obvious to the Hottentots and later to tribes further north, that these white newcomers were not only here to stay, but were multiplying day by day. Inevitably, border confrontations flared up precipitated by the increasing livestock theft perpetrated mainly by the Hottentots. Then the security situation worsened due to the persistent incursions by the Xhosa. The British government, who by this time had occupied the Cape Colony, encouraged settlement in this region as a buffer between the settlers and their neighbors, and about 5,000 settlers arrived from various parts of England, Scotland, Ireland, and Wales as the '1820 Settlers.'

As their numbers increased, groups of settlers, for a variety of reasons, began migrating into the interior. By now, they no longer regarded themselves as colonial interlopers settling and farming land for a company or a distant fatherland. Their umbilical cord with the rest of the world had been severed and, like their American contemporaries on the other side of the globe, they were carving a permanent home from the wilderness for themselves and future generations.

Congratulations! You have just been introduced to the original 'White Tribe of South Africa.' It is from these roots that the characters will emerge larger than life. They are the descendants of these hardy pioneers who prevailed under very harsh conditions to establish a place in the sun for themselves and their children. Through all their hardships, they remained refined and religious folk, who never neglected the education of their children. They labored long and hard, but never lost their sense of humor. Many stories revolve around these folk, who work hard, play hard, and have a unique sense of humor!

While my main focus is on the white community, we must not lose sight of the fact that they only constitute a minority group in this multi-ethnic society. To understand what makes this society 'tick' or more correctly, function, it is imperative that we carefully examine the other groups to learn all we can about their roots and how they too fit into this human jigsaw.

To achieve this, it is necessary for us to delve into the political history of South Africa inasmuch as it affects this story line.

Much has been written, in recent years, about the manner in which the pervious white minority government had unsuccessfully endeavored to evolve a society made up of basically four main 'race groups,' who were to be physically separated by legislation, called Apartheid.

The four main groups included: Blacks, Whites, Coloreds, and Asians. As one or more of these designations could be construed as offensive to some, I shall endeavor to define them in the context of the proposed legislation.

Blacks - The indigenous people, the 'Africans.'

Coloreds - Two separate groups emerged over the years. The first, quite naturally, in and around the Cape Colony. The second, much smaller group has its origins in the Natal Province further northeast, which was served by the thriving harbor of Durban.

The Cape Coloreds - As they are still referred to, to date, include two sub-cultural groups, the Griquas and the Cape Malays. The Griqua, mainly of Hottentot-European ancestry settled in the northwestern and northeastern areas of the Cape. They developed their own culture and were characterized linguistically by a broken style of Dutch-Afrikaans maintaining a peculiar, but dignified power of expression. They remained committed to their religion and are best remembered for their loving and enthusiastic renditions of sacred songs by groups and choirs. These colorful and happy-go-lucky people are dwindling in numbers and are gradually being absorbed by the rest of the 'Colored' population. The Cape Malays, by far the largest group, live in the Cape Peninsula, mainly in the well-known Malay Quarter in Cape Town…not unlike the French Quarter in New Orleans in the USA. They are the descendants of early Muslim slaves introduced to the Cape by the Dutch East India Company and comprised of Indians, Chinese, Cingalese, Indonesians, and Malagasy. Despite their isolation and bondage, they remained faithful to Islam and steadfastly adhered to the Islamic faith. This is manifest in all their traditional ceremonies, at weddings, feasts, and funerals, and Holy pilgrimages to their beloved Mecca. Many of their number are highly talented craftsmen and artisans whose skills and reliability have always been much sought after. In recent times, the majority of these skilled individuals have been lost to factory work, due to the labor demands of industrial development.

The other smaller group in the Natal Province are descendants of three main sub-groups, comprising Euro-Africans, St. Helenans, and Mauritians. Generally speaking, in religion, language, and general lifestyle, this unique and talented society has always been closely associated with Whites. Their culture and values are distinctly Western. About 80 percent are believed to be Christian, the others mainly Muslims, and some 70 percent speak Afrikaans and the rest speak English. They have distinguished themselves in fine arts, drama, ballet, and many are successfully employed in the professions or in managerial or executive positions in both the public and private sectors.

Asians - All but 1 percent are of Indian descent, the others, Chinese. In 1860, the British government instituted a scheme to indenture Indian labor to assist in the newly established sugar plantations in the then British colony of

Natal. On November 16 of that year, the first party of 330 laborers, mainly Hindus, arrived from Madras in Durban Harbor aboard the *Truro*. They were contracted for five years. When this period was complete, they were free to return to India at government expense or accept a piece of crown land equal in value to the cost of a return passage. The majority chose land on which to farm, others took up professions, and some were content to work as laborers in various sectors of the economy.

During the 1870s, these indentured laborers were followed by other groups referred to as 'passenger' Indians, because they paid their own passage. They were British subjects who had free access within the Empire who chose to settle in Natal Province and became tradesmen and merchants. For many decades afterward, official policy was that as many as possible, if not all, of this alien community should eventually be repatriated to India. It was not until 1961 after South Africa had become a Republic that they were finally accepted as a permanent component of the multicultural population and the repatriation policy was finally abandoned. The Indian community has never been culturally homogeneous. The main distinctions are religious and to some extent, linguistic, but although some of the older generations still speak Tamil, Telugu, Hindustani, and Gujarati, their main medium of communication is now English. The majority of Indians, about 80 percent, live in the Province of Natal within a 150 km radius of Durban, the busiest port in South Africa.

The very small Chinese component of the Asians, about 1 percent, have a different history. At the conclusion of the Anglo-Boer War (1899-1902), in which a young war correspondent named Winston Churchill was taken prisoner by the Boers, some 50,000 laborers were recruited from China by the gold mining industry. The authorities reluctantly gave approval because of the shortage of African labor at that time but stipulated that repatriation would be instituted once the local labor situation was able to cope with labor demands. Thus, it transpired that in 1906, Chinese laborers, mostly illiterate, arrived from Shantung Province and after laboring hard and honestly, were repatriated between 1908 and 1910. However, a handful did manage to stay! The next influx of Chinese into South Africa commenced in the 1920s, but, unlike those previous uneducated laborers, these men and women came from a higher social background in China. They, like many others from the four corners of the world, were lured by the opportunities generated by the gold and diamond industries.

This concludes my personal understanding of the general history of the influx of foreigners into the southern areas of Africa now known as South Africa.

It is now the time to look more closely and compassionately at the Black peoples of the region, who during those times were powerless to prevent the influx and subsequent growth of the white man and his buddies in their land– …foreigners who with the advantage of education and the technology of the time slowly took control over their land and destiny. At first glance, this statement seems too simplistic, but when you realize that, at that stage of their history, when the foreigners landed, they found no 'wheel,' not unlike early American History.

Let us take a fresh look at the Africans of the region, the indigenous people who were referred to by the politicians, as Blacks, whose African roots go way, way back in time to the Stone Ages nearly two million years ago!

When the first white man stepped onto the beaches of South Africa, the region was inhabited by over a million black people made up of many tribes, the largest two being the Zulu and Xhosa as they are referred to now. Between them, they represent roughly 80 percent of today's black population and are of similar numbers. The history of all the tribes and their various affiliations is obviously not a subject that can be readily researched for this book, so I will, at this juncture, concentrate mainly on their present language diversity. This information should help the reader to appreciate the complexity and diversity of the Black population of South Africa, and like race, different languages also divide.

Generally speaking, the African population can be subdivided into the following four major language groups: Nguni, Sotho, Tsonga, and Venda. However, they are mutually unintelligible. Within this complex language situation, nine Black languages are officially recognized by the South African government. They are Zutu, Xhosa, Swazi, and Ndebele of the NGUNI tribes; Northern, Western, and Southern Sotho of the SOTHO tribes; Venda, and Tsonga.

Now, to complete the South African language recipe, we slowly add English, with a little heat, followed by a similar amount of Afrikaans with the burner on high, stir well the result. Today, South Africa has one of the most complex and diversified population mixes in the world, a rich mosaic of distinctive minorities, but without any cultural common denominator. This is underscored by the fact that not one of South Africa's eleven official languages is spoken by a majority of all their people! South Africa is a microcosm of the whole world…its peoples reflect both the ethnic diversity and the disparities in social and economic development of the globe. It can be said, therefore, that no other country mirrors the ethnic and development profile of the world so nearly as reflected in South Africa. America could also be thus compared, except that the percentage ratios of various races are out of balance with the world percentages, e.g., African Americans are in the minority. Unfortunately, due to this most complex and disparate population mix, this largely misunderstood society, has no common 'South African' identity with universally accepted cultural and political norms.

Having digested the foregoing, it soon becomes obvious that communications between the various folk presented problems, some serious, many perplexing, others confusing but, as always, plenty filled with humor…and pity to those who can't learn to laugh at themselves! Imagine, on the one hand, Europeans trying to master any of the African dialects, and on the other hand, the poor Africans, not only having to learn the Queen's English, but also confronted with Afrikaans, a language in its infancy, derived from Dutch and believed to be the only Germanic language to have originated outside Europe.

The obvious question now is, what about Apartheid? Once again, in my defense, has anybody every really successfully explained how Apartheid was supposed to work? Even the very architects of this infamous legislation were divided on certain of its aspects. In view of the very complicated nature of the subject, I will restrict my comments to my personal understanding of how it evolved.

In 1948, the National Party, which very successfully identified itself with the Afrikaans speaking public, narrowly defeated the opposition. The victory came as a surprise, even to their leaders! Many factors contributed to this swing, among them the disenchantment of the returning WW II soldiers, acute housing shortages, memories of earlier food shortages, and to a degree, the ineptness of the previous mainly English speaking administration.

The very next year, 1949, saw the first of the Apartheid laws passed…among them, the Group Areas Act, which was implemented to stop the gradual integration of the racial groups. From this point, a system of segregation by race was vigorously and ruthlessly enforced on all the population to the distinct advantage of the Whites. The rest is history!

A point of interest, the word 'Apartheid' in Afrikaans means 'the state of being apart,' but unfortunately, outside of Afrikaans, it is pronounced and sounds like 'apart-hate!' Unfortunate choice of word!

This now concludes my personal rendition of South African history, looking very broadly at the origins of the various population groups, which now have to somehow learn to co-exist.

I trust that you have enjoyed this candid rendition, which was intended not only to enlighten you, but also help to understand the culture of immigrants, heading out to start new lives in distant countries.

Author with South African President P.W. Botha.

Flat Head Action

Hudson Against Gravity

Packard Wins